*Daniel Defoe
and the
Supernatural*

Rodney M. Baine

Daniel Defoe
and the
Supernatural

University of Georgia Press · *Athens*

Preface

THIS STUDY of Daniel Defoe and the supernatural is intended to
illuminate an important aspect of Defoe's thought and art—his
belief in an unseen world and his employment of occult materials in his writings. The supernatural was highly important to
the author and to his protagonists. In his autobiographical *Appeal
to Honour and Justice* and elsewhere he acknowledged that he received spiritual promptings and that after suffering disastrous consequences upon ignoring them, he finally learned to heed them. A
familiarity with his occult ideas is essential for the reader fully to
understand and appreciate in *Robinson Crusoe* and *Moll Flanders*,
for example, supernatural materials which to a casual reader might
seem superficial or even meretricious.

In all his occult writings, *A True Relation of the Apparition of
one Mrs. Veal* (1706), "A Vision of the Angelick World" (1720),
The Political History of the Devil, *A System of Magick* (both
1726), and *An Essay on the History and Reality of Apparitions*
(1727), Defoe, like Meric Casaubon, Henry More, and Joseph
Glanvill in the previous century, was striving in an age of sensu-
ous epistemology to re-establish the reality of an unseen world. As
early as May 30, 1706 Defoe, as editor of the *Review*, branded the
rejection of the supernatural as a sort of atheism; and in 1720, in
his "Vision of the Angelick World," he castigated those who reject,
first, apparitions, then all spirits, and finally God himself.

Most of Defoe's contemporaries saw, as he did, daily manifestations of the Devil's assaults upon man and God's continuing care

for him. The supernatural, or unseen world, ceaselessly permeated the natural, or seen world. In the next century it became fashionable to ignore or to be amused at belief in the supernatural, and this aspect of Defoe's belief and artistry received little attention and less respect. In the last few decades of the present century, however, it has again become permissible to discuss seriously belief in the supernatural. Few, perhaps, believe in the Devil, and probably even fewer seriously acknowledge the ministry of the blessed angels. But after careful scientific study in England and America by societies for psychical research it has again become possible in scholarly circles to discuss apparitions and other supernormal phenomena.

Apart from *The Apparition of Mrs. Veal,* Defoe's occult writings have never received adequate attention. In 1830 Walter Wilson discussed briefly this aspect of Defoe's mind and art, and some of the later nineteenth century biographers did not altogether ignore it. But in his *Daniel Defoe: Citizen of the Modern World* (1958), John Robert Moore did not see fit to devote even two sentences to the occult books, perhaps because they do not fit in with his thesis of Defoe's modernity. Even more disappointingly, G. A. Starr in his recent *Defoe and Spiritual Autobiography* (1965) has failed to treat seriously this area of Defoe's concern and has not cited a single one of the supernatural works to illuminate the spiritual patterns in Defoe's fiction. On the other hand, in his *Reluctant Pilgrim* (1966), J. Paul Hunter fully recognizes Crusoe's supernatural guidance, but cites only the popular *Apparition of Mrs. Veal* as evidence of Defoe's work in the "spectral" (or occult) tradition. To find a study of the supernatural in Defoe it is necessary to turn abroad—to the quite inadequate article by Defoe's French biographer, Paul Dottin, "Daniel Defoe et les sciences occultes," in the *Revue Anglo-Americaine,* December 1923, or to R. G. Stamm's *Der Aufgeklärte Puritanismus Daniel Defoes* (1936). But these studies do not reveal the complexity and significance of Defoe's occult ideas.

The examination of Defoe and the supernatural demands more than a thorough analysis of these ideas as they are found in the occult works and in the fiction. It demands that some of the occult works hitherto attributed to Defoe be re-examined carefully for evidences of authorship. Such a re-examination shows that several occult works in the Defoe canon—*The Dumb Philosopher, The Life and Adventures of Duncan Campbell,* and *The Friendly Dae-*

mon—were not written by Defoe. The necessity of this re-examination is patent: if Defoe wrote meretricious occult material like *Duncan Campbell*, he was capable of using the supernatural for its sensational appeal, not its spiritual value. He was prostituting his pen to praise and advertise what he was elsewhere attacking as foolish and vicious. Much confusion in Defoe studies has resulted from the too ready acceptance of the traditional attributions made by the Defoe bibliographers, for these attributions would seem to exhibit in Defoe's occult works spiritual principles which are mutually discordant and contradictory. Admittedly Defoe sometimes wrote on both sides of a political issue. But this fact would not justify the assumption that he would risk his soul's salvation by assuming a similar freedom with religious or spiritual issues. When he is exonerated from the charge of writing such work as *Duncan Campbell*, his beliefs in the supernatural assume consistency and cogency.

In the preparation of this study I have been indebted to a number of institutions, librarians, and colleagues. I have enjoyed several travel grants and the University of Georgia provided several quarters free for research. In the final stage of preparation I was encouraged by receiving the Michael Award for research for the academic year 1966–1967. For their assistance I am indebted to the Boston Public Library and Mr. John Alden, Keeper of Rare Books, and Miss Ellen N. Oldham; to the Harvard College Library and especially to Miss Carolyn Jakeman and Miss Anna Marie Decker; to the Barrow Library of the Columbia Theological Seminary; to Mrs. Nancy R. Braun of the Library of the Austin Presbyterian Theological Seminary; to the University of Indiana Library; and to the Library of the University of Georgia, and especially to Mrs. Christine Burroughs and Mr. John Marshall, who helped to secure Defoe materials.

For reading chapters and offering helpful advice I am grateful to my colleagues William Thurman, Robert H. West, and especially the late Edd W. Parks, who generously read the entire book. Mrs. Barbara Sullivan checked through the *Review* for pertinent information; Miss Carla Anderson corrected a number of errors in typing the book; and Aline Everitt Baine eliminated scores of them in various stages of preparation. Most of all, I am indebted to my wife, Mary Rion Baine, for reading typescript, the proof in all its stages, and helping to prepare the index.

I wish to thank the American Philosophical Society for permission to reprint much of my article "Daniel Defoe and *The History and Reality of Apparitions,*" *Texas Studies in Literature and Lan-*

guage for permission to reprint a revised version of "Defoe and the Angels," and *Philological Quarterly* for permission to reprint parts of "Mrs. Bargrave's Story" and for cancelling "Dickory Cronke: the Dumb Philosopher" which had already been typeset so that it could be included here.

Rodney Baine

Texts and Abbreviations

Spelling, capitalization, and punctuation of quotations follow the editions noted. References to Defoe's fiction cite the Shakespeare Head edition published by Blackwell in 1927–1928. Otherwise the standard edition is that printed by Tegg at Oxford in 1840–1841—*The Novels and Miscellaneous Works of Daniel De Foe*. An exception is *The Consolidator*, which is cited in the edition of Henry Morley, in *The Earlier Life and Chief Earlier Works of Daniel Defoe* (London, 1899). For *Serious Reflections of Robinson Crusoe*, including "A Vision of the Angelick World," the edition cited is that of George A. Aitken, in *Romances and Narratives by Daniel Defoe* (London, 1895).

ABBREVIATIONS

CJ   *The History and Remarkable Life of the truly Honourable Col. Jacque.*

CS   *The Life, Adventures, and Pyracies, of the Famous Captain Singleton.*

DC   *The History of the Life and Adventures of Mr. Duncan Campbell.*

FA   *The Farther Adventures of Robinson Crusoe.*

HA   *An Essay on the History and Reality of Apparitions.*

HD   *The Political History of the Devil.*

JP   *A Journal of the Plague Year.*

MF   *The Fortunes and Misfortunes of the Famous Moll Flanders.*

RC   *The Life and Strange Surprizing Adventures of Robinson Crusoe.*

SM   *A System of Magick.*

SR   *Serious Reflections during the Life and Surprizing Adventures of Robinson Crusoe.*

To Aline

Contents

Part One

The Supernatural:
The Real Defoe

Introduction:
Patterns of Providence

IN HIS JOURNAL for July 6, 1781, John Wesley recorded gloomily that "the doctrine of a Particular Providence (and any but a Particular Providence is no Providence at all) is absolutely out of fashion in England."[1] In Defoe's day this doctrine was beginning to weaken; but Puritans like William Turner and the Mathers and Defoe were doing their best to demonstrate its reality, for they had no more doubt of God's special and particular intervention than of his general direction and general providential care.

Throughout the seventeenth century, even the scientists defended this doctrine, "more ready to compromise a scientific principle than to surrender an essential religious belief." Robert Boyle came close to rejecting the belief in a particular providence; and privately Isaac Newton evidently did reject God's immediate and special intervention. But presumably unwilling to disturb popular faith on this point, Newton left it to his successors like Edmund Halley to question the miracles; and even Halley was reverent or circumspect enough to delay publication of his attacks until 1724— far into the eighteenth century.[2] That same year, in his *Discourse of the Grounds and Reasons of the Christian Religion*, Anthony Collins attacked another major evidence of providential intervention, the evidence offered by the scriptural prophecies. Gradually the attacks of freethinkers, deists, and skeptics began to undermine faith. "Whilst belief in the miraculous nature of the Bible history still survived," Leslie Stephen remarked, "belief in the continued agency of the supernatural powers was daily growing fainter."[3]

To combat disbelief in God's intervention, Puritans were on the alert for notable phenomena which could be interpreted as providential mercies or punishments. This pious view of God's intervention permeated Puritan moral and spiritual guidebooks and sermons. As Increase Mather remarked in his *Doctrine of Divine Providence,* "*This subject of* Divine Providence *has been largely and Elaborately handled by others.*"[4] It also prompted collections of accounts which cumulatively proved God's providential direction and care. In his *Of Credulity and Incredulity in Things Natural, Civil, and Divine* (1668), Meric Casaubon remarked, "I wish we had yearly, an account of all memorable things, that happen in this kind, in all parts of England. I doubt not, if performed by such as are creditable, and juditious; but good use might be made of it" (pp. 171–172). In the same year, in his *Blow at Modern Sadducism,* Joseph Glanvill suggested a "*Cautious,* and *Faithful History* made of these *certain* and *uncommon appearances*" (p. 117), a project which was to be realized in *Sadducismus Triumphatus.* Meanwhile, the suggestion had been made and put into practice by Matthew Poole; and Increase Mather evidently used Poole's collection in his own *Essay for the Recording of Illustrious Providences* (1684). Here Mather suggested that he might later "publish a Discourse of *Miscellaneous observations, concerning things rare and wonderful; both as to the works of Creation and Providence.*"[5] Finally, in 1697 the Poole manuscript provided for William Turner a nucleus for his monumental *Compleat History of the most Remarkable Providences,* which enlisted the aid of many Puritan divines and laymen in England and America and reprinted part of Defoe's recent *Essay upon Projects.* As John Ryther remarked in his "Sea-Dangers and Deliverances Improved," "The Lord doth not give us our Deliverances to cast them at our heels, nor brings us out of our Dangers, that we might forget them, as though we never had been in any of them. God expects that we should faithfully Register and Record them. . . ."[6] Defoe himself published a collection in this tradition—*The Storm: or a Collection of the most Remarkable Casualities and Disasters which Happen'd in the Late Dreadful Tempest, both by Sea and Land* (1704). Based largely upon and incorporating reports from clergymen and laymen throughout England concerning the great tempest of 1703, this considerable collection included an extensive section "Of Remarkable Deliverances." The Preface announced the intent of the collection: "*The main Inferences I shall pretend to make or at least venture the exposing to publick View, in this case, is, the strong Evidence God has been pleas'd to give in this terrible manner to his own Being. . . .*"[7]

Defoe's conviction that the supernatural permeates the natural life—that God in his infinite wisdom and through his general and special providence impinges upon, enters into, and guides, or tries to guide man through various ways and that the Devil similarly attempts to assail and seduce him—this conviction is apparent throughout Defoe's writings, especially in the occult works and, most important, in his fiction. In his *Little Review* for August 21, 1705, Defoe at the same time professed his belief in providence and warned against too facile interpretation:

> It has always been the Societies Opinion, That we are by the Error of Custom and Temper, so fond of believing things Supernatural, that are not so, that we make more Miracles in our own mistaken Whymsies, than ever God Almighty works himself.
> At the same time they are far from prescribing this Invisible Power, absolutely to second Causes, and locking up all Supernatural Operations.
> The falling off the Man's Hair at the time of his rash Imprecation, may very well be allow'd to be a Judgment of Providence, to shew the Power of an Invisible Hand, which can take us at our words.[8]

In his autobiographical *Appeal to Honour and Justice* (1715), Defoe demonstrated that he accepted supernatural guidance in the conduct even of his mundane affairs. In 1694, for example, he refused an attractive offer to settle at Cadiz because Providence "placed a secret Aversion in my Mind to quitting *England* upon any account."[9] Time and again, Defoe felt celestial warning or celestial prompting in the conduct of his life.

In Defoe's fiction these patterns of divine providence are manifestly important. Almost at the outset of *Robinson Crusoe* God sends warning to the errant Crusoe, who ignores the monitory implications of "two such visible Instructions as [he says] I had met with in my first Attempt" at seafaring, though his even more hardened companion is concerned: "*Young man, says he, you ought to take this for a plain and visible Token that you are not to be a Seafaring Man.*" The companion "told me [Crusoe explains] I might see a visible Hand of Heaven against me."[10] As J. Paul Hunter has demonstrated in his *Reluctant Pilgrim*, the supernatural furnishes the pattern for the novel. Crusoe's vision of the angel serves as the "pivot"; and "The pattern of the novel is consistent: when Crusoe obeys his supernatural promptings . . . , he progresses toward ultimate deliverance. . . ."[11] In the *Farther Adventures of Robinson Crusoe* an older and wiser protagonist suggests that "as human Prudence has the Authority of Providence to justify it, so it has, doubtless, the Direction of Providence to set it to Work; and would we listen carefully to the Voice of it, I am fully persuaded we might prevent many of the Disasters, which our Lives are now, by our own Negligence, subjected to."[12]

To Defoe's employment of Providence in *Robinson Crusoe*, Charles Gildon strenuously objected: "... I cannot pass in Silence his Coining of Providences; that is, of his making Providence raise a Storm, cast away some Ships, and damage many more, merely to fright him from going to Sea. If this be not a bold Impiety, I know not what it is. . . ."[13] As usual Gildon's attack had no effect upon Defoe. He continued to demonstrate providential intervention in the lives of his later heroes. Thus late in life Colonel Jack is converted by his "tutor" to perceive that Providence has been responsible for the pattern of his career: "It occurr'd to me presently, that if none of all these Things befall us without the Direction of a Divine Power, as my new Instructor had told me at large; and that God had order'd every Thing, the most Minute and least Transaction of Life, insomuch *That not a Hair of our Head shall fall to the Ground without his Permission*, I say, it occurr'd to me, that I had been a most unthankful Dog to that Providence that had done so much for me. . . ." By the end of the story, he maintains, "... in collecting the various Changes and Turns of my Affairs, I saw clearer than ever I had before, how an invincible over-ruling Power, a Hand influenced from above, governs all our Actions of every Kind, limits all our Designs, and orders the Events of every Thing relating to us."[14]

But it is perhaps in the *Journal of the Plague Year* that the pattern of Providence is most frequently felt and most variously apprehended. Defoe's persona, H. F., recognizes that the plague has secondary, physical causes: "... when I am speaking of the Plague, as a Distemper arising from natural Causes, we must consider it as it was really propagated by natural Means, nor is it at all the less a Judgment for its being under the Conduct of humane Causes and Effects; for as the divine Power has form'd the whole Scheme of Nature, and maintains Nature in its Course; so the same Power thinks fit to let his own Actings with Men, whether of Mercy or Judgment, go on in the ordinary Course of natural Causes, and he is pleased to act by those natural Causes as the ordinary Means; excepting and reserving to himself nevertheless a Power to act in a supernatural Way when he sees Occasion. . . ."[15]

H. F. is shocked at those who deny the hand of God in the plague, "making a Jest at me calling the Plague the Hand of God, mocking, and even laughing at the Word Judgment, as if the Providence of God had no Concern in inflicting such a desolate Stroke; and that the People calling upon God, as they saw the Carts carrying away the dead Bodies, was all enthusiastick, absurd, and impertinent" (p. 81). "... I look'd upon this dismal Time to be a particular Season of Divine Vengeance, and that God would, on this Occasion, single out the proper Objects of his Displeasure, in a more special and remarkable Manner, than at another Time; and that, tho' I did not believe that many good People would, and did, fall in the common Calamity, and that it was no certain Rule to judge of the eternal State of any one, by their being distinguish'd in such a Time of general Destruction, neither one Way or other" (pp. 83–84). Yet he finds it difficult to understand how God should spare blasphemers, and he finds it fitting that the plague has not spared any of the astrologers or mountebanks who took advantage of the people's credulity.

Man's duty to heed God's visible signs, Defoe expressed clearly through the persona, H. F. The "best Method" one can take in any important decision in life, he suggests, "especially, if he be one that makes Conscience of his Duty, and would be directed what to do in it, [is] namely, that he should keep his Eye upon the particular Providences that occur at that Time, and look upon them complexly, as they regard one another, and as altogether regard the Question before him, and then I think, he may safely take them for Intimations from Heaven of what is his unquestion'd Duty to do in such a Case . . ." (p. 12).

In determining the course of his own conduct, H. F. heeds seemingly trivial and insignificant events. "It came very warmly into my Mind, one Morning," he relates concerning his leaving or remaining behind in London, "as I was musing on this particular thing, that as nothing attended us without the Direction or Permission of Divine Power, so these Disappointments [at not leaving London] must have something in them extraordinary; and I ought to consider whether it did not evidently point out, or intimate to me, that it was the Will of Heaven I should not go" (p. 12). In addition to these seemingly trivial events, he mentions "the strong impressions which I had on my Mind for staying" and "the Intimations which I thought I had from Heaven" (pp. 14–15). These indications seem to be reinforced when he resorts to bibliomancy.

But Providence works not only by plagues and miracles and portents which the prayerful can perhaps interpret, but by patterns which can be perceived and pointed out for the benefit of the spiritually unperceptive. Especially does God, some thought, use day fatalities to indicate his pleasure or his anger—patterns in coincidence or recurrence of days or places. This was evidently the second type of work from Defoe's pen—his unpublished and now unlocated "Historical Collections; or Memoirs of Passages and Stories Collected from Several Authors. 1682."[16] According to the Reverend John Duncan, it was signed "Bellmour F[oe]." and had been "corrected for the press."[17] It was evidently not extensive. "Should the historical collections be thought worth printing," Duncan wrote to T. Chapman on August 23, 1783, "I have 91. others which have been printed many years ago of the same nature & tendency, & none of which are in the Manuscript, I think—which might be added to the Manuscript to make up the Vol^m. else it will be small." As Dr. John Robert Moore has conjectured, Defoe may have used some of these at the conclusion of his *Memoirs of a Cavalier*, and he may have drawn upon them also for his *Review*. Defoe's first published collection of day fatalities appeared in a series of articles which he published in the *Review* about the same time that he published his *Apparition of Mrs. Veal*—early in July 1706. The evidence that God manifests himself in day fatalities is so powerful, Defoe thought, that to deny it "must be prodigious Hardness, and that Men, that attempt it, must declare War against their own Understandings, when they go about to lessen the invisible Agency of supernatural Operations" (III, 313):

> I place no Extraordinaries upon Days and Hours, Eclipses and Parallels; but I cannot believe, but they are sometimes directed; and I could give such a Train of clashing Hours, concurring Minutes, and the Harmony of Circumstances, both as to Time, Place, and Action, as would make a very pleasing and diverting Account to any body that is curious in these Observations.
>
> I have collected these Coherences back to the Beginning of the Reformation in *England*, and could fill 2 or 3 of these Papers with but a few of them; but 'tis foreign to the purpose, the present Case fills us with just Acknowledgments of the remarkable Circumstance, as to Time.
>
> . . . .
>
> Really, Gentlemen, you that can look neither up nor down for these things, are strangely short-sighted—This can never be human Direction, it must certainly come from God, or Devil; choose you whether; you must give it to one of them, and the Necessity is remarkable. (III, 314–315)

As Defoe remarked in the *Review* for November 19, 1706, ". . . tho' I take great Notice of the Concurrence of Circumstances, and the strange Revolutions of Time, yet does my Observation of Days lead to no Superstition, or at all bind up the Providence of GOD to such Circumstances—" (III, 551).

These patterns are particularly noticeable in *Robinson Crusoe*, and they occur with full force to the repentant Crusoe after his conversion:

> . . . I remember that there was a strange Concurrence of Days in the various Providences which befel me; and which, if I had been superstitiously inclin'd to observe Days as Fatal or Fortunate, I might have had Reason to have look'd upon with a great deal of Curiosity.
>
> First, I had observed that the same Day that I broke away from my Father and my Friends, and ran away to *Hull*, in order to go to Sea, the

same Day afterwards I was taken by the Sallee *Man of War*, and made a Slave.

The same Day of the Year that I escaped out of the wreck of that Ship in *Yarmouth* Roads, that same Day-Year afterwards I made my escape from *Sallee* in the Boat.

The same Day of the Year I was born on, (viz.) the 30*th* of *September*, that same Day I had my Life miraculously saved 26 Year after, when I was cast on Shore in this Island. . . . (I, 153–154)

In the chapter "Of Listening to the Voice of Providence," in *Serious Reflections of Robinson Crusoe* (1720), Crusoe notes the Roman and the Biblical observance of days and animadverts, "I have seen several collections of such things made by private hands, some relating to family circumstances, some to public. . . ." Crusoe then gives several examples of concurrences of days in the Civil War. These he characterizes as "a kind of silent sentence of Providence."[18]

A few years later, Defoe included most of these same examples, along with many others, in the collection with which he ended his *Memoirs of a Cavalier.* Here, after the autobiographical narrative has been completed and the concerns of the Civil War have been settled, the narrator desires to "leave behind me some of my own Remarks and Observations." It is then with eleven pages of day fatalities that the book is concluded, with "Some Minutes too of Circumstances . . . as to the Fatality and Revolution of Days and Times."[19] Defoe was probably the most notable contemporary collector of day fatalities. Though many collected other evidences of providential direction, the main collectors of this type of evidence seem to have been John Gibbon, John Aubrey, William Turner, and Defoe. In 1678 Gibbon published his *Day-Fatality, or Some Observation of Days Lucky and Unlucky.* The augmented 1686 edition John Aubrey incorporated in his *Miscellanies* (1696), adding perhaps half as much again. The Gibbon collection Turner also reprinted, from Aubrey, in his *Compleat History.*[20]

These are all insights into and interpretations of the past. Requesting signs of the future most Christians regarded as an invasion of God's prerogative denied even to the blessed angels. The practice of palmistry, judicial astrology, and other forms of divination Defoe roundly condemned and ridiculed. However, two forms of divination which ordinarily were not practiced professionally, second sight and bibliomancy, occasionally appear uncondemned in Defoe's fiction.[21] From early in the Middle Ages the Bible had been used in the practice of divination—deliberately opening the Bible and relying upon God to direct the fingers and eyes to the appropriate page and verse. Even though various Councils had condemned bibliomancy, some Catholics still practiced it even in Defoe's day, for in 1722, evidently, Bishop De Langle vainly attempted to abolish the practice in the Cathedral of Boulogne.[22] Among the Protestants, for whom the Bible was the sole avenue for the interpretation of God's plan and guidance, bibliomancy also persisted, and was occasionally even defended, despite condemnation by Sir Thomas Browne in his *Pseudodoxia Epidemica, or Vulgar Errors* (1646) and, in Defoe's day, by Thomas Woodcock, or whoever wrote *An Account of Some Passages in the Life of a Private Gentleman.* George Berkeley, first Earl of Berkeley, for example, was "willing to decline superstition upon all occasions." Nevertheless he thought himself "obliged to make use of such a providential piece of Scripture" as he turned to when "Being sick, and under some dejection of spirit, opening my Bible to see what place I could light upon, which might administer comfort to me, casually I fixed upon the sixth of Hosea."[23] But the Private Gentleman could testify to the dangers attending the practice: "when terrible expressions happen'd, or I dip'd upon them, as I did often to my unspeakable Terror: For when I met with them, I was persuaded God pointed to my Fate, so concluded my self under unavoidable Wrath. This is a usual, but dangerous Practice with many on the like Occasion; avoid it therefore as a Snare and a Temptation; Sometimes Success has follow'd, but much oftener it has prov'd pernicious. . . ."[24] Even later, so pious a minister as John Wesley seems to have made frequent recourse to bibliomancy. "Begging God to direct me," he recorded in his Journal for June 6, 1738, "I opened my Testament . . ." (I, 105).

Although bibliomancy was regarded as a superstitious practice, one should not condemn as equally superstitious the conviction that God sometimes directs a seemingly chance hearing, reading, or remembering of a particularly appropriate passage of Scripture. Though John Bunyan did not, at least in his *Grace Abounding to the Chief of Sinners,* exhibit himself as practicing bibliomancy, yet he frequently recalled Biblical passages as personal answers to his problems. Nor should Robinson Crusoe be accused of "biblical lottery" for taking unto himself a passage which he meets soon after his conversion.[25] But after he finds the ominous footprint in the sand, Crusoe does seem to have almost resorted to bibliomancy: "I was guided and encourag'd to pray earnestly to God for Deliverance: When I had done praying, I took up my Bible, and opening it to read, the first Words that presented to me were, *Wait on the Lord, and be of good Cheer, and he shall strengthen thy Heart; wait, I say, on the Lord*: It is impossible to express the Comfort this gave me. In Answer, I thankfully laid down the Book, and was no more sad, at least, not on that Occasion" (I, 182).

As one might expect, Gildon objected strongly to this passage: ". . . he makes a Kind of *Sortes Virgilianae* of the Bible, by making *Crusoe* dip into it for Sentences to his purpose" (p. 104). Perhaps more annoyed than chastened by Gildon's objection, Defoe later made another hero engage in similar practice. In the *Journal of the Plague Year*, when the narrator is undecided as to whether he should remain in London, as he is prompted to do, or leave, as his brother urges, "turning over the Bible, which lay before me, and while my Thoughts were more than ordinarily serious upon the Question, I cry'd out, WELL, *I know not what to do, Lord direct me!* and the like; and at that Juncture I happen'd to stop turning over the Book at the 91*st Psalm*, and casting my Eye on the second Verse, I read on to the 7th Verse exclusive," placing in God trust for deliverance even from the Plague. ". . . From that Moment I resolv'd that I would stay in the Town . . ." (p. 15).

Instead of relying upon any of these forms of divination, Defoe advocated that men should listen for the promptings and hints of the blessed angels, hear and question the apparitions which are not of the Devil, and reject all forms of diabolical communication. In order to make clear Defoe's ideas here, separate chapters delineate his views of the ministry of the blessed angels, the power and temptations of the Devil, and the medium of the apparition, as it was used not only by these angelic powers, but by inferior spirits. Subsequent chapters deal with the two most famous ghost-stories attributed to Defoe, consider his prophecies, and show that he did not write *The Life and Adventures of Duncan Campbell* or any of the Campbell tracts still attributed to him, or *The Dumb Philosopher*. Only after these clarifications are made can the pattern of Defoe's religious thought in the belief and practice of the supernatural emerge clearly in his works, particularly in his fiction.

I | Defoe and the Angels

IT IS NO LONGER NECESSARY or perhaps even proper to apologize for an historical study in angelology. Today even Protestant theology has resumed this study, partly because of the example set by Karl Barth, who in his *Church Dogmatics* devoted to the subject more than a hundred pages. Perhaps the influence of Barth has made the ministry of the angels a more meaningful explanation of some aspects of man's psychic experience than extrasensory perception seems to be. It may, however, come as a mild surprise to find a study in angelology centered upon Daniel Defoe. But the popular portrait of Defoe as the worldly, practical London merchant and political timeserver is best corrected by a study of his occult works, especially of his views of angelic ministry. "A Vision of the Angelick World" was a serious attempt in an increasingly skeptical age to advance angelology as a handmaid to religion. Appended to his *Serious Reflections during the Life and Surprizing Adventures of Robinson Crusoe* in 1720, this tract was certainly free from any meretricious appeal. Indeed so earnest were the *Serious Reflections* and "A Vision" that the publisher, Taylor, could not sell even the first thousand copies, despite the use of Crusoe to popularize old as well as new materials; and evidently no subsequent English edition of *Robinson Crusoe* included the "Vision" until it was reprinted in 1790.[1] Material from the *Serious Reflections* was incorporated in the various condensed versions of *Robinson Crusoe*, but not material from the "Vision." Yet, oddly enough, there were several unabridged editions of the French translation of the "Vision," including a reprinting in the 1787 *Voyages Imaginaires*, two editions of the Dutch translation, and a German translation. Likewise serious and almost as unsuccessful financially was Defoe's *Essay on the History and Reality of Apparitions* (1727), which was centered upon angelology.

An understanding of Defoe's angelology in these two works will help to clarify his religious interests and purposes, purposes which we sometimes only vaguely appreciate or even quite misunderstand when we meet them in *Robinson Crusoe* and the *Farther Adventures of Robinson Crusoe*, in *Moll Flanders*, *The Fortunate Mistress*, and *Captain Singleton*. Such an understanding will reveal a sincere Puritan trying both in his occult works and in his fiction to retain and strengthen all meaningful and credible evidence of Providence, of an invisible world of spirits, and of a communion thereby with God.

During his lifetime Defoe had witnessed the gradual dispelling of legal and philosophical belief in contemporary witchcraft and had, about the turn of the century, seen Balthazar Bekker and Laurent Bordelon, on the Continent, ridiculing belief in apparitions more effectively than Reginald Scot and John Webster (the Puritan) had previously managed to do in England. Though these skeptics did not attack belief in angels *per se*, nevertheless they did discourage too implicit a reliance upon dreams and other angelic agencies; and in 1709 John Trenchard in his *Natural History of Superstition* suggested that all beliefs in such supernatural agencies were delusions. Many Protestants, jealous of any intermediary between God and man, were only too willing to ignore this supernatural ministration. Some divines, like Richard Baxter and Joseph Glanvill, had attempted to rehabilitate all these beliefs, including even that in witchcraft, compiling and publishing evidential accounts and accusing all those who disbelieved of veering toward Sadducism or atheism. In his *Certainty of the Worlds of Spirits* Baxter was concerned "to note how little Sence most Protestants shew of the great Benefits that we receive by Angels: How seldom we hear them in publick or private, give thanks to God for their Ministry and Helps? And more seldom pray for it?" (London, 1691, pp. 222–223). And Glanvill complained, "*Heaven* and *Hell* are become words of sport: and *Devils* and *Angels*, *Fairyes* and *Chimaera's*: 'Tis *Foppish* to *speak* of *Religion*, but in *Railery*. . . ."[2]

Although Milton had seen angelology flourish, discussion in England had gradually languished. Angelology occasionally furnished subjects for a series of sermons, like those of George Bull or Thomas Shepherd; and several works devoted considerable sections to the subject: Richard Baxter's *Certainty of the Worlds of Spirits* (1691), Richard Burthogge's *Essay upon Reason, and the Nature of Spirits* (1694), John Aubrey's *Miscellanies* (1696), William Turner's *Compleat History of the most Remarkable Providences* (1697), and John Beaumont's *Gleanings of Antiquities* (1724). But few books were devoted completely or even largely to angelology. Two tracts developed the subject of guardian angels: the brief, anonymous *Scala Naturae* (1695), defending the theory, and the likewise anonymous and even briefer *Modest Enquiry into the Opinion concerning a Guardian Angel* (1702), possibly a posthumous work by Richard Saunders (d. 1692), or perhaps by George Hamond. If one may begin with an American example by an author well known to Defoe, the major offerings were Increase Mather's *Angelographia, or Discourse of the Holy Angels* (1696), which reprinted some of Mather's sermons on angels and added a disquisition concerning angelical apparitions; Richard Saunders's posthumous *Angelographia, or Discourse of Angels* (1701), edited by George Hamond, the last thorough treatise published in England in the tradition of the previous century; John Beaumont's learned and original, but indiscriminate and credulous *Historical, Physiological and Theological Treatise of Spirits* (1705); and John Reynolds's *Inquiries concerning the State and Oeconomy of the Angelical Worlds* (1723), essentially a theological work which avoids most of the basic questions of angelology and shows little knowledge of the pneumatic tradition.

To these Defoe made a considerable addition, especially with his "Vision of the Angelick World" (1720) and his *History of Apparitions* (1727). The "Vision" is the broader in scope. It develops rather fully the general view of Providence advanced in the chapter "Of Listening to the Voice of Providence," in *Serious Reflections*, and the ideas on angelic communication suggested that same year in three letters written for the *Weekly Journal*.[3] The vision framework itself is of little significance, and it was used for only a sixth of the entire work. It was a favorite device: Defoe had adopted it earlier in his *Consolidator, or Memoir of Sundry Transactions from the World in the Moon* (1705) and, specifically to describe the empire of the Devil, in three successive numbers of *The Review*, from January 11 to January 16, 1711. Here in the "Vision" Defoe employed it for a brief glimpse of the Devil and his work. In the greater part of the tract, however, Defoe discussed the ministry of the angels. Although he made no attempt to illustrate all the media of their communion with man, he did include several, especially those of angelic dreams and promptings, which he himself experienced. In his *History of Apparitions* he developed his theory of beneficent spirits or angels and treated at length his theory of angelical apparitions, including those which appear in dreams. From these sources it is possible to educe an extensive angelology. It resembles in many ways the systems of his predecessors; but it exhibits also many unorthodoxies, and it is striking in its rational control, its dramatic vividness, and its use of personal examples. To discriminate between Defoe's conventionalities and his heterodoxies, we must place his ideas in the context of Protestant angelology of the seventeenth century and against current philosophical and religious thought as it affected these traditional beliefs.

Like most Protestant theologians from John Calvin to Karl Barth, Defoe was often cautious and tentative in his angelology. Moreover he was in 1720 genuinely puzzled concerning some aspects of angelic ministry: ". . . it is not so easy to inquire into the world of spirits," he confessed, "as it is evident that there are such spirits and such a world. We find the locality of it is natural, but who the inhabitants are is a search of still a sublimer nature, liable to more exception, encumbered with more difficulties, and exposed to much more uncertainty."[4] Here Defoe was of course following not merely Calvin, but practically all the Puritan angelologists. In his *Ministration of and Communion with Angels*, for example, Isaac Ambrose had quoted Peter Martyr *"that to enquire of the Angels accurately and subtilly is,* magis ad curiositatem nostram quam ad salutem."[5] In his *Christian Directory* Richard Baxter recommended, " 'Be satisfied in knowing so much of angels as God in nature and Scripture hath revealed; but presume not to inquire further, much less to determine of unrevealed things.' " The anonymous author of *A Modest Enquiry into the Opinion concerning a Guardian Angel* (1702) insisted that such speculation as his must not be allowed "to disturb the Churche's Peace, which is a thing so sacred and inviolable, that all Theories and Speculations ought to yield the greatest deference to it" (p. 1). Even in our own day Karl Barth has warned, "The dogmatic sphere which we have to enter and traverse in this section is the most remarkable and difficult of all," and he cautiously entitled his discussion of angels "The Limits of Angelology."[6]

The distinction between good and evil angels Defoe kept quite clear. ". . . The word angel is to be understood of good angels," he explained; "for the devils . . . are also angels: Satan is called an angel of light; but the evil angels I shall always treat with their new surname, devil; so that when I speak of angels I am always to be understood of the good angels."[7] In his angelology Defoe consistently observed this distinction between good and evil angels; and he devoted to the Devil his quite separate and distinct treatment in *The Political History of the Devil* and its sequel *A System of Magick* (both 1726). Thus it is convenient to follow his own separate treatment and to discuss here only the nature and ministry of the blessed angels.

In their consideration of angelic order, or hierarchy, almost all the Protestant theologians attacked the scholastic angelology based upon Dionysius the Areopagite. "It must needs disgust a sober Man," commented George Bull from his pulpit, "to read the many nice and idle Questions they [the Catholic schoolmen] have started, and taken a great deal of Pains to resolve."[8] Some Protestants insisted that all angels of whatever rank are ministering spirits, subject to dispatch to this world upon God's commands.[9] Others thought that the higher orders remain in the presence of the Most High and that only the subordinate orders are sent to this world. But practically all of them admitted that some sort of order must exist among the angels—and here the doctrine of Divine Plenitude operated—for few were Levellers of angels.[10]

On this point Defoe's angelology shows an interesting development. In 1720, in the "Vision," he had taken considerable pains to explain the apparent ineffectiveness of angelic ministry—in man's failure to understand and heed angelic warnings. Defoe was troubled, later, to account for the frequency and ineffectiveness of benign apparitions; and in his *History of Apparitions* he adopted a theory of intermediate spirits, not immediately heavenly. This spiritual communion could not be diabolical in origin, since it was benign; and only on extraordinary occasions could it be angelical, according to Protestant theology, for the Gospel had largely replaced angelic apparitions and the persisting type of ministry was usually ineffectual and thus imperfect. Citing as his precedent the adoption of the New Philosophy to replace the cumbersome Ptolemaic system by its greater efficacy and ease in explaining observed phenomena, Defoe suggested a theory of intermediate spirits: "Is it at all irrational to suppose, or improbable to be," he asked, "that God may have made a degree of angels or of ministering spirits (whether they are angelic, or of another species, is not for us to determine) who may be of a differing degree, appointed for a differing residence, and to different employments from the superior angels, for a season?" (p. 55). Concerning their origin and nature he remained, however, tentative and cautious: ". . . there are a certain middle species of spirits in being; let them be what they will, let them be employed, directed, limited, and restrained, how and in what manner he pleases who is their Maker, and who ought to be their guide and director . . ." (p. 74).

Although in some ramifications of these suggestions of intermediate spirits Defoe was unorthodox, many angelologists, strictly Puritan as well as Neo-Platonic, had suggested the communion of benign spirits not immediately heavenly in their origin. Defoe was certainly not identifying them with the "fairies, nymphs and spirits of the Gentiles," which, as Miss Briggs has pointed out, were widely regarded as "an intermediate creation between humanity and pure spirits, of an ethereal body."[11] Nor was he borrowing them from the earthly spirits of Cornelius Agrippa, though the Defoe-Farewell Library included copies of *De Occulta Philosophia* and *The Vanity of the Arts and Sciences*.[12] Defoe may have developed his theory from the suggestions of Joseph Glanvill and Henry More. Some benign communications, Glanvill thought, though not "*immediately* from *Heaven*, or from the *Angels*, by *extraordinary Commission* and *Appointment*," doubtless emanate from these good Genii.[13] Why, Glanvill asked, "should they not believe that the *Air* and all the *Regions* above us, may have their *invisible intellectual Agents*, of *nature* like unto our *Souls*, be *that* what it will; and some of them at least as much *degenerate* as the *vilest* and most *mischievous* among *Men*. This *Hypothesis* will be enough to secure the *possibility* of *Witches* and *Apparitions*." These spirits, More agreed, are "the benign Eyes of God, running to and fro in the world, with love and pity beholding the innocent endeavours of harmless and single-hearted men, ever ready to do them good, and to help them."[14] Increase Mather seems at times to have agreed, though Mather found it "not easy to determine of what sort those *Genii* are."[15]

In the "Vision" Crusoe places the abode of the angels conventionally: "infinitely higher" than the evil spirits of the air (p. 274). In the *History of Apparitions* the abode of the angels is still Heaven, but that of the spirits "the unknown mazes of the invisible world, those coasts which our geography cannot describe" (p. 4), but which is elsewhere identified as the solar system, where they are "placed by their merciful Maker as an advanced body" for our protection (p. 179). They must indeed exist in a place, Defoe agreed with the pneumatologists, for otherwise they would be omnipresent.

But neither angels nor spirits are, he thought, corporeal. Like Baxter and many other Protestants, he preferred to avoid controversy on this point. In 1704, moreover, not well grounded in pneumatics, he had been quite unconvincing in a discussion of spirit.[16]

But in the *History of Apparitions* Defoe aligned himself with the philosophers like LeClerc and contemporary angelologists like Shepherd against Milton and many other Protestant predecessors. He maintained quite firmly, ". . . bodies they are not, and cannot be, neither had they been ever embodied. . ." (p. 36). But a spirit "may assume shape, may vest itself so with flesh and blood, that is seemingly, so as to form an appearance" (p. 31).

Concerning the freedom and independence with which angels or spirits act, Defoe was inconsistent and sometimes vague. At times he stated, conventionally, that the angels act only as God directs: ". . . as we may have reason to believe that they all act by commission, it is also most certain that they cannot go an inch, no, not an hair's breadth beyond that commission . . . and thence we are to infer that they do not give further or more frequent notices to us, because they are not permitted. . ." (*HA*, p. 261). Even the intermediate spirits "do heaven's work, are under his immediate government and direction, and are honoured with his special commission" (p. 53). But Defoe introduced this subordinate species into his angelology partly to explain why, acting on their own initiative, spirits sometimes fail in their purposes, as, he felt, they would not do if they were acting at God's proper command. Thus in the "Vision" he had a friendly clergyman, in answering some of Crusoe's doubts, suggest that the angels might be left relatively free, that "spirits unembodied had it left to them to converse as they thought fit, how, where, and with whom they would" (p. 257). In the *History of Apparitions* he several times reiterated this suggestion: ". . . they are free agents, as well in their motions as actings" (*HA*, p. 60). He evidently felt that if the intermediate spirits were free to act upon their own initiative, the inadequacy of their performance would not reflect upon Divine Providence. These spirits might do good "with a sort of an imperfection and manifest debility; so as sometimes to act, as it were, to no purpose; being not able to make the good they aim at effectual, and therefore cannot be from heaven" (p. 32). Perhaps Defoe came nearest to reconciling his divergent positions in this compromise: ". . . though these spirits may have leave to give such notice and such warnings to some particular persons for the saving their lives, yet we are not to suppose it is placed in their power to contravene the determination of Heaven, and to act contrary to appointments of his providence, especially in things of general import . . ." (p. 261).

Doubtless because of his view that angels are now denied freedom to warn communities of general dangers, Defoe had "H. F.," his persona of the *Journal of the Plague Year*, reject as hypochondriac or spurious all the alleged angelic warnings of the coming plague, whether delivered by angelic apparition, dream, voice, or professional conjurer.

> Next to these publick Things, were the Dreams of old Women: Or, I should say, the Interpretation of old Women upon other Peoples Dreams; and these put abundance of People even out of their Wits: Some heard Voices warning them to be gone, for that there would be such a Plague in *London,* so that the Living would not be able to bury the Dead: Others saw Apparitions in the Air; and I must be allow'd to say of both, I hope with out breach of Charity, that they heard Voices that never spake, and saw Sights that never appear'd; but the Imagination of the People was really turn'd wayward and possess'd: And no Wonder, if they, who were poreing continually at the Clouds, saw shapes and Figures, Representations and Appearances, which had nothing in them, but Air and Vapour. . . .
> . . . One time . . . I join'd with them to satisfy my Curiosity, and found them all staring up into the Air, to see what a Woman told them appeared plain to her, which was an Angel cloth'd in white, with a fiery Sword in his Hand, waving it, or brandishing it over his Head. . . . I look's as earnestly as the rest, but, perhaps, not with so much Willingness to be impos'd upon; and I said indeed, that *I could see nothing,* but a white cloud, bright on one side, by the shining of the Sun upon the other Part. (pp. 26–27)

In his view that angels are for individual men sometimes allowed freedom of action, Defoe was unorthodox, for Protestants held that angels act only as God's messengers or agents, not as independent beings. Hardly ever did the discussion of their freedom involve anything but their freedom to sin. In theory they may be free, but not to act independently. Increase Mather was in his *Angelographia* very clear on this point: "The Angels are not at their own Dispose, but follow the direction of the Eternal Spirit . . ." (p. 19). And Shepherd was even more specific: "The greatest Angel in Heaven does nothing of his own head, but acts as he is sent forth and commissioned by Jesus Christ . . .: They see many things out of order here, that need their helping Hand; yet do nothing till they have advices and directions from Heaven. . . ." But perhaps Defoe had at least an implied precedent in the theory that guardian angels, whom Shepherd would not even recognize, are delegated some initiative in guarding their charges. Moreover, Glanvill again furnished a precedent. These spirits, according to Glanvill, evidently possess a measure of free will: ". . . it seems to me not unreasonable to believe, that *those officious spirits* that oversee our affairs, perceiving some *mighty and sad alterations* at hand, in which their *Charge* is much concerned, cannot chuse, by reason of their *affection* to us, but give us some *seasonable hints* of these *approaching Calamities . . .*" (*Blow,* pp. 56–57). Glanvill was not alone. In his *Antidote against Atheism* Henry More had already made a similar suggestion; and Hallywell re-echoed More and Glanvill. Richard

Baxter (*Certainty*, p. 4) accepted the possibility, and Thomas Tryon used the theory to explain premonitions of approaching death.[17]

The angels are endowed by God with comprehensive knowledge, and from Him they receive divine illumination. According to Defoe, they possess "vast capacious understanding" and "extensive knowledge"; "they are necessarily to be supposed to know all things needful to be known, relating to us, as well as to other things; . . . they can take cognizance of human affairs . . . by their own angelic and spirituous penetration" (*HA*, pp. 59–60). Protestant theologians agreed that although the angels are not omniscient, they know everything which happens on earth and within the universe, that by their long experience they are very skillful in predicting future contingencies based upon natural law, but that they do not know the heart of man—his "thoughts, affections, or desires"—except by God's illumination or by inferences drawn from man's actions, his features, and his fancy, or imagination, to which faculty they have access.[18]

Not only are the angels vastly superior to man in knowledge and understanding; according to Defoe, they possess foreknowledge. Here especially Defoe was unorthodox. Satan, he held, has no power to know the future, except that his predictions prove more probable than do ours. But even the intermediate spirits evince this power. In the *Review* for May 18, 1706, he had been hesitant on this point: "I should perhaps yet doubt their being able to foretell," he wrote, "what shall come to pass for the future" (III, 240). But in the "Vision" Crusoe is quite certain of angelic foresight: the angels "foresee what concerns us"; there are "undeniable testimonies that they [warnings] proceed from some being, intelligent of those things that are at hand, while they are yet to come" (pp. 282, 284–285). And Crusoe narrates an incident to demonstrate the peril with which one ignores such intimations (pp. 285–286). In his *History of Apparitions* Defoe frequently reiterated this doctrine. "Now by what agency must it be that we have directions for good or foreboding thoughts of mischief which attend us, and which it is otherwise impossible we should know anything of, if some intelligent being who can see into futurity had not conveyed the apprehensions into the mind, and had not caused the emotion which alarms the soul?"[19]

Concerning the foreknowledge of the angels, orthodox Christian doctrine sternly denied any such possibility, except as the future was revealed to the angels by God. Popular belief still credited oracles, soothsayers, and fortune tellers with somehow coming at the knowledge of the future, though it was not always clear by what agency. At the head of his section on prophecies, John Aubrey translated Cicero's *De Divinatione*: "I know of no Country either so Polished and Learned, or so Rude, Barbarous and Unciviliz'd, but what always allowed that some particular Persons are gifted with an insight into Futurity, and are endued with a Talent of Prediction."[20] But whatever may have been true of divine prophecies and angelic warnings in the past, orthodoxy taught, these were now ceased or were so rare as to constitute modern miracles. The oracles had been discredited by Van Dale, Fontenelle, and Bekker. As Heywood stated, angels

> . . . understand no further than reveal'd
> By the Creator: else 'tis shut and seal'd.[21]

Nevertheless some Christian angelologists allowed an insight into futurity. Although John Beaumont generally gave credit for enlightenment to his genii, in his *Treatise of Spirits* he suggested that "the Imaginative Faculty comes sometimes to the Knowledge of future things." And in his *Gleanings of Antiquities* he approached the parapsychological theory of preperception, of the power of the sensitive mind sometimes to foresee the future: "And as common Dreams, according to what many Persons may observe in themselves, often carry in them a prophetick Energy, so that what they dream comes to pass; so it's no wonder, if in this extatick State of Dreaming (during which the Astral Impulses are incomparably stronger than in common Dreams, or in the ordinary Course of Life) that prophetick Energy more efficaciously exerts itself, so that Persons then, both sleeping and waking, surprizingly see, foresee, and predict what the Mind of Man in a common state cannot bear to."[22] Such a theory Crusoe specifically rejects in the "Vision" (p. 288). Heydon thought that the withdrawn mind is sometimes enlightened by God or the angels with premonitions of the future; and Shepherd thought that angels "know many things to come, tho' not all, there are some *Arcana Divinii Imperii*, some Secrets which God keeps lock'd up."[23] Glanvill, however, in *Sadducismus Triumphatus*, is once again nearer Defoe: "For if it be supposed, that there is a Sort of Spirits over us, and about us, who can give a probable Guess at the more *remarkable Futurities*, I know not why it may not be conjectur'd, that the Kindness they have for us, and the Appetite of foretelling strange Things, and the putting the World upon Expectation, which we find is very grateful to our own Natures, may not incline them also to give us some general Notice of those uncommon Events which they foresee. And yet I perceive no Reason why we have to fancy, that whatever is done in this kind, must needs be *immediately* from *Heaven*, or from the *Angels*, by extraordinary *Commission* and *Appointment*" (p. 28).

Much more important for our understanding than the nature of the angels is their function—the modes of their ministry. For it was in demonstration rather than in theory that Defoe was interested. The function of the angels of whatever rank, Defoe agreed with all the authorities, Catholic and Protestant alike, is twofold, worship and service of God. Concerning their worship he had nothing to say; he was concerned rather with the reality and implications of angelic ministry.

Concerning one particular aspect of angelic ministry—the question of the guardian angel—there was agreement only among the Catholics. Noel Taillepied, for example, asserted dogmatically, "All the Fathers and Catholic Doctors are of the same opinion, and thus disprove the blind errors of Bodin and his *Demonomania* and Calvin in his *Harmonie.* . . , who are both audacious enough to write that it is not certain that each man has a Guardian angel."[24] In his *Consolidator* Defoe himself seemed rather inclined to accept the theory of the guardian angel: "Nor can I see a reason why embodying a spirit should altogether interrupt its converse with the world of spirits from whence it was taken; and to what else shall we ascribe guardian angels, in which the Scripture is also plain? And from whence come secret notices, impulse of thought, pressing urgencies of inclination to or from this or that, altogether involuntary, but from some waking kind assistant wandering spirit, which gives secret hints to its fellow-creatures of some approaching evil or good which it was not able to foresee."[25] By the time he wrote his "Vision," however, he had evidently rejected individual assignment of guardian angels; and in his *History of the Devil* he was outspoken on this point: ". . . as to this story of good and evil angels attending every particular person, it is a good allegory, indeed . . . ; but as to the rest, the best thing I can say of it is, that I think it is a fib."[26] Again in his *History of Apparitions* he condemned the idea of individual assignment but commended the general principle: "Thus they are guardian angels really, and in the very letter of it, without being obliged to attend at every particular man's ear or elbow. Mankind are thus truly said to be in the hands of God always; and Providence, which constantly works by means and instruments, has the government of the world actually in his administration, not only by his infinite power, but by immediate deputation, and the subdued Devil is a prisoner of war both chained and restrained" (p. 58).

On this point of the individual guardian angel the Protestants were not nearly so united in opposition to Catholic doctrine as is sometimes contended. Some Protestants, like Reginald Scot, Samuel Freeman, and Thomas Shepherd, did oppose the doctrine; and Benjamin Camfield was "dubious." Others, like Joseph Hall, Joseph Glanvill, and John Reynolds left it a matter of uncertainty. But still others, like Henry Lawrence and Increase Mather, thought such guardianship probable; and many definitely accepted the doctrine: John Salkeld, John Pordage, Henry Hallywell, Robert Dingley, John Heydon, Matthew Smith, Mrs. Chudleigh, and John Beaumont.[27] *A Modest Enquiry into the Opinion concerning a Guardian Angel*, a brief Protestant tract of 1702, undertook to prove the ministry of guardian angels from reason, Scripture, the doctrines of philosophers and the Church Fathers, and "some credible Stories of Relations" (p. 10).

In their ministry the angels, Defoe thought, do not intervene physically to alter the course of nature. In the *History of Apparitions* he stated that the angels "cannot act so upon material objects, as to interfere with our affairs, overrule our fate" (p. 60). But God may use angelic ministry to utilize physical phenomena, "may appoint instructions to be given by fortuitious accidents, and may direct concurring circumstances to touch and affect the mind as much and as effectually as if they had been immediate and miraculous" ("Vision," p. 313). The story which Crusoe tells to illustrate—how a seemingly supernatural warning reforms two members of an Atheistical Club at Oxford—provides the main dramatic incident of the "Vision." Like many of the other examples in the "Vision" and the *History of Apparitions*, this story Defoe evidently had first-hand.[28]

The physical extent to which angels intervene in their ministry was not generally agreed upon by Protestant theologians in Milton's day. Some divines placed angelic ministry entirely upon a spiritual plane, and indeed most emphasized this aspect of their service. For Lawrence angelic ministry comprised instruction, admonition, and encouragement. But Isaac Barrow included also such physical activity as protecting man from danger, rescuing him from mischief, and aiding him in his undertakings.[29] Baxter and many others agreed that the angels are concerned about and active in all the affairs of our daily lives.

But there was a shift of opinion during Defoe's lifetime away from the belief in direct, physical intervention. It was a common belief among many Protestants like Joseph Hall that angels are able to control the forces of nature, in Addisonian imagery to "ride in the whirlwind and direct the storm"; and even in the eighteenth century Shepherd could still maintain that the angels "Purvey and Cater for us."[30] But the advance of science—especially the work of the Royal Society and the growth of meteorology—dampened the enthusiasm of dissenters after Richard Baxter, Robert Wodrow, William Turner, Matthew Poole, and the Mathers from collecting physical data exhibiting God's providential care. Moreover in the very year which saw the publication of the *History of Apparitions* (1727) Thomas Woolston began his shocking attack upon the miracles of Christ (a mainstay to demonstrate God's Providence). As contraventions of natural order Woolston found them unbelievable, but accepted them as allegories. A position which was perhaps generally acceptable was that stated in the anonymous *Devils of Delphos, or the Prophets of Baal* (1708), a copy of which was in the Defoe-Farewell Library: "It is indeed credible, that this Order is never broke, by the Angels, but by the Command and peculiar Permission of God. For it wou'd be unworthy its Author to have that Order most wisely establish'd by the Supream Lord of all Things, rashly, and frequently chang'd by his Creature" (p. 81).

Instead of violating the order of nature, Defoe thought, angels center their ministry upon the mind and soul of men by apparition, voice, dream, and other, even more subtle media. Concerning apparitions as a medium of angelic ministry, Crusoe is undecided in the *Farther Adventures of Robinson Crusoe*: "For my Part, I know not to this Hour, whether there are any such Things as real Apparitions, Spectres . . . (*FA*, II, 112). Later, as narrator in Defoe's "Vision of the Angelick World," Crusoe refuses to discuss apparitions, partly because so much discredit attached to unauthenticated collections of ghost and apparition stories. Moreover, "the glorious angels of heaven are very seldom allowed, at least not lately, to appear in the glorious forms they formerly took, or, indeed, in any form, or with a voice" (pp. 249, 274). To demonstrate his own reliability as an authority on the occult, Crusoe employs the standard technique of the apparition writer by admitting that most apparently occult phenomena are the result of hypochondria or delusion, and he cautions his readers specifically against accepting too readily just any apparitional evidence. "I must be allowed to leave this where I find it," Crusoe comments. "There are some difficulties which I am not yet got over in it . . . and shall not venture to decide it without more certainty than I am yet arrived to" (p. 293). Seven years later, in his *History of Apparitions*, Defoe got over this difficulty by means of his intermediate spirits, and the angelic apparition became for him an important medium of angelic communication: "almost all real apparitions are of friendly and assisting angels," Defoe assured, "and come of a kind and beneficent errand to us" (p. x). To illustrate the frequency and importance of this medium Defoe offered dozens of examples from Biblical, classical, and fresh, contemporary sources. Several of these accounts came from the percipient himself, and they are related with a scrupulous care for accuracy and a dramatic vividness which have made several of them, like the *Apparition of Mrs. Veal*, classic examples of apparitions.

Only one example of an apparition seems to have come from Defoe's own experience, from his earlier, mercantile years; and this apparition of the living, of his apprentice Beacon,[31] evidently seemed to Defoe so meaningless at the time that he did not seriously consider all the implications of this sort of evidence until he came to reflect upon the incident (in *HA*, pp. 167–171) after publishing his "Vision" in 1720. Upon deliberation, Defoe decided that the weight of testimony in all ages, of reliable and well-known men in his own day, of his own acquaintances, and of his own eyes constituted an overpowering attestation of this form of spiritual communion. He was by this time convinced that the ghosts of the departed do not return or, like that of Mrs. Veal, pause in transit. Moreover he was, like most other Protestants, reluctant to give credit to contemporary angelical apparitions.[32] But since most apparitional communications are benign in intention and effect, he was thus forced to evolve a theory of friendly angelic apparitions which emanate neither from the departed nor immediately from Heaven.

According to the "Vision," angelical communication is managed by voices, noises, dreams, impulses, hints, and apprehensions (p. 249). The only "angelic" voice heard in the "Vision" is the spurious one which converts the Oxford atheists. Less than a year and a half later, however, Defoe used such a voice in *Moll Flanders*. After Moll and her favorite husband, James, separate, Moll is almost frantic with grief. ". . . After Dinner I fell into a violent Fit of Crying," she recalls, "every now and then, calling him by his Name, which was *James; O Jemy!* said I, *come back, come back, I'll give you all I have; I'll beg, I'll starve with you. . . .*" When they meet again, Moll relates, "I told him how I had pass'd my time, and how loud I had call'd him to *come back again*: he told me he had heard me very plain upon *Delamere Forest*, at a Place about 12 Miles off: *I smil'd*: Nay says he, *Do not think I am in Jest, for if ever I heard your Voice in my Life, I heard you call me aloud, and sometimes I thought I saw you running after me*; Why said I, what did I say? for I had not nam'd the Words to him, *you call'd aloud*, says *he, and said*, O Jemy! O Jemy! come back, come back."[33] This episode Defoe surely did not intend to be merely a supernatural sauce to season Moll, to make her more palatable to the squeamish taste. Nor did he use it merely to indicate spiritual sensitivity in both Moll and James, the greater of course in the highwayman, though the incident does perform this function and would doubtless to the modern reader serve as an interesting anticipation of extrasensory perception. But for Defoe and for many of his readers the incident evidently suggested angelic concern for Moll, concern based upon angelic foresight of the life in store for her after her separation from her Jemy. Since a number of writers, like Aubrey, Turner, Mather, and Beaumont, gave examples of communion with the invisible world by means of voices, the contemporary reader would not have found in the incident in *Moll Flanders* an inexplicable novelty, as readers today doubtless find it.[34]

The dream as a medium of angelic communication most Protestant theologians found quite unexceptionable. Moses Amyraldus had devoted a book to the analysis of divine, angelic, and natural dreams, and the work had been translated in 1676. Already, in 1658, Philip Goodwin had published his *Mystery of Dreams, Historically Discoursed*. Ambrose discussed this medium at some length. George Bull himself experienced such dreams. Saunders believed that now that apparitions and voices were no longer the usual media of angelic communication, "they reveal things to Men in *Dreams*." John Beaumont devoted a considerable chapter to dreams and suggested that his own genii would communicate with him only when, on their instructions, he went to sleep.[35]

In the *Review* for May 17, 1711, Defoe was reluctant to emphasize the medium of the angelic dream: "I might descend to Dreams—," he suggested hesitantly. "But I refrain this, purely on account of the poor distemper'd People, who running into the other Extreme, are always Dreaming and Interpreting—And even Dream they are Dreaming, till they disorder their Heads, and the Heads of those about them, whose Errors, however I pity, yet I cannot from thence reject all the warnings God is pleasd to give us in the Visions of the Night—" (VIII, 96).

Angelic ministration through the medium of dream is especially important, however, in both the "Vision" and the *History of Apparitions*. It is indeed the very first medium which Crusoe discusses; and Defoe had him devote to it considerable space and dramatize his implications through an argument between a layman and a clergyman (pp. 250–258). Although no personal examples appear in the "Vision," Defoe had Crusoe comment, "If I may speak my own experience, I must take leave to say, that I have never had any capital mischief befall me in my life but I have had notice of it by a dream . . ." (p. 251). In the *History of Apparitions* Defoe included many examples, some of them probably from his own experience. Unmistakably autobiographical is the dream which warned him of impending arrest after he had published his *Shortest Way with the Dissenters*. The account he presented as a "relation of fact, which also I take upon me to vouch the reality of, having been present, at the very instant, of every part of it" (*HA*, p. 219). "The night before he had appointed to come to London . . .," Defoe wrote, "being in bed with one Mr. R—[obert] D—[avis], he dreamed that he was in his lodgings at London, where he had been concealed as above, and in his dream he saw two men come to the door, who said they were messengers, and produced a warrant from the secretary of state to apprehend him, and that accordingly they seized upon and took him" (*HA*, p. 220). Awaking, the percipient aroused his brother-in-law and related the dream, but, calmed, was persuaded to go back to sleep. The dream then recurred exactly as before, and "he saw the very men that apprehended him, their countenances, clothes, weapons, &c., and described them in the morning to his said brother, D—, in all the particulars." In spite of this reiterated warning, however, the narrator persisted in ignoring it, "and the next morning was taken by the messengers, just in the very manner as he had been told in his dream, and the very same two men whose faces he had seen, and with the same clothes on, and weapons, exactly as he had described" (pp. 221, 222).

In Defoe's fiction, angelic dreams are surprisingly frequent. In *Captain Singleton* he seems to have employed angelic ministry by dream for merely worldly purposes. After the Quaker William and the cockswain both dream the same night that enormous wealth awaits them if they will only put ashore on Madagascar, William importunes the skeptical Singleton, who records,

> His Dream was, he said, that he went on Shore with 30 Men, of which the Cockswain he said was one, upon the Island, and that they found a Mine of Gold, and enrich'd them all; but this was not the main thing he said, but that the same Morning he had dreamt so, the Cockswain came to him just then, and told him, that he dreamt he went on Shore on the Island of *Madagascar*, and that some Men came to him and told him, they would shew him where he should get a Prize would make them all rich. The upshot of the adventure of course bears out the veridity of the dreams and justifies the Quaker's comment: ". . . *my Dream is fully made good, and the Cockswain's too.*"[36]

Angelic dreams in *Robinson Crusoe* are more frequent and varied. Obviously benign and supernatural is a monitory dream

27

which Crusoe has after a very agitating experience. He is careful first to explain that the dream could not be natural in origin:

> ... one would have thought, I should have dream'd of it: But I did not, nor of any Thing relating to it; but I dream'd, that as I was going out in the Morning as usual from my Castle, I saw upon the Shore, two *Canoes,* and eleven Savages coming to Land, and that they brought with them another Savage, who they were going to kill, in Order to eat him; when on a sudden, the Savage that they were going to kill jumpt away, and ran for his Life; and I thought in my Sleep, that he came running into my little thick Grove, before my Fortification, to hide himself; and that I seeing him alone, and not perceiving that the other sought him that Way, show'd my self to him, and smiling upon him, encourag'd him; that he kneel'd down to me, seeming to pray me to assist him; upon which I show'd my Ladder, made him go up, and carry'd him into my Cave, and he became my Servant. . . . (*RC,* I, 230)

This dream, calculated for Crusoe's personal safety and eventual escape, is realized a year and a half later, though not precisely as dreamed. When Friday gets away from his captors, Crusoe records, "I was dreadfully frighted, (that I must acknowledge) when I perceived him to run my Way; and especially, when as I thought I saw him pursued by the whole Body, and now I expected that part of my Dream was coming to pass, and that he would certainly take shelter in my Grove; and I could not depend by any means upon my Dream for the rest of it, (*viz.*) that the other Savages would not pursue him thither, and find him there" (I, 234). Not fatalistic, Crusoe kills one pursuer and helps to turn back the others.

Obviously angelic is the dream apparition which visits the hardened Crusoe on June 27 with a far more important mission—the salvation of his soul:

> ... In this second Sleep, I had this terrible Dream.
>
> I thought, that I was sitting on the Ground on the Outside of my Wall, where I sat when the Storm blew after the Earthquake, and that I saw a Man descend from a great black Cloud, in a bright Flame of Fire, and light upon the Ground: He was all over as bright as a Flame, so that I could but just bear to look towards him; his Countenance was most inexpressibly dreadful, impossible for Words to describe: when he stepp'd upon the Ground with his Feet, I thought the Earth trembl'd, just as it had done before in the Earthquake, and all the Air look'd, to my Apprehension, as if it had been fill'd with Flashes of Fire.
>
> He was no sooner landed upon the Earth, but he moved forward towards me, with a long Spear or Weapon in his Hand, to kill me; and when he came to a rising Ground, as some Distance, he spoke to me, or I heard a Voice so terrible, that it is impossible to express the Terror of it; all that I can say I understood, was this, *Seeing all these Things have not brought thee to Repentence, now thou shalt die:* At which Words, I thought he lifted up the Spear that was in his Hand, to kill me.

This angelic ministry marks the turning point in Crusoe's spiritual history.[37] ". . . Conscience that had slept so long," Crusoe comments, "begun to awake . . ." (I, 100, 103).

A somewhat similar monitory dream Colonel Jacque experiences one night after a successful haul, near the close of his criminal career:

> . . . at last being overcome with Sleep, I drop'd, but was immediately rous'd with Noise of People knocking at the Door, as if they would beat it down, and crying and calling out to the People of the House, rise, and let in the Constable here, we come for your Lodger in the Garret.
>
> I WAS frighted to the last Degree, and started up in my Bed; but when I was awake, I heard no Noise at all, but of two *Watch-men* thumping at the Doors with their Staves, and giving the Hour past Three o'Clock, and a rainy wet Morning, *for such it was*: I was very glad when I found it was but a Dream, and went to Bed again, but was soon rouz'd a second Time, with the same, very same Noise, and Words: Then being sooner awak'd than I was before, I jump'd out of Bed, and run to the Window, and found it was Just an Hour more, and the *Watch-men* were come about past Four o'Clock, and they went away again very quietly; so I lay me down again, and slept the rest of the Night quietly enough.
>
> I LAID no Stress upon the Thing call'd a Dream, neither till now did I understand that Dreams were of any Importance. . . . (*CJ*, I, 87–88)

That morning, however, he finds that his "old Comrade and Teacher" in crime has been apprehended and carried to Newgate Prison, and soon afterwards Jacque himself is arrested and carried before a Justice. The monitory dream in particular and the experience which it illuminates soon lead him to renounce his career of theft.

Regarding hints, or impulses as a medium of angelic ministry, there was perhaps less agreement among angelologists, for obviously it would be difficult to weigh these hints and to ascertain their origin. George Bull, however, set great store by such impulses: "We may trace the Footsteps of this secret Providence over us in many Instances. . . . How often may we have observ'd strong, lasting, and irresistible Impulses upon our Minds, to do certain things we can scarce for the present tell why or wherefore? The Reason and good Success of which we afterwards plainly see. So on the contrary, there are oft-times sudden and unexpected Accidents, as we call them, cast in our way to divert us from certain Enterprizes we are just ready to engage in, the ill Consequence whereof we do afterwards, but not *till then* apprehend. . . . *How strange many times are our present Thoughts and Suggestions in sudden and surprizing Dangers!*"[38]

Here perhaps best of all one can perceive Defoe's intense conviction of supernatural ministry. The extent to which Defoe himself let his critical decisions be guided by these hints and aversions appears perhaps earliest in his rejection of a lucrative post in Cadiz: "Misfortunes in Business having unhing'd me from Matters of Trade, it was about the Year 1694 when I was invited by some Merchants, with whom I had corresponded abroad, and some also at home, to settle at *Cadiz*, in *Spain*, and that with Offers of very good Commissions, but Providence, which had other Work for me to do, placed a secret Aversion in my Mind to quitting *England* upon any account, and made me refuse the best Offers of that kind. . . ."[39]

At least as early as *The Consolidator* he was advocating that we listen to this voice: "And what if I should say that the notices of these things are not only frequent, but constant, and require nothing of us but . . . to keep our eyes, our ears, and our fancies open to the hints, and observe them?"[40]

In course of a discussion concerning his *British Visions*, Mr. Review, in his issue for May 17, 1711, states fully his belief in angelic hints:

> I firmly believe, and have had such convincing Testimonies of it, that I must be a confirm'd Atheist if I did not—A Converse of Spirits, I mean between those unimbodied, and those call'd Soul, or incas'd in Flesh—Whether the first Act in their Pre-existent State, or otherwise, I think (and am thankful for it) is as needless, as it is impossible to know; but that such a Converse of Spirits is in Nature, I say, I am fully satisfy'd; from whence *else* come all these private Notices, strong Impulses, pressings of Spirit, involuntary Joy, Sadness, and foreboding Apprehension, *and the like*, OF, and ABOUT Things immediately and really attending us, and this in the most Momentous Articles of our Lives. . . . It would be endless to fill this Paper with the Testimonies Learned and Pious Men of all Ages have given to this; I could add to them a Volume of my own Experience, some of them so strange, as would shock your belief; tho' I could produce such Proofs as would Convince any Man—I have had, perhaps, a greater Variety of Changes, Accidents, and Disasters in my short and unhappy Life, than any Man, *at least than most Men* alive; yet I had never any considerable Mischief or Disaster attending me, but sleeping or waking I have had Notice of it before-hand, and had I listened to these Notices, I believe might have shunn'd the Evil—*Let no Man think this is a Jest*—I seriously acknowledge, and I do believe, my neglects of these Notices have been my great Injury, and since I have ceased to neglect them, I have been guided to avoid even Snares laid for my Life, by no other Knowledge of them, than by such Notices and Warnings—And more than that, have been guided by them to discover even the Fact and the Persons.
>
> I acknowledge, that the very Time, Persons, Circumstances, &c. of such Things, have been in this manner discover'd to me—I have living Witness to produce, to whom I have told the Particulars in the very Moment, and who have been so affected with them, as that they have press'd me to avoid the Danger, to retire, keep myself up, and the like—Whose Advice, if I had not as well as the Notice aforesaid, entirely neglected, I believe, as I said above, I had been safe; which omitting and slighting, I went on, and have fallen into the Pit, exactly as describ'd to me— (VIII, 94, 95)

In his *Serious Reflections of Robinson Crusoe* Defoe in his fifth chapter, "Of Listening to the Voice of Providence," suggested that in communicating with man, God now acts largely by "notices, omens, dreams, hints, forebodings, impulses, &c., which seem to be a kind of communication with the invisible world, and a converse between the spirits embodied and those unembodied" (p. 186): ". . . though I abhor superstitious and sceptical notions of the world of spirits, of which I purpose to speak hereafter, either in this work or in some other by itself . . . yet I cannot doubt but that the invisible hand of Providence, which guides and governs this world . . . may, and I believe does, direct from thence silent messengers on many occasions—whether sleeping or waking, directly or indirectly, whether by hints, impulses, allegories, mysteries, or otherwise, we know not: and does think fit to give us such alarms, such previous and particular knowledge of things that, if listened to, might many ways be useful to the prudent man to foresee the evil, and hide himself" (p. 183).

In the "work by itself," "A Vision of the Angelick World," Defoe placed the major emphasis in angelic communion upon impulses and hints. ". . . I lay a greater weight upon these," he had Crusoe declare, "than upon any of the other discoveries of the invisible world, because they have something in them relating to what we are about, something directing, something to guide us in avoiding the evils that attend us, and to accepting, or rather embracing, opportunities of doing ourselves good when they present. . . ." "I seriously advise all sober-thinking persons [Crusoe suggests] not to disregard those powerful impulses of the mind in things otherwise indifferent or doubtful, but believe them to be whispers from some kind spirit, which sees something that we cannot see, and knows something that we cannot know" (pp. 283, 280). "As to my own experience," he comments, "I waive saying much of it, but that in general I never slighted these impulses but to my great misfortune: I never listened to and obeyed them, but to my great advantage . . ." (p. 284).

To illustrate and confirm this type of angelic communication, Defoe had Crusoe offer several stories, of which two may have been from his own experience. The first example concerns a man who, living six or seven miles from London, receives a strong and reiterated impulse to go to London. Answering it, he is there rewarded with a particular business opportunity which gains him £1000 (pp. 279–280). The unspectacular, business nature of this instance, along with the opening formula, "I know a man," suggests strongly that the man was Daniel Defoe.

The second example has already been identified, by Wilson, Lee, and Aitken, as probably Defoe's own experience.[41] Crusoe relates how a man of his acquaintance, who had been convicted of a misdemeanor at King's Bench Court, was tempted to fly from England rather than face utter ruin. Awakening one morning under great emotional stress,

> he felt a strong impulse darting into his mind thus, Write a letter to them. It spoke so distinctly to him, and as it were forcibly, that, as he has often said since, he can scarce persuade himself not to believe but that he heard it; but he grants that he really did not hear it too.
>
> However, it repeated the words daily and hourly to him, till at length, walking about in his chamber, where he was hidden, very pensive and sad, it jogged him again, and he answered aloud to it, as if it had been a voice, Who shall I write to? It returned immediately, Write to the judge. This pursued him again for several days, till at length he took his pen, ink, and paper, and sat down to write, but knew not one word of what he should say; but, *dabitur in hac hora,* he wanted not words. It was immediately impressed on his mind, and the words flowed from his pen in a manner that even charmed himself, and filled him with expectations of success.
>
> This letter was so strenuous in argument, so pathetic in its eloquence, and so moving and persuasive, that as soon as the judge read it he sent him word he should be easy, for he would endeavour to make the matter light to him; and, in a word, never left till he obtained to stop prosecution, and restore him to his liberty and to his family. (p. 281)

This same reliance upon angelic ministry of impulse, Defoe exhibited in his hero in *Robinson Crusoe* and the *Farther Adventures of Robinson Crusoe.* Concerning the ministry of secret hints or impulses, Crusoe is early convinced by his own experience:

> . . . I began to see the merciful Dispositions of Heaven, in the Dangers we run through in this Life. How wonderfully we are deliver'd, when we know nothing of it. How when we are in (a *Quandary,* as we call it) a Doubt or Hesitation, whether to go this Way, or that Way, a secret Hint shall direct us this Way, when we intended to go that Way; nay, when Sense, our own Inclination, and perhaps Business has call'd to go the other Way, yet a strange Impression upon the Mind, from we know not what Springs, and by we know not what Power, shall over-rule us to go this Way; and it shall afterwards appear, that had we gone that Way which we should have gone, and even to our Imagination ought to have gone, we should have been ruin'd and lost: Upon these, and many like Reflections, I afterwards made it a certain Rule with me, That whenever I found those secret Hints or pressings of my Mind, to doing, or not doing any Thing that presented; or to going this Way, or that Way, I never fail'd to obey the secret Dictate; though I knew no other Reason for it, than that such a Pressure, or such a Hint hung upon my Mind: I could give many Examples of the Success of this Conduct in the Course of my Life. . . . and I cannot but advise all considering Men, whose lives are attended with such extraordinary Incidents as mine, or even though not so extraordinary, not to slight such secret Intimations of Providence, let them come from what invisible Intelligence they will, that I shall not discuss, and perhaps cannot account for; but certainly they are a Proof of the Converse of Spirits, and the secret Communi-

cation between those embody'd and those unembody'd; and such a Proof as can never be withstood: Of which I shall have Occasion to give some very remarkable Instances, in the Remainder of my solitary Residence in this dismal Place. (I, 202–204)

After such hints providentially caution Crusoe not to reveal himself at the arrival of a ship, he later returns to explain:

> ... I had some secret Doubts hung about me, I cannot tell from whence they came, bidding me keep up my Guard. ...
> Let no Man despise the secret Hints and Notices of Danger, which sometimes are given him, when he may think there is no Possibility of its being real. That such Hints and Notices are given us, I believe few that have made any Observations of things, can deny. . . . (II, 41)

This secret admonition to be on guard keeps Crusoe from grave danger when the supposed English ship arrives. When, at the end of the book, Robinson Crusoe returns to England, he is again preserved by such hints, for he is providentially warned by such admonitions that he must travel from Lisbon to London by land rather than by sea. Even though he once ships his baggage to go by sea, he changes his mind, to find later that two of the very ships which he had successively chosen to board had suffered disaster.

In the *Farther Adventures of Robinson Crusoe* the Spaniard whom Crusoe leaves as governor of the Island also learns that such promptings should not be ignored. He "found himself very uneasy in the Night, and could by no Means get any Sleep. . . . His Mind run upon Men fighting, and killing of one another, but was broad awake, and could not by any Means get any Sleep; in short, he lay a great while, but growing more and more uneasy, he resolv'd to rise." He discovers nothing, but still cannot sleep and accidentally awakens another Spaniard, to whom he then explains his restlessness. "Say you so, says the other *Spaniard*, such Things are not to be slighted, I assure you; there is certainly some Mischief working, says he, near us. . . . Well, says the *Spaniard*, there is something in it, I am persuaded from my own Experience; I am satisfied our Spirits embodied here have a Converse with, and receive Intelligence from the Spirits unembodied and inhabiting the invisible World, and this friendly Notice is given for our Advantage, if we know how to make Use of it." Going to the top of the hill, they discover just in time that hostile landings are being made (*FA*, II, 164–166).

Such reiterated insistence upon the efficacy of angelic hints made Crusoe and Defoe natural targets for the ridicule of skeptical critics and furnished ample ammunition for Charles Gildon's burlesque *The Life and Strange Surprizing Adventures of Mr. D ... De F. ...* When Defoe appears there and unhappily sees Crusoe, he laments,

"Bless my Eye-Sight, what's this I see! I was secure too soon here, the *Philistines* are come upon me; this is the Effect of my not obeying the *Secret Hint* I had not to come Home this Night." Gildon returned to comment upon Crusoe's "secret Impulse to a Seafaring Life, to which Impulse you so often recommend a blind Obedience, whether grounded on Reason or not, and would perswade us that it proceeds from the secret Inspiration either of Providence or some good Spirit. . . ." Later, Gildon continued, "he [Defoe] presses very earnestly our serious Regard to the secret Hints and Impulses of the Mind, of which we can give no Rational Account. But I must tell him, that this is only the Effect of a blind superstitious Fear, which ought not to be minded by any Man of common Sense or Religion." ". . . But for a Protestant to recommend this Superstition, is something extraordinary: But here the Dregs of Popery still hang about Mr. *Crusoe*." Gildon's final flirt regards Defoe's continuation of the theme in the *Further Adventures*: ". . . nor shall I stop long upon the *Spaniards* Prognosticating Humour, from Dreams and unaccountable Whimsies, because the *Spaniard* seems to have learnt this by dwelling so long in *Crusoe's* Habitation; for he has the same Notion of secret Correspondence betwixt unbodied and embodied Spirits, which *Crusoe* every where avows."[42]

Gildon's attack may have helped to prompt a chapter concerning providential care in *Serious Reflections of Robinson Crusoe* and surely suggested an accompanying tract of some one-hundred pages detailing the means of angelic ministry. Gildon's ridicule, moreover, did not prevent Defoe from endowing later heroes and heroines, like Singleton, Moll Flanders, and Roxana, with this same sensitivity to angelic ministry. In Roxana this faculty is combined with some of the qualities of second sightedness, possibly suggested to Defoe by his reading of William Bond's recent biography of Duncan Campbell, the Scottish seer who claimed the gift of the second sight.[43] In *The Fortunate Mistress* (1724) Roxana has a fearful premonition concerning a journey of her beloved first "keeper": "I told him I did not know what might be the reason, but that I had a strange Terror upon my Mind about his going, and that, if he did go, I was perswaded some Harm wou'd attend him. . . ." His attempt to reassure her does not comfort her. "I stared at him as if I was frighted, for I thought all his Face looked like a Death's-Head; and then immediately I thought I perceiv'd his Head all Bloody, and then his Cloaths look'd Bloody, too; and immediately it all went off, and he look'd as he really did. Immediately I fell a-crying and hung about him, My Dear, *said I*, I am frighted to Death, you shall not go; depend upon it, some Mischief will befall you. I did not tell him how my vapourish Fancy had represented him to me; that, I thought, was not proper; besides, he would only have laugh'd at me. . . ." But this "vapourish fancy" was actually a second sight. That very day he is set upon and stabbed to death. Roxana is grief-stricken: "Then the Manner of his Death was terrible and frightful to me, and, above all, the strange Notices I had of it; I had never pretended to the Second Sight or anything of that Kind, but certainly, if any one ever had such a thing, I had it at this time, for I saw him as plainly in all those terrible Shapes as above, *First*, as a Skeleton, not Dead only, but rotten and wasted; *Secondly*, as kill'd, and his Face bloody; and *Thirdly*, his Cloaths bloody, and all within the Space of one Minute, or indeed of a very few Moments."[44]

Several years later, in his *System of Magick*, Defoe recounted an incident which may have served to inspire this part of his story. Here the narrator recounts an incident from a walk in a "friend's garden near London," where a gentleman present asks concerning a young lady whom he sees walking in an adjacent garden:

> Has she been sick? said he. Now it was true, that the lady had been very ill, and was come into the country for air, and we told him how it was. Well, said he, the air won't recover her, for she will die within a very few days. I earnestly pressed him to tell us how he knew it; he answered ambiguously a good while, but as I pressed him with great importunity, he told me seriously: said he, You cannot see it as I do, I wish I could not see things so as I do, but her face now at this instant is to me exactly what you call a death's head; that is, the skeleton of a head or scull, and no other.
>
> The thing was right, and the young woman died within a week after. (*SM*, p. 327)

From the earnestness with which Defoe continually insisted upon his spiritual guidance and from his persistence, even after Gildon's attack, in bestowing upon his heroes and heroines this angelic ministry, in its various forms, it would seem quite clear that he was serious in his use of angelic communion. Understanding this angelic ministry thus becomes necessary not only for the full understanding of Defoe's heroes and heroines, but for the understanding of the writer's serious themes and purposes in his fiction. His willingness in an increasingly skeptical generation to insist upon angelic converse between the two worlds, visible and invisible, helps to show the supposedly meretricious journalist really a serious Puritan concerned to demonstrate God's persisting care, through angelic ministry, to reclaim and guide lost man.

II | The Devil and Daniel Defoe

UNFORTUNATELY FOR MANKIND, as Defoe believed, angelic ministry is not the only avenue of supernatural converse between the seen and unseen worlds. Throughout Defoe's fiction—especially in *Robinson Crusoe, Captain Singleton, Moll Flanders,* and *The Fortunate Mistress*—the Devil looms as a very real and potent force. It is impossible to appreciate truly the fall and subsequent redemption of Defoe's heroes and heroines without understanding the strength of the Tempter. Fortunately Defoe's portrait of the Devil in the occult works helps us to understand their spiritual experience.[1]

Such an appreciation is not difficult for the imaginative reader to recapture. Although man has at some stages of his sophistication been inclined to ignore the guardianship or even the reality of the blessed angels, he has never managed completely to shrug off the Devil. In Milton's day and earlier, Satan had received perhaps overmuch attention; and even after Defoe's day Isaac Watts warned the young and the melancholy to "avoid the reading or hearing of frightful stories of witches and devils . . . for these things will hang about the imagination, and perplex the mind with foolish terrors."[2] As Karl Barth has suggested, "It has never been good for anyone . . . to look too frequently or lengthily or seriously or systematically at demons. . . ."[3] But by the second quarter of the eighteenth century this morbid fascination no longer continued to exercise a danger in intellectual circles. Most people were doubtless as terrified as their ancestors had been by fears of the Devil; but if one is to believe Richard Baxter and Joseph Glanvill, even in Defoe's child-hood people were becoming Sadducees and atheists, convinced that the Devil was dead or impotent. Writing in 1713, Anthony Collins maintained, "THUS the Devil is intirely banish'd the *United Provinces*, where *Free-Thinking* is in the greatest perfection; whereas all round about that *Commonwealth*, he appears in various shapes: sometimes in his own, sometimes in the shape of an old black Gentleman, sometimes in the shape of a dead Man, and sometimes in that of a Cat."[4]

The persistance of popular and serious interest in the Devil is demonstrated by the rich and varied literature published on the subject after the Glorious Revolution. The numerous books and pamphlets devoted to witchcraft evince perhaps best of all the con-tinuing power and proximity of the Devil. In addition to these, many of the classics of the preceding period, like Glanvill's *Sad-ducismus Triumphatus*, were reprinted. An impressive list of dia-bolica was added, including Nathaniel Crouch's *Kingdom of Dark-ness, or the History of Daemons, Spectres, Witches and Super-natural Delusions, Mischievous Feats, and Malicious Impostures of the Devil* (1688); Richard Baxter's "Of the Malice and Misery of the Devil," in his *Certainty of the Worlds of Spirits* (1691); Bryan Turner's *De Primo Peccati Introitu, seu de Angelorum et Homi-num Lapsu* (1691); Cotton Mather's "The Devil Discovered," in his *Wonders of the Invisible World* (1692); Increase Mather's *Sin and Misery of the Fallen Angels*, in his *Angelographia* (1696); John Aubrey's *Miscellanies* (1696); William Turner's *Compleat History of the Most Remarkable Providences* (1697); Richard Stafford's *Discourse of the Miseries of Hell* (1697) and his sermon (penned in Bedlam) *Of the Devil's Devices* (1699); Charles Leslie's *History of Sin and Heresie* (1698); and Thomas Shepherd's sermon on the power of Devils, in his *Several Sermons of Angels* (1702). John Trenchard's skeptical *Natural History of Superstition* (1709) did not appreciably slow the stream: it continued with Tobias Swin-den's *Inquiry into the Nature and Place of Hell* (1714); Richard Boulton's compilation *A Compleat History of Magick, Sorcery, and Witchcraft* (1715–1716); Francis Hutchinson's *Historical Essay con-cerning Witchcraft* (1718), which contained a sermon on evil angels as well as other material on the Devil; Thomas Lewis's *Nature of Hell, the Reality of Hell-Fire, and the Eternity of Hell-Torments* (1720); Boulton's *Possibility and Reality of Magick, Sorcery, and Witchcraft, demonstrated, or a Vindication of the Compleat His-tory of Magick, Sorcery, and Witchcraft* (1722), in reply to Hutchin-son; and John Reynold's theological *Inquiries concerning the State and Oeconomy of the Angelical Worlds* (1723). Thus interest in the

Devil was far from dead or dormant when Defoe published, in 1726, his *Political History of the Devil* and its sequel, *A System of Magick, or a History of the Black Art.*

In 1726, at this "most turbulent period of the deistic debate,"[5] Defoe felt called upon to defend the reality of the Devil and at the same time combat the superstitious fears of the unsophisticated. "This, indeed, is in part the benefit of the Devil's history, to let us see that he has used the same method all along; and that ever since he has had anything to do with mankind, he has practiced upon them with stratagem and cunning . . . " (*HD*, p. 158). In a way, Defoe was carrying out a promise which he had made as early as June 6, 1705; in his *Little Review* he had proposed "to make due Inquisition after the Improvement the Devil makes in the Manufacture of Vice, and to discover him as far as possible, in all his Agents, and their Meanders, Windings and Turnings in the Propagation of Crime."[6] *The Political History of the Devil* appeared anonymously on May 7, 1726, published by T. Warner. Though postdated 1727, *A System of Magick*, the sequel to *The Political History of the Devil*, appeared late the same year.[7]

In these two occult books Defoe discussed at some length the number and order of the fallen angels, their habitation and domain, their corporeity and form, their power, especially their knowledge or foreknowledge, the modes of their attack upon mankind, and their unwitting human tools and their knowing accomplices; and in the first book he embodied a highly dramatic version of Satan's Fall and his subsequent attack upon man.

The name "Devil" Defoe used indiscriminately for God's adversary or for his subordinate angels who fell with him: "the Devil signifies Satan by himself, or Satan with all his legions at his heels, as you please" (*HD*, p. 17). The numbers of these are "infinitely great"; but any attempt to be more precise led Defoe into a burlesque of scholastic precision. In one estimate he humorously suggested $10,511,675\frac{1}{2}$ as the total number of devils; and in another, calculating the devils in three lines of dust, "ten hundred times a hundred thousand millions of the first line, fifty millions of times as many in the second line, and three hundred thousand times as many as both in the third line" (*HD*, pp. 78, 79).

Of this host, Satan, or the Devil, is head. "Satan, the leader, guide, and superior, as he was author of the celestial rebellion, is still the great head and master-devil as before; and under his authority they still act . . ." (*HD*, p. 31). He has "sovereignty of the whole army of Hell, . . . making all the numberless legions of the bottomless pit servants" (*HD*, p. 38). Not even worth debate are the "enthusiastic and visionary . . . notions of a parity of devils, or making a commonwealth among the black divan" (*HD*, p. 26).

Protestant theologians had never been as interested as had their Catholic brothers in the exact constituency of the fallen host— whether all nine orders were represented or three entire orders— and whether the fallen angels were now organized on the basis of their relative sinfulness. Defoe was doubtless satisfied with the succinct statement of Joseph Glanvill, "that the *Devil* is a name for a *Body Politick*, in which there are very different *Orders and Degrees* of *Spirits*, and perhaps in as much *Variety* of *Place* and *State*, as among our selves."[8]

These fallen angels now dwell in the upper regions of the air. The notion that they inhabit hell as a place of torment in the center of the earth Defoe rejected as "infinitely absurd and ridiculous" (*HD*, p. 190). Where Satan's future abode would be located he did not pretend to guess: ". . . of this hell, its locality, extent, dimensions, continuance, and nature, as it does not belong to Satan's history, I have a good excuse for saying nothing, and so put off my meddling with that, which if I would meddle with, I could say nothing to the purpose" (*HD*, p. 85). Though Protestant theologians were generally reticent upon such scholastic questions, Defoe must have been tempted to ridicule a recent original attempt to locate Hell on the surface of the sun—Tobias Swinden's *Inquiry into the Nature and Place of Hell* (1714).

Instead of a Hell of physical torture, Defoe believed in a spiritual Hell within the damned soul. This idea he had already suggested in his "Vision of the Angelick World":

> A heaven of joy must in His [God's] presence dwell,
> And in His absence every place is hell.   (p. 277)

Defoe also cited Sir Thomas Browne's " 'The Devil is his own hell' " and suggested that rage and envy constitute "part of his hell, which . . . is within him, and which he carries with him wherever he goes; nor is it so difficult to conceive of hell, or of the Devil either, under this just description. . ." (*HD*, pp. 188–189). "In all these notions of hell and devil," Defoe continued, "the torments of the first, and the agency of the last, tormenting, we meet with not one word of the main, and perhaps only, accent of horror which belongs to us to judge of about hell, I mean the absence of heaven; expulsion and exclusion from the presence and face of the chief ultimate, the only eternal and sufficient Good; . . . these people tell us nothing of the eternal reproaches of conscience, the horror of desperation, and the anguish of a mind hopeless of ever seeing the glory which alone constitutes heaven, and which makes all other places dreadful, and even darkness itself" (*HD*, p. 191).

In the doctrine that Hell is essentially separation from God, Defoe was of course following theologians as well as poets like Marlowe:

> *Me[phistopheles]* Why this is hel, nor am I out of it:
> Thinkst thou that I who saw the face of God,
> And tasted the eternal ioyes of heauen,
> Am not tormented with then thousand hels,
> In being depriv'd of euerlasting blisse:

In his *Enchiridion* Erasmus had maintained, ". . . the torments of hell . . . are nothing else but the perpetual anxiety of mind which accompanies habitual sin."[9] And Charles Leslie had recently agreed: ". . . Sin and Hell are in effect the same. There is Hell, that is Misery, involv'd in the nature of every Sin. . . ."[10] John Dennis had concurred, in *Priestcraft Distinguish'd from Christianity* (1715): ". . . their Pride, their Hatred and the rest of their tormenting Passions, became at once their Transgression and their Hell" (p. 7).

But even though Hell is primarily spiritual, devils inhabit space, concentrating their attacks upon man from the regions surrounding the earth: "Satan has no particular residence in this globe or earth where we live; . . . he rambles about among us, and marches over and over our whole country, he and his devils, in camps *volant*; but . . . pitches his grand army or chief encampment in our adjacencies, or frontiers, which the philosophers call atmosphere, and whence he is called the prince of the power of that element or part of the world we call air . . ." (*HD*, pp. 70–71). Thus Defoe imagined "the Devil sitting in great state, in open campaign, with all his legions about him, in the height of the atmosphere; or if you will, at a certain distance from the atmosphere, and above it" (*HD*, p. 323).

In giving locality to the Devil, Defoe was of course quite orthodox, for pneumatologists agreed that the Devil would otherwise be omnipresent; and the idea that the demons or devils occupy the lower air was a view commonly accepted ever since the early centuries of Christianity. Certainly most of Milton's contemporaries put the empire of Satan in the airy regions. Isaac Ambrose commented, "The Air is his own element, wherein now he reigneth: he is *Prince of the power of the air* (i. e.) of the airy Dominion or Princedom. The Jews have a tradition, that all the space between the Earth and the Firmament is full of Troops of evil Spirits. . . ."[11]

Though the Devil is "a spirit incorporeal, an angel of light, and consequently not visible in his own substance, nature, and form" (*HD*, p. 42), he can nevertheless assume shape. But contrary to Protestant demonologists of Milton's day, Defoe insisted that the Devil does not actually possess or really assume a material body: "We have divers accounts of witches conversing with the Devil; the Devil in a real body . . . ; also of having a familiar, as they call it, an incubus, or little devil, which sucks their bodies, runs away with them into the air, and such like; much of this is said, but much more than it is easy to prove, and we ought to give but a just proportion of credit to those things" (*HD*, p. 42). Defoe also ridiculed the monstrous bogey form long associated with the Devil, "with bat's wings, horns, cloven foot, long tail, forked tongue, and the like" (*HD*, p. 202). "Children and old women have told themselves so many frightful things of the Devil, and have formed ideas of him in their minds, in so many horrible and monstrous shapes, that really it were enough to fright the Devil himself to meet himself in the dark, dressed up in the several figures which imagination has formed for him in the minds of men; and, as for themselves, I cannot think by any means that the Devil would terrify them half so much if they were to converse face to face with him" (*HD*, p. 1).

To the figure of Satan as goat, with cloven hoof, Defoe devoted a humorous and at the same time thoughtful chapter, "Of the extraordinary appearance of the Devil, and especially of his cloven foot," reducing the picture to its proper simplicity, as Increase Mather had already done in his *Angelographia*.[12] The actual form of Satan is, instead, that of a glorious original so disfigured by sin that Satan is now restrained from appearing in his own shape: ". . . God has, for a protection and safeguard to mankind, limited the devil from afrighting him by visible appearances in his native and hellish deformity, and the horrid shape he would necessarily bear . . ." ("Vision," p. 274). Like Baxter, Defoe believed that such an appearance was extremely rare, for "it would render him so frightful to his emissaries, and even his best friends and most useful servants would be terrified, and would run away from him instead of conversing with him."[13]

Although orthodox theologians agreed that Satan acts only by God's permission, they varied widely in interpreting the degree of this permissiveness; and many, in an age when medicine and meteorology were in their virtual infancy, were still inclined to give the Devil credit for vast physical powers. Luther was of course especially prone to do so. Devils, he thought, are "in the thick dark clouds, which cause hail, lightnings, and thunderings, and poison the air, the pastures and grounds."[14] In England, Isaac Ambrose also assigned the Devil vast meteorological powers: "Now if there they are as Princes, and have Power, no wonder if they can violently move the air, and cause tempests and storms. . . ." Moreover "The water is an Element commanded by him. . . ."[15]

Much of the attack upon this exaggerated notion of the Devil's physical prowess came, before the scientific onslaught upon this area of diabolic power, from the disbelievers in witchcraft. One of the most effective of these in Defoe's youth was N. Orchard, with his *Doctrine of Devils proved to be the grand Apostacy of later Times; with an Essay tending to rectifie those undue Notions and Apprehensions Man have about Daemons and Evil Spirits* (1676). Orchard maintained that devils "have not such an unlimited, irrestistible, and omnipotent power, as Demonologers idolatrously attribute to them; especially in Physical or natural things, whatever their power may be in respect of Morals."[16] Defoe would have agreed heartily with John Spencer's pronouncement: "The biggest works the Devil doeth, have but a tympany of greatness. . . ." God "*onely doeth* great wonders."[17] Even England's latest defender of witchcraft realized how dangerous this inflated concept of the Devil's power could be. "Thus we are too ready," Francis Bragge complained, "to make him our God, and comply with his temptations, and enslave ourselves to his cursed will. . . ."[18]

As early as June 12, 1708, in his *Review*, Defoe had challenged the concept of Satan's almost limitless physical might: "The Prince of the Air was not let loose to affright or amuse the People . . . ; if he has the Power to raise Storms, Tempests, Thunders and Lightning, *as some say he can, tho' I do neither grant or believe it*, yet he has been restrain'd from doing it here. . . ." And in a subsequent vision of the Devil's empire, Defoe failed to find this power: "And I found he had very great Power to raise Storms . . . among the Affairs of Nations and Kingdoms, tho' his Power of raising ordinary Storms . . . did not appear" (V, "132" [131]; VII, 502). In his "Vision" Defoe had Crusoe remark upon the popular exaggeration of Satan's might: "If Satan or his instruments had one tenth part of the power, either of the air, or in the air, or over the elements, that we give them in our imaginations, we should have our houses burnt every night . . . but he can do nothing by violence, or without permission" (p. 291). Even if Satan were able to fall upon man with violence, it would not be to his advantage so to act, as Defoe makes clear time and again, but to proceed by craft. But Satan has no choice: ". . . with his fall from heaven, as he lost the rectitude and glory of his angelic nature, I mean his innocence, so he lost the power too that he had had before; and that when he first commenced devil, he received the chains of restraint too, as the badge of his apostacy, viz. a general prohibition to do anything to the prejudice of this creation, or to act anything by force or violence without special permission" (*HD*, p. 88).

Though Satan lacks independent power, he possesses knowledge, through his own nature and experience and the virtual omnipresence of his devils. Satan is "as near being infallible as any of God's creatures" (*HD*, p. 53); and some of his angels are almost always in our company (*HD*, p. 285). He "has very much of the attribute of omnipresence, and may be said, either by himself or by his agents, to be everywhere, and see everything; that is to say, everything that is visible" (*HD*, p. 201). "The Devil," Defoe clarified, "is not omniscient; he cannot, at the distance of his airy dwelling, know the thoughts of the agent . . ." (*SM*, p. 379). The orthodox position concerning Satan's knowledge was put clearly by Joseph Hall, who maintained that devils "cannot but know the natures and constitutions of the creatures, and thereby their tempers, dispositions, inclinations, conditions, faculties; and therewith their wants, their weaknesse and obnoxiousnesse; and thereupon strongly conjecture at their very thoughts, and intentions, and the likelyhood of their repulses or prevailings: out of the knowledge of the causes of things they can foresee such future events as have a dependance thereon."[19]

Such a position Defoe was at times willing to hold, though it granted the Devil more knowledge than at other times he was willing to admit. But Defoe certainly did not assign the Devil power greater than that of the blessed angels, as did some of the witchcraft writers and Samuel Freeman, who suggested, "Tho it be granted that the Devil knows the Actions of Men, it does not follow that the Saints or Angels must do so too; he being a little nearer to Man on Earth than Angels and Saints in Heaven are; *He is called the Prince of the Power of the Air*, and . . . is often so near as to see and hear Men, tho he is invisible himself. . . ."[20]

Of all the attributes of Satan, Defoe was especially sure of one—he does not have foreknowledge. ". . . Satan has not a more certain knowledge of events than we; . . . that he may be able to make stronger conjectures and more rational conclusions from what he sees, I will not deny; and that which he most outdoes us in is, that he sees more to conclude from than we can, but I am satisfied he knows nothing of futurity more than he can see by observation and inference . . ." (*HD*, p. 119).

A few Protestant divines, like Martin Luther, were so obsessed with the Devil that they thought that he "declared what shall happen and come to pass."[21] And Increase Mather recorded that in a conversation in Cambridge, England, John Spencer "said to me, that his Judgment was, *That the Evil Angels had* Praenotions *of many Future Things, and did accordingly give strange* Praemonitions *of them.*"[22] But orthodox Christian divines, Catholic and Protestant alike, agreed with Defoe that the Devil is not allowed revelation or foreknowledge. So spoke Thomas Cooper, Philip Goodwin, Richard Saunders, and, at least in his book, John Spencer.[23]

The media through which the Devil exercises his powers upon mankind are thus largely spiritual. The ability of the Devil to assume apparitional form in order to converse with man, orthodox demonologists acknowledged; and they agreed that Satan frequently appeared in borrowed guise. Having rejected the appearance of ghosts, or revenants, Protestant theologians especially credited the diabolical apparition. At the end of the century William Turner offered twenty-five examples in his *Compleat History*.[24] Increase Mather continued to manifest the old beliefs, in his *Angelographia*: ". . . Evil Angels do appear more often than good Ones. No wonder, because they are of more Earthly Inclinations, than those Spirits, that dwell above. Evil Angels do often appear . . ." (pp. 63–64). Even in the following century John Beaumont and some others held on to the now discredited belief. But attacks of Reginald Scot and John Webster had long since undermined credulity in Satanic apparitions as well as in witchcraft; and as early as 1646 the angelologist Henry Lawrence thought that the devils appeared "almost as seldome now a dayes" as did the blessed angels (p. 45). After the attacks upon apparitions by Balthasar Bekker and Laurent Bordelon in 1694 and 1710, disbelief accelerated. Defoe's son-in-law, Henry Baker, writing in his *Universal Spectator* for October 7, 1732, gave the verdict which Defoe had helped to popularize: with only one exception, Baker commented, "there is no Instance of his [the Devil's] appearing among us."[25]

Defoe acknowledged that Satan has assumed apparitional guise in the past and could do so again, that "the Devil had certainly power to assume . . . a human shape" (*HD*, p. 262). "That some extraordinary occasions may bring these agents of the Devil, nay, the Devil himself, to assume human shapes, and appear to other people, we cannot doubt . . ." (*HD*, p. 326). "But in these modern ages of the world," Defoe added, "he finds it much more to his purpose to work under ground . . . and to keep upon the reserve; so that we have no authentic account of his personal appearance, but what are very ancient or very remote from our faith, as well as our inquiry" (*HD*, p. 326). Only one appearance, "I had so solemnly confirmed by one that lived in the family, that I never doubted the truth of it" (*HD*, p. 265).

The more subtle media through which the Devil now exercises his power, it seemed to Defoe's predecessors and contemporaries, are far more effective; and gradually writers came to center almost exclusively upon such subtle temptations as the Devil effects in dreams, evil impulses, and passions. Though Martin Luther gave the Devil credit for great physical powers, he also recognized the Devil's shifts: "Satan plagues and torments people all manner of ways. Some he affrights in their sleep, with heavy dreams and visions, so that the whole body sweats in anguish of heart."[26] In *Paradise Lost* (IV, 801–809) Milton had suggested that Satan had made his first attempt upon Eve in the form of a dream; and Defoe accepted the suggestion as very likely (*HD*, pp. 94–95). Baltus summarized, ". . . it is certain the Devil can cause Dreams. 'Tis the Doctrine of all the Divines, who after *Tertullian*, distinguish three sorts of Dreams [divine, Satanic, and natural]."[27]

"Nor is it clear to me," Defoe commented, "that the Devil had any other way, but by dream or apparition, to come at the intelligent faculties of man. It is evident he does suggest evil; now he must do it sleeping or waking; if sleeping, it must be by a dream, in which he does but imitate the good spirit, which, as the Scripture says plainly, and gives a multitude of instances of it, opens the understandings of men in the night visions, and seals their instructions; nor is it a new practice of Satan to mimick and imitate his Maker, in the measures and operations of his wisdom with mankind" (*SM*, p. 96). ". . .Nothing is more sure," Crusoe comments in the "Vision", "than that many of our dreams are the whispers of the devil . . ." (p. 272). Dreams Defoe accepted as "the second best of the advantages the Devil has over mankind" (*HD*, pp. 331–332); and in his *System of Magick* he suggested that by it Satan first tempted Cain to murder and subsequently used it to introduce the practice of magic.

Two of Defoe's examples of Satan's assaults by dream may be autobiographical. The first, introduced by Defoe's formula "I knew a person," delineates a man continuously afflicted by lascivious dreams:

> I knew a person who the Devil so haunted with naked women, fine beautiful ladies in bed with him, and ladies of his acquaintance too, offering their favours to him, and all in his sleep, so that he seldom slept without some such entertainment; the particulars are too gross for my story, but he gave me several long accounts of his nights' amours, and being a man of a virtuous life and good morals, it was the greatest surprise to him imaginable; for you cannot doubt but that the cunning Devil made everything he

acted to the life with him, and in a manner the most wicked; he owned with grief to me, that the very first attack the Devil made upon him, was with a very beautiful lady of his acquaintance, who he had been really something freer than ordinary with in their common conversation. This lady he brought to him in a posture for wickedness, and wrought up his inclination so high in his sleep, that he, as he thought, actually went about to debauch her, she not at all resisting; but that he waked in the very moment, to his particular satisfaction. (*HD*, p. 329)

This same temptation Defoe recounted briefly also in his *History of Apparitions*. Here again the Devil tempts the sleeper with "beautiful women, sometimes naked, sometimes even in bed with him, . . . but the case has, on two or three occasions, been mentioned by other hands, and the person is much too known to allow the further description of it without his consent" (pp. 210–211).

The second diabolical dream appears so often that one wonders whether the dreamer might have been Defoe himself. Here the dreamer strips a child of its jewelry and considers killing it:

I knew another, who, being a tradesman, and in great distress for money in his business, dreamed that he was walking all alone in a great wood, and that he met a little child with a bag of gold in its hand, and a fine necklace on its neck; upon the sight, his wants presently dictated to him to rob the child; the little innocent creature, (just so he dreamed,) not being able to resist, or to tell who it was, accordingly, he consented to take the money from the child, and then to take the diamond necklace from it too, and did so.

But the Devil, (a full testimony, as I told him, that it was the Devil,) not contented with that, hinted to him, that perhaps the child might some time or other know him, and single him out, by crying or pointing, or some such thing, especially if he was suspected and showed to it, and therefore it would be better for him to kill it for his own safety, and that he need do no more but twist the neck of it a little, or crush it with his knee; he told me he stood debating with himself whether he should do so or not; but that in that instant his heart struck him with the word murder, and he entertained a horror of it, refused to do it, and immediately waked. (*HD*, pp. 330–331)

The same diabolical temptation reappears, in a slightly fuller version, in *The History of Apparitions*, again as taking place in a dream:

The Devil, subtle in his contrivance, as well as vigilant in application of circumstances, knows a man to be in perplexed circumstances, distressed for want of money, a perishing family, a craving necessity; he comes in his sleep and presents him with a little child dressed up with jewels of a great value, and a purse of gold in its hand, and all this as happening in a place perfectly opportune for the purpose, the nurse having negligently left the child out of her sight.

. . . .

I could give this in the form of a relation of fact, and give evidence of the truth of it; for I had the account of it from the person's own lips, who was attacked in sleep; and (as he said with a sincere affliction) yielded to the temptation; and I committed the barbarous robbery, said he, with the utmost resentment; I plundered and stripped the poor smiling infant, who innocently played with me when I took off its ornaments, gave me the purse of gold out of its little pocket, and bid me keep it for her to play with. (pp. 208–209)

In *Moll Flanders* the dream had earlier been presented as an even more vivid reality:

> . . . going thro' *Aldersgate-street*, there was a pretty little Child had been at a Dancing-School, and was a going home all alone, and my Prompter, like a true Devil, set me upon this innocent Creature; I talk'd to it, and it prattl'd to me again, and I took it by the Hand and led it along till I came to a pav'd Alley that goes into *Bartholomew-Close*, and I led it in there; the Child said that was not its way home; I said, yes, my Dear, it is, I'll show you the way home; the Child had a little Necklace on of Gold Beads, and I had my Eye upon that, and in the dark of the Alley I stoop'd, pretending to mend the Child's Clog that was loose, and took off her Necklace, and the Child never felt it, and so led the Child on again: Here, I say, the Devil put me upon killing the Child in the dark Alley, that it might not Cry, but the very thought frighted me so that I was ready to drop down, but I turn'd the Child about and bad it go back again, for that was not its way home. . . . (II, 7)

The frightful dream which Captain Singleton experiences towards the close of his adventures and details to his Quaker friend, William, is also evidently diabolical in origin: "Why, *said I*, I had frightful Dreams all Night, and particularly I dreamt that the Devil came for me, and asked me what my Name was? and I told him, then he askt me what Trade I was? Trade, *says I*, I am a Thief, a Rogue, by my Calling; I am a Pirate and a Murtherer, and ought to be hanged; Ay, ay, says the Devil, so you do, and you are the Man I look'd for, and therefore come along with me, at which I was most horribly frighted, and cried out, so that it waked me, and I have been in a horrible Agony ever since" (p. 325). The Quaker persuades Singleton "that to despair of God's mercy was no Part of Repentance, but putting my self into the Condition of the Devil . . ." (p. 326). The Devil had obviously not counted on William. The Devil, Singleton commented, "followed his Work very close with me, and nothing lay upon my Mind for Several Days, but to shoot my self into the Head with my Pistol" (p. 323).

So also, Defoe thought, does Satan seduce by hints and impulses, as in *Moll Flanders*. Part of his devilism is the "capacity for conveying itself, undiscovered, into all the secret recesses of mankind, and the same secret art of insinuation, suggestion, accusation, &c., by which he deludes and betrays mankind . . ." (*HD*, p. 44). ". . . when he has designed the delusion, or the perplexing of mankind, or any other of his infernal infatuations, he has brought them to pass by the injection of evil thoughts or other dark means, moving his passions and affections, instilling all the hellish imaginations that are requisite to the mischiefs he designs" (*SM*, p. 116).

Here Defoe was orthodox. Glanvill, for example, had explained, ". . . there is little Doubt, but that *Spirits, good or bad*, can so move the *Instruments of Sense* in the *Brain*, as to *awake* such *Imaginations*, as they have a Mind to *excite*; and the Imagination having a mighty *Influence* upon the *Affections*, and *they* upon the *Will* and *external Actions*, 'tis very easy to conceive how *good Angels* may stir us up to *Religion* and *Virtue*, and the *evil Ones tempt* us to *Lewdness* and *Vice*, viz. by *Representments* that they make upon the *Stage of Imagination*, which *invite* our *Affections*, and *allure*, though they cannot *compel*, our *Wills*."[28] Isaac Ambrose specifically detailed Satan's media: "He can work on the understanding: he can penetrate into the fancy, which is the Organ of the internal senses, and move those Phantasms he finds there, and by that means excite various thoughts in the understanding, and perswade to this or that."[29] In his study of *Paradise Lost* Patrick Hume suggested "That the Devil, by his great sagacity, may be able so to distemper the humours of human Bodies, to heat and inflame the Blood and animal Spirits, and by them so to disorder the Fancy, that many evil thoughts, inductive of sinful desires, may assult us, is not to be doubted. . . ."[30]

But "the devil's best handle, and by which he takes fastest hold of us all,"[31] is the passions. To know when the Devil is at us, Defoe suggested:

> you have no more to do but look a little into the microcosm of the soul, and see there how the passions, which are the blood, and the affections, which are the spirit, move in their particular vessels; how they circulate, and in what temper the pulse beats there, and you may easily see who turns the wheel. . . .
>
> But on the other hand, if at any time the mind is ruffled, if vapours rise, clouds gather, if passions swell the breast, if anger, envy, revenge, hatred, wrath, strife; if these, or any of these, hover over you; much more, if you feel them within you; if the affections are possessed, and the soul hurried down the stream to embrace low and base objects; if those spirits, which are the life and enlivening powers of the soul, are drawn off to parties, and to be engaged in a vicious and corrupt manner . . . the case is easily resolved, the man is possessed, the Devil is in him. . . . (*HD*, pp. 366–367)

". . . How effectually they [the passions] form a hell within us," Defoe exclaimed, "and how imperceptibly they assimilate and transform us into devils, mere human devils, as really devils as Satan himself, or any of his angels; and that, therefore, it is not so much out of the way as some imagine, to say, such a man is an incarnate devil; for, as crime made Satan a devil, who was before a bright immortal seraph, or angel of light, how much more easily may the same crime make the same devil, though every way meaner and more contemptible, of a man or a woman either!" (*HD*, p. 189). ". . . Every vice is the Devil in a man; lust of rule is the devil of great men, and that ambition is their devil, as much as whoring is father . . . . . 's devil; one has a devil of one class acting him, one another, and every man's reigning vice is a devil to him" (*HD*, p. 368).

That Satan employs man's passions as avenues of temptation was generally recognized by Catholic and Protestant divines alike. After naming the Devil as only the external cause of evil, working on man's own corruption, Lawrence listed a number of man's passions and commented, ". . . your carnal lusts, the concupiscence of the flesh, and the boyling and ebullition of the blood to anger, and all passions, it is not so much, or it is not especially against these you wrestle, but rather against him that acts [activates] them, and makes use of them to your ruine and dis-advantage, which is the divell . . ." (p. 4). In his *Daemonologia Sacra* (1677), Richard Gilpin emphasized man's own corruption rather than Satan's power: "The way by which he doth entice, *is by stirring up our minds to lust.*" "By *lust*," Gilpin hastened to explain, "I mean those *general desirings* of our minds after *any* unlawful object. . . ."[32] In his *Angelographia* (1696) Increase Mather suggested that sin "turns men into Devils. There are wicked men who are Devils incarnate" (p. 125); and in his *View of Death* (1725) John Reynolds visualized the devils sewing tares "With pregnant seeds of each enraged lust!" (p. 76). Perhaps the change towards Satan which the deists and the scientists managed to effect during Defoe's lifetime is nowhere more apparent than in a sermon published in 1725 by Jeremy Collier: there he maintained that for evil we should blame not Satan or the Devil, but man's own passions, for the inhabitants of the other world "are far removed from human Converse."[33]

This recognition of the Fifth Column of passions is a commonplace in Defoe's writings. In his *True-Born Englishman*, for example, the passions are delineated as Satan's "Vice-gerents and Commanders":

> Thro' all the World they spread his vast Command,
> And Death's Eternal Empire is maintain'd.
> They rule so politickly and so well,
> As if they were *Lords Justices* of Hell.
> Duly divided to debauch Mankind,
> And plant Infernal Dictates in his Mind.[34]

In *The Consolidator* the passions are metamorphosed into trades-men anxious to advertise and display their goods: "As for the Devil's warehouse, he has two constant warehouse keepers, Pride and Conceit, and these are always at the door, showing their wares and exposing the pretended virtues and accomplishments of the man by way of ostentation" (p. 274). So important is this aspect of the Devil's work that Crusoe takes especial pains to explain to Friday "how he [the Devil] had a secret access to our Passions, and to our affections, to adapt his Snares so to our Inclinations, as to cause us even to be our own Tempters, and to run upon our Destruction by our own Choice" (*RC*, II, 3).

Especially did Defoe suggest that lust is the most common ave-nue to man's domination and that woman is often the devil incar-nate. "Thus if rage, envy, pride, and revenge can constitute the parts of a devil," Defoe whimsically asked, "why should not a lady of such quality, in whom all those extraordinaries abound, have a right to the title of being a devil really and substantially, and to all intents and purposes, in the most perfect and absolute sense . . ." (*HD*, p. 270). "Modern naturalists . . . tell us, that as soon as ever Satan saw the woman [Eve], and looked in her face, he saw it evi-dently that she was the best formed creature to make a fool of, and the best to make a hypocrite of, that could be made, and therefore the most fitted for his purpose" (*HD*, p. 53). The most detailed story incorporated in *The History of the Devil* shows the narrator convincing a she-devil that he has recognized her real nature through her disguise as wife and mother. "I could," commented Defoe, ". . . give you such a list of devils among the gay things of the town, that would frighten you to think of; and you would pres-ently conclude with me, that all the perfect beauties are devils . . ." (*HD*, p. 283). "Nay, . . . if they have not the Devil in their heads or in their tails, in their faces or their tongues, it must be some poor despicable she-devil, that Satan did not think it worth his while to meddle with; and the number of those that are below his operation, I doubt is very small" (*HD*, p. 216). Satan has now changed from employing the ugly witches which formerly he was wont to use: ". . . the Devil has changed hands, and . . . now he walks about the world clothed in beauty, covered with the charms of the lovely; and he fails not to disguise himself effectually by it, for who would think a beautiful lady could be a mask to the devil? and that a fine face, a divine shape, a heavenly aspect, should bring the Devil in her company, nay, should be herself an apparition, a mere devil?"

(*HD*, p. 287). Such an agent of the Devil is one of the wives of Colonel Jack. She is a "Snare" laid in the way "which had almost ruined me" (II, 2). There is "Witchcraft, in the Conversation of this woman" (II, 3) and "much Witchcraft on her Tongue" (II, 9–10).

The recriminatory attitude towards woman, who caused man's first fall and subsequently continued as temptress, an attitude as old as *Genesis,* was still standard in Defoe's day. Indeed among Anglicans as well as Puritans a debate still raged as to whether woman possessed an immortal soul. A pioneer in advocating higher education for women, Defoe was in these passages only partly serious, perhaps using the same comic tone as in Quevedo's *Visions,* of which the Defoe-Farewell Library contained a copy in the L'Estrange translation: "What, (says a Devil) have you so soon forgot the Roguery of these Carrions [handsome women]? Have you not had Tryal enough yet of them; they are the very Poyson of Life, and the only dangerous *Magicians* that corrupt all your Senses, and disturb the Faculties of your Soul; these are they that cozen your *Eyes* with *false Appearances,* and set up your *Wills* in opposition to your *Understanding* and *Reason.*"[35]

The baseness of man's passions, especially his sexual lust, always reminded the orthodox, Calvinist or not, of man's fallen nature, of his depravity. In "A Vision of the Angelick World" Crusoe points out this devilish propensity: ". . . 'tis our own corrupt, debauched inclination, which is the first moving agent; and therefore the Scripture says, 'A man is tempted when he is drawn away of his own lusts, and enticed.' " ". . . our doing evil is from the native propensity of our wills: *humanum est peccare.* I will not enter here into the dispute about original corruption in nature, which I know many good and learned men dispute; but that there is a secret aptness to offend, and a secret backwardness to what is good, which, if it is not born with us, we can give no account how we came by, this I think every man will grant; and that this is the devil that tempts us the Scripture plainly tells us, when it says, 'Every man is tempted when he is drawn away of his own lust and enticed" (pp. 248, 266–267). Thus the first advantage of the Devil, as Defoe asserted in the image popularized by Bunyan's *Holy War,* is "the treachery of the garrison within" (*HD,* p. 332).

In view of Defoe's traditional treatment of the Devil, it is perhaps surprising to find that he also identified poverty and prisons as diabolical agents.[36] Sometimes in the novels a protagonist speaks in terms more familiar to present-day sociology than to traditional theology. Thus Moll Flanders pleads with her Bath lover that he provide for her so that she will not have to combat the "Temptations from the frightful prospect of Poverty and Distress" (I, 131); and in retrospect she explains that "had I not fallen into that Poverty which is the sure Bane of Virtue, how happy had I been . . . but I, prompted by that worst of Devils, Poverty, return'd to the vile Practice" (I, 202–203) of prostitution. "As Covetousness is the Root of all Evil," she remarks, "so Poverty is the worst of all Snares" (I, 203). The same devil of poverty prompts her career as thief: when she sees a neglected bundle, "the Devil, who laid the Snare, prompted me, as if he had spoke, for I remember, and shall never forget it, 'twas like a voice Spoken over my Shoulder, take the Bundle; be quick; do it this Moment . . ." (II, 4). Thus the Devil, Moll comments, "began, by the help of an irresistible Poverty, to push me into this Wickedness" (II, 16). The same Devil of poverty is responsible for Roxana's adulterous conduct: ". . . the Devil, and that greater Devil of Poverty, prevail'd, and the Person who laid Siege to me, did it in such an obliging, and I may almost say, irresistible Manner, all still manag'd by the Evil Spirit; for I must be allow'd to believe, that he has a Share in all such things, if not the whole Management of them; . . . the Devil manag'd, not only to bring me to comply, but he continued them as Arguments to fortify my Mind against all Reflection, and to keep me in that horrid Course, I had engag'd in" (II, 4). "Necessity first debauch'd me," Roxana summarizes, "and Poverty made me a Whore at the Beginning . . ." (II, 5). The same Devil of poverty first debauches Colonel Jack.

Defoe's occult books embody not only an analysis of the Devil's habitat, power, and modes of operating, but a history of his Fall and his subsequent corruptions of man. On the title page of his *History of the Devil*, Defoe indicated fairly accurately the organization and material of Part I as "*Containing a State of the Devil's Circumstances, and the various Turns of his Affairs, from his Expulsion out of Heaven, to the Creation of Man: with Remarks on the several Mistakes concerning the Reason and Manner of his Fall. Also his Proceedings with Mankind ever since Adam, to the first planting of the Christian Religion in the World.*" The preadamite section and that presenting the Fall owe largely to Milton, though Defoe felt that he must, as he suggested in his title, set right Milton's theological unorthodoxies. The subsequent Biblical account is Defoe's dramatic exegesis of Satan's history as the Devil succeeded, time and again, in seducing mankind. Here Defoe relied not only upon the Bible itself, but upon learned commentators like Matthew Poole and historians like Sir Walter Raleigh.

Such a general plan as Defoe followed in this section was certainly no new pattern. General histories of the world, like Sir Walter Raleigh's, quite commonly opened with a preadamite section and continued with some of the very incidents which Defoe selected for dramatic presentation. More important, Milton had stamped this pattern upon the Puritan imagination. *Paradise Lost* embodies in effect a history of the Devil, for in Books XI and XII Milton had Michael reveal to Adam in a vision just such high spots as Defoe covered, leading to the Flood, and had him narrate briefly the sequel, to the Crucifixion. Available to Defoe also were such post-Miltonic patterns as those of Isaac Ambrose, Richard Bovet, and Charles Leslie. Although from its title, Richard Gilpin's *Daemonologia Sacra, or a Treatise of Satan's Temptations* (1677) sounds like an anticipation of Defoe's plan, it is not; and Ambrose's *War with Devils* is chronological only in the sense that it follows the assaults of the Devil upon everyman from birth to death. In the first two chapters of *Pandemonium* Richard Bovet followed an approximately Miltonic pattern, and in the rest of Part I he covered in a haphazard way the material which Defoe later handled in the second part of *The History of the Devil* and in *A System of Magick*. Quite similar to Milton's and Defoe's patterns, though not organized upon the same chronological pattern, is Charles Leslie's *History of Sin and Heresie* (1698).

For the preadamite portion of his *History of the Devil* Defoe seems sometimes engaged rather in a running commentary on and criticism of *Paradise Lost* than an analysis of Satan's generalship or politics.[37] He sometimes had to remind himself of what he was supposed to be doing, "being at this time not writing the history of Mr. Milton, but of the Devil" (*HD*, p. 65). Because of his admiration for the earlier Puritan, it was hard to do so, for his "poetry, nor his judgment, cannot be reproached without injury to our own" (p. 25). *Paradise Lost*, however, was "a fine poem, but the devil of a history" (p. 64). ". . . Mr. Milton's admirers must pardon me if I let them see, that though I admire Mr. Milton as a poet, yet that he was greatly out in matters of history, and especially the history of the Devil . . ." (p. 25). Aside from objecting lightly to some of Milton's poetical liberties, Defoe took Milton to task quite seriously on a number of theological heterodoxies, some of them of cardinal importance.

On the question of how sin was able to enter Heaven, Defoe was far from reproaching Milton with the inadequacy of his poetic presentation, for to Defoe the problem seemed insoluble. Commenting with two pages of original verse on this mystery, Defoe wrote some lines which may have been in the recollection of William Blake when he wrote "The Tyger":

> How didst thou pass the adamantine gate,
>   And into spirit thyself insinuate?
>   From what dark state? from what deep place?
>   From what strange uncreated race?
> Where was thy ancient habitation found,
> Before void chaos heard the forming sound?[38]

Concerning the specific occasion which Milton dramatized to explain Satan's defection, however, Defoe both acknowledged the poetic aptness and attacked the unorthodoxy, which Patrick Hume had ignored, but Leslie had objected to.[39] The announcement of the Messiahship in God's pronouncement "This day have I begotten" was "erroneous," "grossly erroneous": ". . . Mr. Milton is not orthodox in this part, but lays an avowed foundation for the corrupt doctrine of Arius, which says, there was a time when Christ was not the Son of God" (*HD*, pp. 31, 68). In what was evidently one of the earliest criticisms of Milton on this point, Defoe explained, ". . . Christ is not declared the Son of God but on earth; it is true, it is spoken from heaven, but then it is spoken as perfected on earth; if it was at all to be assigned to heaven, it was from eternity, and there, indeed, his eternal generation is allowed. . . . But then the declaring him *that day*, is wrong chronology too, for Christ is declared *the Son of God with power*, only by the resurrection of the dead, and this is both a declaration in heaven and in earth . . ." (*HD*, pp. 66–67). "Satan knows very well, that the Messiah was not declared to be the Son of God with power till by and after the resurrection from the dead, and that all power was then given him in heaven and earth, and not before; so that Satan's rebellion must derive from other causes, and upon other occasions . . ." (*HD*, p. 11).

His next chapter (VI) Defoe devoted to exposing "some more of Mr. Milton's absurdities," concerning the fall of the angels and their temporary imprisonment in hell. Although Milton was unorthodox on this point,[40] his geography of Hell did not bother Defoe as much as did the idea of a physical confinement, which he maintained has not yet taken place. Oddly enough, though Patrick Hume had noticed it but regarded the matter as uncertain (p. 6), Defoe did not object to Milton's unorthodoxy in creating the angels before the Hexameron: "As for the length of the time (between their so flying the face of their almighty Conqueror, and the creation of man), which, according to the learned, was twenty thousand years, and according to the more learned, not a quarter so much, I would not concern my curiosity much about it . . ." (*HD*, p. 74). Regarding Satan's motive in tempting mankind, Defoe again took issue with Milton, maintaining that it was envy rather than any mistaken attempt to "affront God" and "rob him of the glory" (*HD*, p. 52).

In his account of the Devil in Scriptural times, Defoe concentrated, in the main, upon key scenes of the Devil's successes and disappointments, working these up dramatically and in some detail. Throughout he was guided by the twin lights of Scripture and reason, for the light of the second helped to interpret that of the first. As Defoe later remarked in his *History of Apparitions*, "the wisdom of Providence too is not known to act inconsistent with itself; and, which is a sufficient answer to all the rest, we are allowed to judge of all these things by our reasoning powers, nor have we any other rules to judge by; and it can be no crime to reason with calmness, and with due respect to superior power, upon the ordinary administration even of Heaven itself" (p. 98).

In his account of the Fall Defoe did not quarrel with Milton, as he did in that of the prelapsarian period, but followed *Paradise Lost* as a vivid and poetic dramatization of Scripture. Like Milton, Defoe emphasized Satan's appeal to man's passions; and like Milton, again, he centered upon the temptation of Eve and gave even less attention to that of Adam than Milton had done. In the account of Eve's fall Defoe added a whimsical, half-serious comment concerning woman's persistent weakness: "The foolish woman yielded presently, and that we are told is the reason why the same method so strangely takes with all her posterity, viz. that you are sure to prevail with them, if you can but once persuade them that you believe that they are witty and handsome. . . ." ". . . Here," Defoe commented, "began the Devil's new kingdom" (*HD*, pp. 93, 97). But if Defoe seems here to be vulgarizing Milton's account, one must remember that between Milton and Defoe there had intervened not only Dryden's sophisticated *State of Innocence* (1677), but George Powell's marionette version of Dryden, which was popular in the early 1710's.[41]

Despite Satan's success in working Adam's fall, Defoe emphasized, the immediate promise of Divine grace to Adam's posterity showed the Devil that his work was only begun. Satan's politics are thus his continual assault upon the soul of man. In working out his history, Defoe imposed a selective pattern. Like Raleigh he went at once from the Fall to Cain: "The same Pride and ambition which beganne in the Angels, and afterward possest *Adam, Cain* also inherited. . . ."[42] Defoe devoted his first dramatic scene to Cain's murder of Abel, where he developed the envy of Cain as worked up by one of his sons or grandsons. And here is apparent one of Defoe's most obvious techniques—his disposition to create an imaginative dramatic scene to account reasonably for some important development on which Sacred or profane history is silent.

Defoe's next dramatic scene for the Devil's onslaught was the drunkenness of Noah, a scene which Milton had ignored in his sanguine account of Noah and mentioned later only in a single line; but which Bovet had commented on.[43] However trivial the incident might seem, it represented, Defoe thought, the Devil's conquest over the only family surviving the flood. Defoe's selection of this particular event emphasized again his concern with man's moral life. Sin for Defoe was not only any deviation from the Will of God, but any debasement of man's nature. ". . . the Devil certainly made a conquest here," Defoe commented, "and as to outward appearance, no less than that which he gained before over Adam; nor did the Devil's victory consist barely in his having drawn in the only righteous man of the whole antedeluvian world, and so beginning or initiating the new young progeny with a crime; but here was the great oracle silenced at once; the preacher of righteousness, for such no doubt he would have been to the new world, as he was to the old, I say, the preacher was turned out of office, or his mouth stopped, which was worse . . ." (*HD*, p. 126).

Defoe's next major incident was one which fascinated his age and previous generations—the building of the tower of Babel, which seemed to Charles Leslie and to Defoe a masterpiece of the Devil's politics in creating confusion.[44] Historians like Raleigh and Bochart had demonstrated historically and linguistically that the incident resulted in the diffusion of the races and tongues throughout the world.[45] But more important, Defoe thought, through the tower of Babel Satan succeeded in so dispersing mankind that most of the races were left with only a glimmering remains of Revealed religion, devoid of all grace (*HD*, p. 136 ff). Through Abraham, Satan was once again thwarted, but the Devil found proper instruments for his purpose in Lot's two daughters (*HD*, p. 148). Later, in Egypt, God chose Moses to lead his people, but Aaron became Satan's tool. Thereafter Defoe's account became a mere brief selective catalogue of the major flagrant sins of the Jews up to the coming of Christ. And here finally was Satan's worst and permanent defeat since his expulsion from Heaven.

Since that time Satan has been forced to rely for outward aid upon false religions and false prophets. He has encouraged and supported special human agents, "instruments, as well human as infernal and diabolical, and of the human, as well the ecclesiastic as the secular" (*HD*, p. 174). These special agents, like the fallen angels, are likewise numerous and diverse, including groups and individuals, unwitting tools and knowing accomplices. First are those groups which practice ecclesiastical magic and false worship: the pagan priests, the Catholic Church, the Mohammedans. Others, newer instruments of Satan, carrying their defiance of God beyond that of Satan himself, refuse to recognize their Redeemer or even their Maker: Socinians, deists, skeptics, and atheists. Still others—sorcerers, witches, and the like—advanced Satan's kingdom through a supposed covenant with him; and working with or without covenant were augurs, sybils, judicial astrologers, and fortune-tellers.

Though references to the Devil's worship are to be found throughout the occult works and especially throughout the various parts of *Robinson Crusoe*, it is discussed perhaps most comprehensively in two chapters of the *Serious Reflections of Robinson Crusoe*. America, Crusoe found "all wrapt up in idolatry and paganism, given up to ignorance and blindness, worshipping the sun, the moon, the fire, the hills their fathers, and, in a word, the devil" (*SR*, p. 213). The natives possessed "a blind subjection to himself, nay, I might call it devotion, (for it was all of religion that was to be found among them,) worshipping horrible idols in his name, to whom he directed human sacrifices continually to be made . . ." (*HD*, p. 98). Thus when Friday explains to Crusoe his native religion,

> . . . By this I observ'd, That there is *Priestcraft*, even amongst the most blinded ignorant Pagans in the World; and the Policy of making a secret Religion, in order to preserve the Veneration of the People to the Clergy, is not only to be found in the *Roman*, but perhaps among all Religions in the World, even among the most brutish and barbarous Savages.
> I endeavour'd to clear up this Fraud, to my Man *Friday*, and told him, that the Pretence of their old Men going up the Mountains, to say O to their God *Benamuckee*, was a Cheat, and their bringing Word from thence what he said, was much more so; that if they met with any Answer, or spake with any one there, it must be with an evil Spirit: And then I entered into a long Discourse with him about the Devil, the Original of him, his Rebellion against God, his Enmity to Man, the Reason of it, his setting himself up in the dark Parts of the World to be Worship'd instead of God, and as God; and the many Stratagems he made use of to delude Mankind to his Ruine; how he had a secret access to our Passions, and to our affections, to adapt his Snares so to our Inclinations, as to cause us even to be our own Tempters, and to run upon our Destruction by our own Choice. (*RC*, II, 2–3)

One of the most serious and protracted episodes of *Farther Adventures of Robinson Crusoe* is the earnest effort of the formerly hardened Will Atkins to remove the native superstitions of his wife and Christianize her. Before the native wives of the Englishmen can be instructed in Christian belief, indeed, the Catholic priest insists that the women must be reclaimed from "the publick Profession of Idolatry and Devil-Worship" (III, 23). It is, moreover, Christian indignation at devil-worship which prompts the now elderly Crusoe, in his journey home across Siberia and Russia, to risk the safety of the entire party in order to destroy a diabolical idol. Crusoe is spiritually outraged at the spectacle of natives "wrought up into hellish Devotion by the Devil himself; who envying (to his Maker) the Homage and Adoration of his Creatures, had deluded them into such gross, surfeiting, sordid and brutish things, as one would think should shock Nature itself" (III, 182).

Even worse than the pagans are the Mohammedans. The Greek Orthodox Church Defoe regarded as not far superior, but like Cotton Mather, in his *American Tears upon the Ruines of the Greek Churches* (1701), Defoe regarded the Mohammedans as the worse of two possible evils. In *A Supplement to the Advice from the Scandal Club*, in November 1704, Defoe gave it as his considered opinion that although a Papist could be saved, a Mohammedan could not (pp. 10–11). For in Mohammed, Satan "set up the boldest, the grossest, and the most senseless of all impostures that ever was in the world; and which yet at this time, and for a thousand years past, has strangely triumphed over the Christian world, has spread itself over Asia and Africa . . . and it was, till within a few years past, master of a fourth part of Europe besides" (*SM*, p. 346).

Defoe's attitude toward all these religions—the pagan worship of America and Africa, the Greek Orthodox Church, and the Mohammedan worship—was the one common among English Protestants of his day and could have derived in part from Balthasar Bekker or from Alexander Ross, who in his *Pansebeia, or a View of All Religions in the World* maintained that the natives of Virginia "worshipped the Devil" and that those of Paria, in South America, "be very zealous in worshipping of the Devil, and Idols, to whom they sacrifice men, and then eat them."[46] Doubtless Defoe's views derived also in part from his extensive knowledge of missionary accounts and of travel literature like that of Tournefort and Aaron Hill.[47]

In his *Review* for September 16, 1704, Defoe had wondered, "I Confess 'tis a hard Choice; and I hope we shall never be put to that Nicety to determine, whether Christendom shall be devoured by Popery, or Mohametanism; whether *Turkish* or *Popish* Tyranny shall overrun *Europe*" (I, 237). From the worship of Satan in

America and the impostures of Mohammed to Catholic impostures and delusions was for Defoe and his Puritan and Anglican readers a step only too ready and easy. As Frank E. Manuel has remarked, ". . . by the 1680's if one were ensconced behind the ramparts of English or Dutch Protestantism political contengencies made it a patriotic act to equate pagan and papal idolatry."[48]

The very foundation of the Catholic Church, Defoe believed, was the result of a hellish bargain, and it represented for the Devil an important victory: "He had drawn in the bishops of Rome to set up the ridiculous pageantry of the key; . . . a cheat which, as gross at it was, the Devil so gilded over, or so blinded the age to receive it, that . . . all the catholic world went a whoring after the idol; and the bishop of Rome sent more fools to the Devil by it than ever he pretended to let into heaven, though he opened the door as wide as his key was able to do" (*HD*, p. 183). For Defoe, as for other Protestants, the Reformation was "a blow to the Devil's kingdom, which, before that, was come to such a height in Christendom, that it is a question not yet thoroughly decided, whether that medley of superstition and horrible heresies, that mass of enthusiasm and idols, called the catholic hierarchy, was a church of God, or a church of the Devil; whether it was an assembly of saints, or a synagogue of Satan: I say, take that time to be the epoch of Satan's declension . . ." (*HD*, p. 209). Defoe would doubtless have appreciated seeing his *History of the Devil* listed, in 1744, on the Index at Rome.[49]

Defoe's attack in his occult books upon the Catholic Church as the instrument of the Devil was neither his first nor his last. Indeed there were periods in Defoe's productivity when hardly a year passed without some onslaught against the Catholics, involving especially some Jacobite revelation. From his very first poetical satire, which he evidently revised to attack the Jesuits after the recently discovered Preston Plot, he was alive to the dangers of Jacobite plots to bring in Catholic rule. By about 1710 Defoe had been so effective that the author of *Instructions from Rome, in Favour of the Pretender* (Defoe himself, if one can accept the Defoe canon here), was indirectly praising him as the chief defender of the Protestant cause. In this pamphlet the Pope, after acknowledging "*our Grand Patron* Lucifer" (p. 4) and their "Laudable Design of *Atheism*" (p. 10), instructs his pretended Jacobite correspondents: "Endeavour to suppress that Damn'd Review, that's a plaguey Fellow; Nothing but a Miracle wrought by a Power not Related to us, has preserv'd that Wretch to be a Scourge to our Faction" (p. 12). The central period of Defoe's anti-Jacobitism might be said to be the period 1712–1714, when he felt anxiety concerning

Queen Anne's successor and when another Catholic plot was in the offing to invade England from Scotland.

But these works are far more political than theological. He revealed the dangers of the Catholic religion at far greater length not only in his occult works but in his *New Family Instructor* (1727), where he devoted 247 of his 368 pages to dramatizing the dangers of Popery, in a narrative wherein a father reclaims an errant son from Catholic enticements. A number of popes, the father suggests, dealt with the Devil (pp. 134–137), and the practice of worshipping saints and angels "came from the *Devil*" (p. 150). The third son, James, expostulates with the Catholic convert: "I told him that he was gone from Christ to the *Devil*, and that he worshipped the *Devil* . . ." (p. 210). "I told him," he continued, "his Two Saints, St. *Francis*, and St. *Ignatius*, were *Devils*, were gone to the *Devil*, and made *Devils* like himself . . ." (p. 211).

A particular object for horror for Defoe, as for other Protestants, was the Society of Jesus and its founder, Ignatius Loyola. The Inquisition Defoe believed to be "certainly the Devil's master-piece to bring mankind to such a perfection of devilism" (*HD*, p. 218). Although Defoe usually mentioned Loyola in a trilogy with St. Dunstan and St. Francis, he reserved for the place of eminence "the deceiver St. Ignatius, the greatest enthusiastic of the last ten centuries" (*SM*, p. 25). As Donne remarked in *Ignatius his Conclave, or his Inthronisation in a late Election in Hell* (1634), of which there was a copy in the Defoe-Farewell Library, Loyola was "a subtill fellow, and so indued with the Devill, that he was able to tempt, and not onely that, but (as they say) even to possesse the Devill . . ." (p. 14).

Even a cursory glance at the anti-Catholic literature of the day reveals at once that there was nothing distinctive about Defoe's position: an extensive library was available demonstrating Catholic imposture and dealings with the Devil. The classic Foxe's *Acts and Monuments* had been reprinted in a sumptuous edition in 1684; and Thomas Bray's enormous folio, *Papal Usurpation and Persecution, as it has been Exercis'd in Ancient and Modern Times . . . a Fair Warning to all Protestants* (1712) brought Foxe up to date. As Thomas Bennett remarked in his *Confutation of Popery*, "The Nation is plentifully furnish'd with Books against Popery." Even Sir Richard Steele contributed *An Account of the State of the Roman-Catholick Religion throughout the World* (1715), in which the Pope figures as Antichrist. The Defoe-Farewell Library included a rich collection of Catholic and anti-Catholic literature, especially of saints lives.[50]

"But we need not go to America, or to the Inquisition," Defoe admitted, "nor to paganism, or to popery either, to look for people that are sacrificing to the Devil . . . ; are not our churches (aye, and meeting-houses, too, as much as they pretend to be more sanctified than their neighbours) full of Devil-worshippers?" (*HD*, p. 218). Even the Church of England, Defoe intimated, sometimes served as the instrument of the Devil. Since Defoe did not wish to alienate Anglican readers, as some of his Puritan predecessors had done, he was forced to handle his suggestions subtly, to ask whether in their personal lives Anglican clergymen were much better than their Catholic brothers: suggesting that priests "in most parts of the world" were "dealers with the Devil," he qualified with an ironic "(our own, God bless us! always excepted)" (*SM*, p. 191).

Some volunteers in the Devil's service, however, Defoe thought, outgo even Satan himself in their denial of God and their worship of the Devil. Although the Devil never questioned God or the Divinity of Christ, some modern groups and individuals refuse such recognition, varying from Arians, Socinians, deists, and other anti-Trinitarians to downright atheists and their colleagues the Satanists. "We have also some new practioners in magic among ourselves," Defoe commented, "who deal with the Devil in a more exalted sublime way, and who, for aught I know, are able to teach the Devil some new and more accurate ways of managing them, and the rest of the world too, than ever he knew before" (*SM*, p. 223).

Among the various anti-Trinitarian groups which Defoe singled out for attack, the group which seems to have concerned him least were the neo-Arians, brought back into prominence in the eighteenth century by William Whiston and Thomas Emlyn. For both of these men Defoe had occasional scorn, because they "levelled their Saviour with a class infinitely below the Devil" (*SM*, p. 54). But most of Defoe's attack on Arianism comes in his criticism of Milton's seeming Arianism in *Paradise Lost*, V, 603. Far more reprehensible were the Socinians, for the transition thence to atheism was only too easy. ". . . On a sudden you shall find them dip into polemics, study Michael Servetus, Socinus, and the most learned of their disciples; they shall reason against all religion . . . and satirize God and eternity with such a brightness of fancy, as if the soul of a Rochester or a Hobbes was transmigrated into them; in a little length of time they banter heaven, burlesque the Trinity, and jest with every sacred thing, and all so sharp, so ready, and so terribly witty, as if they were born buffoons, and were singled out by nature to be champions for the Devil" (*HD*, p. 307).

Defoe had already glanced at the Arians and Socinians in his *Review* for November 12, 1706, and in his *Serious Reflections of Robinson Crusoe* Crusoe maintains that they "should be punished

... by the judges" (p. 89). They were of course among the anti-Trinitarians who did not come under the Toleration Act of May 24, 1689, but were penalized, in theory, as much as were the Catholics. Robert South as well as Defoe assigned them to the Devil: " 'The Socinians were impious blasphemers, whose infamous pedigree runs back (from wretch to wretch) in a direct line to the Devil himself. . . .' "[51]

The largest and most amorphous group of anti-Trinitarians attacked as the Devil's agents were the deists, of whom many preferred to be known as freethinkers. Although deism and freethought had been popular in the seventeenth century, the deistic debate was even more acute in the eighteenth century, especially after the publication of Anthony Collins's *Discourse of Freethinking* in 1713 and his *Discourse of Grounds and Reasons of Christian Religion* in 1724. The deists and freethinkers Defoe assailed in all his occult works. But particularly in his *New Family Instructor*, Part II, did Defoe attack the incredulity of the freethinkers. The deistic position is voiced by a gentleman "tainted in Principle with the new Errors, as to the Trinity; and, withal, a little of a Deist, or Sceptick, or Free-Thinker, call them what you will" (p. 253). These beliefs, in his appended poem "Trinity, or the Divinity of the Son," Defoe characterized as

> ... Lyes, too gross for *Satan*'s self,
> And Falshoods, Hell it self had never heard of? (p. 379)

Skeptics Defoe also ranked as agents of the Devil. These were of course not the Pyrrhonists or philosophical skeptics like Dryden or even Joseph Glanvill, who himself attacked religious skepticism, but those who doubted God's existence or man's communion with him.

But it was in atheism especially that man had outdeviled the Devil himself; and Defoe, like Henry More, Richard Bentley, and other Boyle lecturers, never tired of accusing the atheist of being an instrument of Satan. In Part II of *The Family Instructor* (1715) Sir Richard's sister, an atheist, "an instrument of the devil" (pp. 112–113), is so identified by her own brother: ". . . you are possessed, that you are given up to Satan" (p. 131). In *The History of the Devil* and *A System of the Magick* Defoe sounded the same theme.

> It may be asked of me, why I will insist upon this matter in a treatise of magic; that this relates to the atheists, not to magicians, and that by the same rule, all enthusiasms, heresies, and mysterious things in religion, as well as in science, may be rated in the same class, and be called by the same name, and so we shall make a magic of religion at last.

But let a short answer suffice to this weak objection; all errors in religion are not equally diabolic, no, nor equally mischievous; and as I have said above, that this seems to be an original deeper than hell, and out of the reach of the Devil; so, as far as it is a crime which derives from the man as an independent, and acting the Devil by himself, I think it must have the height of human imagination and invention in it, and so may be called magical, as magic is a science or art of doing superlative evil. (*SM*, p. 235)

Especially did Defoe concentrate on atheism in *Serious Reflections of Robinson Crusoe*. In his chapter "Of Atheistical and Profane Discourse" Crusoe comments, "The devil himself, who is allowed to be full of enmity against the Supreme Being, has often set up himself to be worshipped as a God, but never prompted the most barbarous nations to deny the being of a God; and 'tis thought that even the Devil himself believed the notion was too absurd to be imposed upon the world. But our age is even with him for his folly, for since they cannot get him to join in the denial of a God they will deny his devilship too, and have neither one nor other" (p. 85). The longest narrative of "A Vision of the Angelick World," moreover, dramatizes the conversion of some of the "hellish society" (p. 298) of Oxford atheists. Paul Dottin, one recalls, believed that Defoe devoted such attention to atheism in his *Serious Reflections* because he was "astonished and not a little troubled to find himself accused [by Gildon] of promoting atheism."[52]

Prominent among these atheistical groups were the Satanists of the Hell-Fire clubs, to one of which Defoe evidently referred in his *System of Magick*: "A bolder Infidel I have not met with since I was last at the pagan circle, near old Charing, where God was owned, sworn by, imprecated, blasphemed, and denied, all in a breath" (p. 71). According to Ned Ward, a Hell-fire club was meeting in a tavern in Westminister as early as 1710; and at the time of their suppression there were at least three Hell-fire clubs in London, "members of which met even in the then royal palace of Somerset House and at houses in Westminister and in Conduit Street."[53] So scandalous did these clubs become that George II by an order in Council directed in 1721 that they be instantly suppressed. Evidently this directive, acted upon in Parliament, drove them underground.[54] Similar clubs apparently operated at both Universities.[55] That at Oxford may indeed be the atheistical club of which Defoe gave a long and dramatic account in his "Vision of the Angelick World" (pp. 296–312). There exists some difference of opinion on the age at which Sir Francis Dashwood, subsequently leader of the infamous Medmenham Monks, became a member of one of these groups; he may have been a member as early as 1725, perhaps of the group "to which Lord Sandwich belonged, and which was painted by Hogarth as *Charity in the Cellar*."[56]

In addition to false religions, involving whole continents in diabolic worship, Satan has used also special human agents to enlarge his kingdom through the employment, or pretense, of magic. In *The History of the Devil* Defoe clearly indicated their services to the Devil, and he devoted to them his sequel, *A System of Magick*. Here, as he indicated in his Preface, he refused to provide "a body of the black art as a science, a book of rules for instruction in the practice, or a magical grammar for introduction to young beginners" (p. ix). Instead he discussed in detail man's willing cooperation with the Devil, especially in the form of a compact. Here in *A System of Magick* Defoe reconstructed what seemed to him on the basis of Biblical references and reasonable conjecture the story of how the Devil seduced mankind into willing cooperation with him. Thus in this sequel Defoe traversed unashamedly some of the same ground which he had already covered in his *History of the Devil*, and basically in the same loose, digressive fashion. For his structure and materials he several times drew not only upon the Bible but upon Sir Walter Raleigh's *History of the World*, as he had done in the earlier book. Like Cornelius Agrippa and Reginald Scot earlier, Raleigh and Defoe both maintained that the early magi, or "magicians," were really men of scientific acquisitions who were superstitiously regarded by the ignorant. In his *History of Magick* (1625, translated in 1657) Gabriel Naude reinforced this view of the early magi and provided a wealth of material to document it. To another learned scholar, Athanasius Kircher, who in his *Oedipus Aegyptiacus* (1652) attributed to curiosity and desire for power the magus's willingness to compact with the Devil, Defoe may have owed some of the inspiration for the two Oriental episodes which he dramatized to account for crucial stages in the diabolical development of magic.[57] More important, perhaps, in providing Defoe's attitude toward his material was the brilliant *Displaying of Supposed Witchcraft* (1677). Between Webster and Defoe intervened a number of interesting and influential attacks upon magic, notably those by Bovet, Bekker, Bordelon, Hutchinson, and St. Andre. Bovet especially may have helped to suggest the material and arrangement for *A System of Magick*, as he probably did for *The History of the Devil*. In his *Historical Essay concerning Witchcraft* (1720) Francis Hutchinson provided almost a chronology of magic as well as of witchcraft (pp. 15–64); and finally, in 1725, in his *Lettres au Sujet de la Magie, des Malefices et des Sorciers* St. Andre retraced the story of the early sages with much the same spirit and general purpose that actuated Defoe.

For Defoe, although there was a wide range in the types of magicians, these might be loosely grouped as sorcerers and soothsayers. The really diabolical type of magic is "by familiar agreement, compact and contract with the brightest men of the times, who he brings over to converse and correspond with him, and who he acts by, and allows them to play their game and his own together, and this is magic" (*SM*, p. 209). These sorcerers are difficult to separate into their Biblical classifications: ". . . in our discoursing with even the most learned men upon this subject," Defoe protested, ". . . it is very hard to bring them to any notions of a difference between magic and witchcraft, between a magician and a sorcerer, between a student in the exalted sciences, a converser with the intellectual world, and a wretch that has a familiar, a wizard or necromancer; but they will, though they may be in the wrong in it too, have them be reckoned all in a class, that they are all practicioners in the diabolical part, and in a word, that they deal with the Devil. . ." (*SM*, p. 275).

"The blackest part of the black art itself" was of course witchcraft. This power witches received directly from the Devil:

1. They have consulted and convenanted with a spirit or devil.
2. They have a deputy devil, sometimes several, to serve and assist them.
3. These they employ as they please, call them by name, and command their appearance in whatever shape they think fit.
4. They send them abroad, to or into persons they design to bewitch, who they always torment, and often murder them, as mother Lakland did several. (*HD*, pp. 332–333)

The covenant, a necessary characteristic of this more hellish magic, according to witch-finders Matthew Hopkins and Robert Hunt, Defoe also regarded as essential. The rest of the qualifications of the witch, particularly the invocation and the familiar, Defoe, obviously disbelieving in the whole business of witchcraft, was inclined to treat lightly: "I find . . . the Devil has appeared to several people at their call. This, indeed, shows abundance of good humor in him, considering him as the devil . . . : nay, some, they tell us, have a power to raise the Devil whenever they think fit; this I cannot bring the Devil to a level with, . . . subjected to every old wizard's call; or that he is under a necessity of appearing on such or such particular occasions, whoever it is that calls him . . ." (*HD*, p. 268). Defoe could not believe

that to whomsoever they should communicate the same tokens, or watchwords, they should have the same power, and that the very words should call him or his agents up to an appearance, whoever made use of them.

This would have been to have the Devil bind himself prentice to them and his heirs for ever; and to have chained himself down galley-slave like, to the sound of the words, which I take to be quite wide of the case. (*SM*, p. 207)

Concerning the invocation, then, Defoe was obviously at one with Marlowe. In *Doctor Faustus,* one recalls, Faustus greets Mephistopholes with the same popular misconception:

> *Fau.* Did not my coniuring speeches raise thee? speake.
>
> *Me.* That was the cause, but yet per accident,
> For when we heare one racke the name of God,
> Abiure the scriptures, and his Sauiour Christ,
> Wee flye, in hope to get his glorious soule,
> Nor will we come, vnless he vse such meanes
> Whereby he is in danger to be damnd:[58]

The rest of the picture of the conjuror amused Defoe too:

> . . . it is not easy to say in what capacity the magician is to be understood to act. 1. Whether with, that is, in concert and agreement, or 2. As we might say, in partnership with the Devil; or whether in a superior orb, as a magician of quality making use of an attendant, obsequious, commanded devil, always at his call, to do what he bids him, jump over his stick, run and go, fetch and carry like a dog, as some eminent magicians of state have been said to act; or, as St. Dunstan, St. Francis, the abbot of Crowland, and others, did by him, who, they tell us, set him to work, sent him of errands, made him ring the bell to vespers, sweep the church, and a thousand good things the servicable devil did for them . . . or, 3. Whether the Devil is master, which I must own is more likely, and the magician servant; and then he does not act the Devil, but the Devil acts him, and makes him do everything he bids him. . . . (*SM,* pp. 150–151)

It should cause no surprise that Defoe, a devout Puritan who accepted the Bible as entirely reliable, should have accepted the historical reality of witchcraft, for the Bible plainly directs that no witch must be suffered to live. "As to witchcraft and possession," Defoe commented, ". . . it is known to be all from an evil spirit, or in plain English, from the Devil. There is no room to dispute it; the wretches employed, acknowledge it, and the hellish things they do discover it; so we need say no more of that . . ." (*SM,* p. 321). The testimony of respected men like Baxter and the Mathers enforced this evidence. As historian of the Devil, Defoe could hardly dismiss the authority of the Bible and the combined weight of demonstration from all ages. But he eyed suspiciously the possibility of contemporary witchcraft: "Not that I am hereby obligated to believe all the strange things the witches and wizards, who have been allowed to be such, nay, who have been hanged for it, have said of themselves; . . . even at the gallows; . . . I may perhaps convince you that the Devil's possessing power is much lessened of late, and that he either is limited, and his fetter shortened more than it has been, or that he does not find the old way . . . so fit for his purpose as he did formerly . . ." (*HD*, p. 365). Defoe could not suppress his incredulity at the outrageous witchcraft accounts, including those from Salem:

> Thus the people of Salem, in New England, pretended to be bewitched, and that a black man tormented them by the instigation of such and such, whom they resolved to bring to the gallows: this black man they would have be the Devil, employed by the person who they accused for a witch: thus making the Devil a page or footman to the wizard, to go and torment whoever the said wizard commanded, till the Devil himself was so weary of the foolish part, that he left them to go on their own way, and at last they overacted the murdering part so far, that when they confessed themselves to be witches, and possessed, and that they had correspondence with the Devil, Satan not appearing to vouch for them, no jury would condemn them upon their own evidence, and they could not get themselves hanged, whatever pains they took to bring it to pass. (*HD*, pp. 343–344)

He was similarly incredulous elsewhere: "The strange work which the Devil has made in the world by this sort of his agents called witches, is such, and so extravagantly wild, that except our hope that most of those tales happen not to be true, I know not how any one could be easy to live near a widow after she was five-and-fifty" (*HD*, p. 315).

At other times Defoe voiced a wry condemnation:

> Then we have a piece of mock pageantry in bringing those things called witches or conjurers to justice; that is, first, to know if a woman be a witch, throw her into a pond, and if she be a witch she will swim, and it is not in her own power to prevent it; if she does all she can to sink herself it will not do, she will swim like a cork: then, that a rope will not hang a witch, but you must get a withe, a green osier; that if you nail a horseshoe on the sill of the door she cannot come into the house, or go out if she be in; these and a thousand more, too simple to be believed, are yet so vouched, so taken for granted, and so universally received for truth, that there is no resisting them without being thought atheistical. (*HD*, p. 319)

Nothing perhaps better illustrates the skeptical change in the temper of the times than does the shift in the fortunes of Faustus, now no longer a fascinating soul damned through diabolic seduction but a lively provider in two theaters of slapstick merriment, a pantomime hit of London in the 1724 season and subsequent seasons. Even Defoe paid Rich homage for deflating the magician, for having "gone further to expose and run down the magic I am speaking of, and cure the world of the hippo, and the vapours, than the whole stage could do before" (*SM*, p. xi).

The less heinous type of magic is divining, or soothsaying. The list of soothsayers would include for Defoe the priests and sybils of the oracles, the augurs, the judicial astrologers, and the fortune-tellers—all those who pretend by any means, diabolical or natural, systematically to see into the future, especially those who make it their profession or craft. All are cheats, for the Devil himself neither possesses nor can communicate any power of foreknowledge. This aspect of man's cooperation with the Devil is not quite so baleful, perhaps, as some other forms are; but it involves misleading others, and the ancient practicioners, at least, believed themselves in league with the Devil.

There is in Defoe's occult books a wealth of material identifying the oracle, "that fraud of all frauds" (*HD*, p. 224), as a diabolical delusion. In the "Vision of the Angelick World," before Defoe seriously considered all the aspects of the problem, Crusoe seems inclined to grant the oracle more than he was later willing to allow: ". . . the devil seemed at that time to have more liberties granted him which it is evident have since been denied him . . ." (p. 276). Later, however, in a considerable chapter of *The History of the Devil*, Defoe exposed "the Devil's management in the pagan hierarchy by omens, entrails, augurs, oracles, and such-like pageantry of hell" (p. xiii). To the older belief that the oracles ceased with the appearance of Christ, Defoe replied, "I will not take upon me to say how far they are really ceased, more than they were before; I think it is much more reasonable to believe there was never any reality in them at all, or that any oracle ever gave out any answers but what were the invention of the priests, and the delusions of the Devil" (*HD*, p. 226).

From classical times a division of opinion existed as to the validity of the oracles in general and the utterances of the Sibyls in particular. The Church Fathers evidently credited all these prophecies to the Devil, but with the advent of the Reformation, some Protestants began to insist that the Oracles, as well as the Popish miracles, were delusions managed by the priests. In adopting the thesis that the oracles were impostures rather than demonic disclosures permitted by God, Defoe was following the line of skeptical inquiry fully argued by Antonius van Dale in his *De Oraculis Ethnicorum dissertationes duae* (1683), popularized by Fontenelle in his *Histoire des Oracles* (1686), and later defended by Le Clerc in the *Bibliotheque Choisis* (XIII, 179–282). Fontenelle, a copy of whose *Histoire* was in the Defoe-Farewell Library, must have appealed to Defoe with his delightfully urbane skepticism regarding the oracles. But Defoe was not merely cribbing from Fontenelle. He was acquainted with the earlier skeptical examinations of pagan religions. Reginald Scot had scoffed at the oracles; and John Webster affirmed "that all these [magicians] mentioned in the Scripture (nay, and that the Priests attending all the so famoused Oracles) were but meer Cheaters and Impostors . . ." (p. 29).[59] And if Defoe read Sir John Floyer, the English translator of Baltus, he found support even in the conservative camp for what mattered most to him—denial to the Devil of the power of prophecy. For a controversy persisted throughout the late seventeenth century and even into the eighteenth concerning the origin of oracular utterance. Bovet in 1684, Aubrey in 1696, Turner in 1697, and Beaumont in 1705 believed in the diabolical validity of the oracles; and even after skepticism had been thoroughly spread—by Bekker, Bordelon, Toland, Trenchard, and Swift (in his *Tale of a Tub*)—the credulous Beaumont as late as 1724 devoted the second section of his *Gleanings of Antiquities* to "A Discourse of Oracles, giving an Account of the Sibylline Oracles." But Defoe's position was by 1726 the normal educated one. Doubtless his readers agreed with Matthew Smith that

> . . . Dark and Double Oracles they told,
> (For th' old Seducer but by Guess projects,
> Comparing former Causes with Effects).[60]

This same type of black magic appears in augury, a more systematic type of prediction. Deriving largely from an examination of sacrifices and the flights of birds, augury had even less chance of retaining credibility after the attacks upon the oracles. Like most Christians Defoe treated it as a division of ecclesiastical and Satanic magic. "The augurs," Defoe explained, "were a sort of Roman priests, who pretended to foretell events by omens, by the chattering of birds, howling of dogs, and other uncouth noises of any kind in the air . . ." (*SM*, p. 203). "Crime did not render the Devil's agents scandalous in their profession, but rather, the wickeder they were, the fitter for the priesthood or augurate" (*SM*, pp. 203–204).

The most pretentious type of divination of Defoe's day was of course judicial astrology. Astrology itself was regarded by Defoe and most of his contemporaries—and perhaps by most of ours—as a valid science. Comprehending but not limited to astronomy, it dealt also with the influences of the heavenly bodies upon earthly bodies—minerals, plants, and animals. Just as the moon exercises a demonstrable pull upon the tides, so do the celestial bodies, many maintained, upon sublunary ones. "That corrupt and horrid imposition, that worst of juggle, the most simple and scandalous of all cheats, called judicial astrology" (*SM*, p. 277); however, Defoe considered the main exhibit of "Artificial or rational magic, in which they included the knowledge of all judicial astrology, the casting or calculating nativities, curing diseases by charms, by particular figures placed in this or that position; by herbs gathered at this or that particular crisis of time, and by saying such and such words over the patient, repeated so many times, and by such and such gestures, stroking the flesh in such and such a manner, and innumerable such-like pieces of mimicry; working not upon the disease itself but upon the imagination of the distempered people . . ." (*SM*, p. 48). A particularly heinous group, termed by the Biblical condemnation as "Observers of times," "by correspondence with an evil spirit, declared such and such days or times to have a particular fatality . . . ; and this part of the black art may take in such as carrying on the study of judicial astrology to the extreme, and to the gates of hell, ascribe events of things to the government and influence of the stars, . . . the practice of judicial astrology, though not a dealing with, or by the help of the Devil, is condemned here, as being a plain robbing divine Providence of its known glory, in directing and disposing both causes and events in all things relating to the government of mankind . . ." (*SM*, pp. 217–218).

Involved often in the practice of judicial astrology was the use of varied talismans and charms. This "kind of astrological magic" the Devil "managed with a great deal of subtlety and art, bringing the stars and planetary influences into play: and by an unpracticed subtlety, the art was then carried on with spell and charm, by words cut in metals, and in stones, divining by the beryl, and the amethyst, by the lustre of the emerald, and the ruby, and by all the old superstitions brought into a new rule of practice. This was called the talismans; or sympathetic conjuring-stone" (*SM*, p. 340).

Under the art of divination or soothsaying Defoe comprehended also "all those lesser pieces of low-prized art, called, telling fortunes, resolving difficulties, finding out and discovering secret things; and perhaps all the juggling part practiced at this time," when, Defoe suggested, it was now "without any correspondence with . . . any other spirit but that of fraud and legerdemain, which the divining or south-saying is only made a cover to" (*SM*, p. 217). ". . . The black art is at end," he maintained; "the Devil having no more need of the magicians, has dropped them, and manages his affairs himself; and the magicians, having no other access to the Devil than what is imaginary and carried on by mere legerdemain, whatever it was formerly, their number is decreased, and, in a manner, worn off by time; so that you have now nothing left but a few jugglers, cunning men, gipsies, and fortune-tellers" (*SM*, p. 372). For these modern fortune-tellers, like Duncan Campbell, whom Defoe never even advertised by a single reference, let alone a biography, he had unmitigated contempt: "there are likewise some other sorts of counterfeit devils in the world, such as gipseys, fortune-tellers, foretellers of good and bad luck, sellers of winds, raisers of storms, and many more. . . ; for it is evident he [the Devil] has little or nothing to do with them . . ." (*HD*, p. 344). But people are credulous: "away they run with their doubts and difficulties to these dreamers of dreams, tellers of fortunes, and personal oracles to be resolved; as if when they acknowledge the Devil is dumb, these could speak; and as if . . . heaven having taken away the Devil's voice, had furnished him with an equivalent, by allowing scolds, termagants, and old, weak, and superannuated wretches, to speak for him . . ." (*HD*, p. 234).

Of the possibility of white witchcraft, or the employment of the supernatural for effecting good, without the intervention of the Devil, Defoe was skeptical. Such a belief was common in his youth. It appears, for example, in Meric Casaubon's *Of Credulity and Incredulity in Things Natural, Civil, and Divine* (1668, pp. 115–117); in Henry More's *Antidote against Enthusiasm* (1662); and especially in his account of Greatrix the stroker, added to the 1726 edition of *Sadducismus Triumphatus* after More's death and obviously ridiculed by Defoe; and in Aubrey's *Miscellanies* (1696). Even in 1724 John Beaumont could in his *Gleanings of Antiquities* assert the mediation of beneficent spirits. To discredit such gullibility Defoe dramatized two considerable episodes. The first deals with a jealous countryman who is seeking to discover, by any means, the identity of his wife's imaginary lover, from a conjuror at Oundle, white or black—dealer with the Devil or no. Doubtless Defoe selected Oundle because it was famous for supernatural activity during his lifetime. In his *History of the Devil* (p. 285) he referred to the famous Northampton well at Oundle whence the sound of a drum beating occasionally emanated. In his *Certainty of the Worlds of Spirits* (1691) Richard Baxter had included a recent letter from Thomas Woodcocke concerning it: "When King *Charles* the Second died," Woodcocke wrote Baxter, "I went to the *Oundle*-Carrier, at the *Ram*-Inn in Smithfield; who told me their Well had drumm'd, and many People came to hear it" (p. 157). More important for the selection of Oundle, Eleanor Shaw and Mary Philips, the last English witches to be executed, were evidently burned at Oundle for witchcraft on March 7, 1705.[61] In his second episode Defoe dramatized another visit to a white magician, an obscure Kentish magician, or "doctor," Thomas Boreman, or Borman, who had lived near Maidstone (*SM*, p. 282). By 1699 Boreman had reprinted his translation of the suppositious compilation called *Aristotle's Legacy, or his Golden Cabinet of Secrets Opened*, in five brief illustrated "treatices" dealing with palmistry, moles, dreams, and day fatalities.[62] In addition, according to Defoe, "There are abundance of books upon this subject [magic] left by Dr. Boreman; and some, as they say, with rules of art, . . . but they are kept so up in private hands, that I do not find they are to be come at, by any means (*SM*, p. 312). Dr. Boreman evidently made his reputation in 1679 as an exorcist in a case reported in *Strange News from Arpington, near Bexly, in Kent, Being a True Narrative of a young Maid who was Possest with several Devils or Evil Spirits, one of which, by the Prayers of a Pious and Religious Doctor, who Came to visit her, was fetcht out of her Body, and appear'd in the Room in the Likeness of a large Snake, and twisted it self about the Doctors Neck, whilst he was at his Devotion.* Defoe must have been intrigued not only by the "eminent Doctor, whom she had long known," "the Maids greatest visitant," who drove out the evil spirits "by the double assistance of his Devotion and Physick," but by the smug opening of the pamphlet: "What Scope and Power the Almighty is pleas'd to allot the *Prince of Darkness, and his Evil Spirits,* would be more becoming the business of a large Volumn, than a little Sheet: some Divines have indeed endeavoured to guess at it, but none of them ever perfectly desided [*sic*] it" (pp. 2, 1). At any rate, *A System of Magick* contains several references to him (pp. 149–150, 377–378) and a long, dramatic episode (pp. 281–315) in which even his benign white magic is discounted. The final impression is that even so apparently innocent and benign a cunning man as Boreman was a hoax, or worse.

III | Defoe and Apparitions

EW, PERHAPS, BELIEVE IN THE DEVIL, and even fewer seriously
admit the service of the blessed angels. But many still believe in
ghosts, and after scientific study in England and America by societies for psychical research it has again become permissable in
scholarly circles to discuss apparitions. Thus in the last few decades
it has become possible to evaluate properly Defoe's ideas concerning and his fictional employment of this supernatural phenomenon.
Serious concern of writers on apparitions became increasingly ur-
gent after about 1660, for waning of belief in witchcraft removed
the most striking manifestation of man's immortality. Demonstration of the reality of apparitions, they thought, would establish
surely the reality of a spiritual world. Thus in 1720, in his "Vision
of the Angelic World" Defoe castigated those who, discrediting apparitions, "persuade themselves there are no spirits at all" and convince themselves that "there is no God, and so atheism takes its
rise."[1] Reserving *A True Relation of the Apparition of Mrs. Veal*
and "A Remarkable Passage of an Apparition" for particular examination in the following chapter, let us here concentrate upon
Defoe's analysis and exempla in his *Essay on the History and Reality of Apparitions* and upon his use of the apparition in his fiction.

Through his *History and Reality of Apparitions* and its frequently reprinted narratives, Defoe helped to shape the popular
thinking of his century concerning apparitions, for his stories were
reprinted, usually without acknowledgment, far into the following

century. The first edition, published by J. Roberts, appeared anonymously on March 18, 1727; and the second, a line for line reprint of the first, appeared in 1735.[2] In 1752, 1770, and again in 1791, there appeared collections which might almost be called new editions of Defoe's book.[3] Indeed for a century most collections of ghost stories included some of Defoe's narratives.[4]

In *The History and Reality of Apparitions* Defoe followed the pattern he had set in *The Political History of the Devil*: he divided his material into sacred and mundane. He first analyzed Scriptural apparitions, the Biblical appearances of God, Satan, and the angels. Then in the second and larger portion of the book he told scores of apparition stories, most of them new, and discussed on secular grounds the reality and origin of apparitions. Finally he advised on how to distinguish between good and evil spirits and how to demean oneself in their presence.

Defoe's division of material into sacred and profane was conventional, but awkward. Because of it, he repeated what he had earlier said concerning ghosts, or revenants. Moreover, he asked his reader to peruse sixty pages before he found a single extra-Scriptural ghost story. Such a division clearly suggests the author's sincere belief in the Bible as the supreme and final authority. Defoe was indeed so conscious of his own piety and his reader's probable lack thereof that he inserted mock apologies for moral and religious discussions and citations of Scripture: "And though I shall trouble my readers with as little as possible out of Scripture, especially at the beginning of my work, because I am unwilling they should throw it by before they read it out, which there would be some danger of, if I should begin too grave; yet, as I cannot go back to originals, or begin at the beginning, without a little history out of those ancient times, you must bear with my just naming the sacred historians. I will be as short as I can" (p. 8).

The division of material was by no means unusual: sacred evidence was frequently separated from the mundane, for apparitions as well as for other phenomena. To argue from the Revealed Word of God in the Holy Scriptures was of course then considered acceptable, and precedence for Scriptural narratives seemed only proper because of their priority and reliability. Defoe was also following the pattern of Joseph Glanvill in *Sadducismus Triumphatus*. In Part II, which comprises the narratives, Glanvill devoted a considerable section to "Proof of Apparitions, Spirits, and Witches, from Holy Scripture" before he went on to his "Choice Collection of Modern Relations."

Though in *The Political History of the Devil* Defoe had taken

Scriptural hints and dramatized them into veritable short stories, in the Biblical section of his *History and Reality of Apparitions* he permitted himself little original treatment and amplification. The only Scriptural apparition which he developed at any length, the spirit called up for Saul by the Witch of Endor, had been given at least a chapter by most writers on apparitions; Glanvill had alloted the incident more than half of his Scriptural space.

Among his extracanonical instances, Defoe used classical examples, modern classics, and—most important of all—a wealth of new stories. His classical offerings he severely restricted to three favorites briefly told: the apparition to Julius Caesar at the Rubicon; the appearance to Brutus on the eve of Phillipi of an unidentified spirit, previously identified in *The History of the Devil* in Shakespearian fashion as the ghost of Caesar (pp. 262–263); and the apparition which urged Alaric to conquer Rome.

Among the modern classics Defoe retold the spectral warning to "Charles VII" of France, properly narrated in *The History of the Devil* (p. 263) as of Charles VI; that to James IV of Scotland; and the apparition of James Haddock to Francis Taverner, where Defoe freely compressed the account in *Sadducismus Triumphatus*. From John Aubrey's *Miscellanies* (1721) Defoe quoted, occasionally smoothing the phraseology, the stories of the haunting of Caisho Borough, the specter appearing to Dr. Turberville's sister, the visit paid in transit by the departing soul of a lady just dead of the smallpox, and the popular story of the ghost of George Villiers, which Defoe appended in Clarendon's version as well as Aubrey's. Publication of variant accounts was not new to compilers of apparition stories: for this last, notorious apparition even Richard Boulton had offered the Clarendon and William Lily versions.[5] But Defoe carefully compared the credibility of the two accounts.

The contemporary stories in the *History of Apparitions* are numerous and professedly new. The original title page advertises "a great variety of surprizing and diverting examples, never publish'd before." In discussing dream visions Defoe promised "some account . . . within the compass of our own times; in which, . . . I do as much as possible, as I have done all along, omit all those accounts which others have published, referring you to those publications for the particulars, and only give you new and more modern accounts. . . . If I find it needful to quote what others have published, you shall have it justly marked as a quotation, that you may search for the truth in its original" (p. 204). When he was three quarters through his book he claimed, "I have hitherto studiously avoided giving you any accounts, however extraordinary, that have been already made public" (pp. 279–280).

For his sources it is not always easy to determine whether Defoe intended to suggest personal information from an eye or ear-witness, a manuscript, or a printed account. In his very first secular story, for example, the apparition of Owke Mouraski, he was far from consistent. "I have heard of a man who travelled four years ...," he began (p. 61). Later he remarked, "I have seen it in manuscript many years ago ..." (p. 74). Elsewhere he noted, "I have had it by me many years ..." (p. 61).

One source upon which Defoe must have relied for his material was oral report. For more than a score of years as a professional journalist he was especially interested in the supernatural. On January 25, 1705, as secretary of the Scandalous Club, he replied at some length in his *Review* to queries concerning apparitions; and the following year he published the best and best-selling ghost story of the century—*A True Relation of the Apparition of Mrs. Veal.* Some of these apparition narratives are second-hand stories. "I have heard a story," he remarked as he began the story of the murderer at the bar whose conscience evokes the apparition of his victim (*HA*, p. 102). The story of the young man who takes a fatal captaincy in the army despite the warning apparition of his dead father came to Defoe from the young man's lieutenant (p. 226). Other stories are professedly first-hand. The narrative of Captain Thomas Rogers, Defoe asserted (p. 213) that he had from the captain himself. A dream concerning a dead mistress, similarly, he had "from the person himself" (p. 209).

Some of these supposedly ear-witness narratives may have been taken from the author's own experience. As was seen earlier, a dream of a gentleman's stripping a little child of her jewels and purse, a story which Defoe asserted that he had from the dreamer's own lips (p. 209), he had already detailed in *The History of the Devil* (pp. 330–331), where he had attributed it to a distressed tradesman; and he had used the dream as a reality in the vivid incident where Moll Flanders plunders a trusting child.[6] A story of a man tormented by reiterated lascivious dreams Defoe had already used in *The History of the Devil* (pp. 329–330), where the dreamer is represented as an intimate friend of the author; and the same story reappears in *The History and Reality of Apparitions* as "on two or three occasions ... mentioned by other hands" (p. 211). And if these were not the dreams of Defoe himself, surely his was the admonitory dream, about the year 1701, of the "party man" concerning the arrest impending if he returned to London. The original was evidently a dream forecasting arrest after the publication of *The Shortest Way with the Dissenters* (1702), and the brother-in-law R—D— in the dream was probably Defoe's sister's husband

Robert Davis.[7] Similarly, in "A Vision of the Angelick World" (pp. 280–281) Defoe included the personal experience, as has been suggested above, of a supernatural intimation concerning a subsequent arrest. And certainly Defoe was the London merchant A. B. who witnesses a phantasm in his counting house one evening (*HA*, pp. 167–169).

Other narratives in the *History of Apparitions* were evidently based upon manuscript accounts. Some of these doubtless were sent him by the readers of his *Review*. Moreover, he might well have had access to a commonplace collection of such stories. In *Serious Reflections*, for example, Crusoe remarks, "I have seen several collections of such things made by private hands, some relating to family circumstances, some to public . . ." (pp. 189–190). The Dr. Scott story, for example, Defoe remarked, "My author assures me" was "never yet published in print" (*HA*, p. 293); and concerning another story he cited "My author" (p. 246) as his unpublished source.

Of all the narratives in the *History of Apparitions* which came to Defoe in manuscript, the relation of Joseph Beacon is the most interesting and important; for it demonstrates again the striking reality which supernatural communication exhibited in Defoe's own experience and observation:

> This young man had an elder brother, who lived in London; he was a fine gentleman, and a scholar, and was at that time studying physic. He was also a stout, brave gentleman, and in particular understood a sword, that is to say, how to use a sword, as well as most gentlemen in England.
>
> He had an accidental re-encounter with a gentleman in the street, in that short street which goes out of Fleet-street into Salisbury-court; and being so complete a master of his weapon, he wounded his antagonist, and drove him into a tavern in the street, from whence came out two more men upon him with their swords, but both of them found the gentleman so much an over-match for them, that they left him as fast as the first; whereupon a fourth came out, not with a sword, but a fire-fork taken hastily out of the tavern kitchen, and running at this gentleman with it, knocked him down, and broke his skull, of which wound he afterwards died.
>
> While this was done in London, his brother, as far off as Boston in New England, writing to his master the merchant, (and who gives this account of it,) after other business, writ this postscript.
>
> Sir,
> I beg you will be pleased in your return to this to let me have some account, as much as conveniently may be, of how my brother does, and what condition he is in, which you will excuse my importunity for, when you read the following account, viz.:
> The 20th of——last, about six o'clock in the morning, lying in my bed, and broad awake, my brother, or an apparition of my brother, came to the bed's feet, and opened the curtain, looking full in my face, but did not speak. I was very much frighted, and however I so far recovered as to say to him, Brother, what is the matter with you?

> He had a napkin-cap on his head, which was very bloody, he looked pale and ghastly, and said, I am basely murdered by——, (naming the person,) but I shall have justice done me; and then disappeared.
>
> Now this letter was so dated, that it was impossible any account could be sent of the disaster, that could reach thither in that time; for it was not dated above fourteen days after the fact was committed in London; and that it was genuine I am well assured, because I saw the letter within an hour after it was received in London, read it myself, and knew the young man's hand, and the young man also, perfectly well, as I did his brother that was killed also, very intimately.
>
> The young man was sober, religious and sensible, not given to whimsey, or lightheaded fancies, not vapourish or distempered, not apt to see double, or to dream waking, as many of our apparition-making people are. . . . (pp. 169–171)

Now this same story, taken from the percipient, Joseph Beacon, a respected member of his congregation, had already been published by Cotton Mather in his *Wonders of the Invisible World* ([London, 1693] pp. 79–81). Mather's version, which concentrates more on the apparition and the epilogue than on the actual encounter, was reprinted in Turner's *Compleat History* (pp. 34–35) and in Richard Boulton's *Compleat History* (I, 254–255) and was the subject of several queries in John Dunton's *Athenian Mercury* for March 21, 1693 (vol. IX, no. 29). At first blush it would seem the source of Defoe's account, and Defoe's claim that his stories of recent apparitions were all fresh would then be patently false. But by a curious coincidence, Defoe had the story from the percipient himself. Evidently Defoe was himself "A. B.," "his master the merchant (and who gives this account of it)," (p. 170), and Joseph Beacon was his agent in Boston.[8] Thus Defoe was not retelling a familiar tale, but narrating a vivid dream apparition to the veridity of which he could himself attest.

Of the allegedly new stories, however, at least two were definitely in print, and perhaps others were. One, the story of the conscience-stricken traveler, drawn back to his own betrayal at the scene of his crime, was a common example of the guilty conscience. In Thomas Taylor's *Second Part* of Thomas Beard's *Theatre of God's Judgement* (4th ed. [1648], pp. 69–70), where it is briefly told, the details of the murder itself, ignored by Defoe, are given as much attention as is the final episode, and the torments of conscience are only briefly touched upon. Nor were they developed in the brief version by Francis Kirkman in his continuation of William Head's *English Rogue* (Part IV, ch. xvii). To prepare for the crucial scene where the murderer, returned after almost a score of years of wandering to the scene of his crime, takes alarm of his conscience and flees at the shouts of "Stop him, stop him!" (*HA*, p. 108), Defoe evidently transferred to this story the wanderings of the peregrine who, like Francis Cartwright, had been driven about continually in search of peace of conscience (Turner, ch. cxii). In Beard's version the story is a factual narrative; in Defoe's it is a brief drama where the motivation and mood are carefully built up to prepare for the climactic scene.

Even though the original murder, according to Beard, had been committed in Queen Elizabeth's time, Defoe could, as he alleged, have "had the substance of this relation from an ear-witness" (p. 110). Moreover, since this story does not involve an actual apparition, he must have felt freer here to borrow and elaborate. He may have felt similarly free in his story of the murderer at the bar—one of three or four stories for which analogues are apparent. This story, which boasts the distinction of being still current,[9] concerns "a certain man who was brought to the bar of justice on suspicion of murder" (*HA*, p. 102) and, seeing the ghost of his victim ready to take the witness stand, remonstrates, "My lord, says he aloud, that is not fair, 'tis not according to law, he's not a legal witness" (p. 103). Now in the trial of G. B. at Salem in 1692, according to Cotton Mather (pp. 62–63) and Deodat Lawson,[10] ghosts appeared, but to the witnesses rather than to the accused; but since this was not a real apparition, Defoe may conceivably have used this tense courtroom setting to heighten the effect of his story.

For the story of the discovery made by an apparition to Dr. Scott of a secreted conveyance, a narrative which Defoe's booksellers even advertised on the revised title page, an analogue exists in a story of a ghost appearing on behalf of abused orphans to inform a particular clergyman "*In such a Room in the house they should finde in a certain Chest the Will and Other Writings to pass away the Estate.*"[11] But this type of specter appearing on behalf of orphans was so popular that it is unnecessary to suppose that Defoe altered the above original to the Scott narrative.

Wherever he may have found his materials, in adapting them Defoe was dramatic and realistic. He used conversation, frequently paragraphed as dialogue, sometimes identified speakers in playbook fashion; employed details which were sometimes deliberately inconsequential and realistic; frequently interrupted to explain or enter a caveat; and almost always commented, finally, concerning the credibility and significance of each narrative.

His remarkable gift of dramatizing expository materials Defoe had already exhibited in such a sober work as *The Family Instructor* (1715, 1718). In the *History and Reality of Apparitions* the use of dialogue is especially characteristic of Defoe's style. In a dozen stories borrowed with little or no alteration, dialogue appears in less than half. In the thirty-two which Defoe told in more or less his own way, dialogue appears in two thirds, and this dialogue is usually spaced in playbook fashion. Sometimes, moreover, the names of the speakers are prefixed in playbook style—a feature of Defoe's narrative style familiar to readers of *Farther Adventures of Robinson Crusoe*.

A stylistic device which Defoe used to increase verisimilitude is the employment of minute, sometimes inconsequential details. This facility is evident in the story of the conscience-stricken peregrine:

> When he arrived at London, intending to land at Westminster, he took a wherry at Billingsgate, to carry him through bridge. It happened, that two lighters loaden with coals, run foul of the boat he was in, and of one another, over-against Queenhithe, or thereabouts; and the watermen were so very hard put to it, that they had much ado to avoid being crushed between the lighters, so that they were obliged to get into one of the lighters and let the boat sink.
>
> This occasioned him, contrary to his design, to go on shore a little to the eastward of Queenhithe: from thence he walked up on foot toward Cheapside, intending to take a coach for Westminster.
>
> As he passed a street which crosses out of Bread-street into Bow-lane, being almost night. . . . (*HA*, p. 108)

Another excellent example is to be found in the story of Dr. Scott, where inconsequential dialogue helps to make the story credible and serves, as do the comic comments of Juliet's nurse, tantalizingly to defer the denouement. Dr. Scott and his host come finally to the chest which according to the apparition would contain the conveyance: "The gentleman looks at the chest smiling; I remember opening it very well; and turning to his servant, Will, says he, don't you remember that chest? Yes, sir, says Will, very well; I remember you were so weary you sat down upon the chest when everything was out of it; you clapped down the lid and sat down, and sent me to my lady to bring you a dram of citron; you said you were so tired you was ready to faint" (p. 303).

Because of their greatest detail and dramatic qualities, such stylistic devices as these naturally demanded more space than was ordinarily accorded such narratives. Witchcraft relations were of course sometimes lengthy and detailed indeed, and poltergeist stories often extended to considerable length, as does the story of the Drummer of Tedworth. But most ghost stories, ancient or modern, are quite short. The average ghost story in *Sadducismus Triumphatus* runs to little more than two pages; the apparition stories in George Sinclair's *Satan's Invisible World Discovered* (1685) average below three small pages; and those in Aubrey's *Miscellanies* are even briefer. Defoe's new stories, on the other hand, average about five and a half pages, and four narratives run above sixteen pages each. For a similarly well-developed apparition story one must go back to the *Apparition of Mrs. Veal* (1706).

Another characteristic device of Defoe in the *History and Reality of Apparitions* is his adoption of the editorial role. Frequently he interrupted dialogue with an editorial comment, introduced with an asterisk or an "N. B.," indented, and italicized. These brief comments, which are almost always used with dialogue, shorten, explain, or object. But even more characteristic is the editorial comment at the close of each narrative. In all the forty-four relations it is only twice omitted. In most stories it is given at some length; and in some the relation consists largely of the final comment. This practice was not entirely new with occult writers. In his *Pandemonium* (1684), for example, Richard Bovet appended a commentative Advertisement to most of his relations. Throughout his book, Defoe insists, "I choose . . . to insist upon the moral of every story, whatever the fact may be, and to enforce the inference, supposing the story to be real, or whether it be really so or not, which is not much material" (*HA*, p. 337). The moral, then, is central in the *History and Reality of Apparitions*, and the stories are exemplary demonstrations of the ideas which Defoe was illustrating and dramatizing.

Of the pertinent philosophical and theological controversies concerning apparitions, Defoe was certainly aware, and he did not in the *History and Reality of Apparitions* eschew philosophical and theological argument, where, in approved Protestant fashion, he utilized the twin lights of Reason and Revelation. But he recognized that an extended disquisition on "pneumatics," or spiritual forms, would provide but a dull inception. Moreover, why argue about the philosophical possibility that spirit exists independent of body when "the evidence will amount to a demonstration of the facts, and demonstration puts an end to argument" (p. 7). Thus Defoe refused to argue the philosophy of spirit: "I shall therefore spend but little time to prove or to argue for the reality of apparition. Let Mr. Glanville and his antagonists, the Hobbists and Sadducees of these times, be your disputants upon that subject . . ." (p. 5). Defoe was not by a journalistic subterfuge avoiding an essential duty. Even the learned Sinclair similarly introduced his *Satan's Invisible World Discovered*: "My purpose is only by some few *Collections* to prove the existence of *Devils, Spirits, Witches,* and *Apparitions*. The *Philosophical Arguments*, which are brought for this end, though very cogent, yet many of them are so profound and speculative, that they require a greater attention and sagacity, than many learned men, that are not used to consider, will allow"

([Edinburgh, 1871] Sig. A recto). And in the Epistle Dedicatory to his *Late Memorable Providences relating to Witchcrafts and Possessions,* Cotton Mather apologized: "Had I on the Occasion before me handled the *Doctrine of Demons,* or launched forth into Speculations about *Magical Mysteries,* I might have made some Ostentation, that I have *read* something, and *thought* a little in my time, but it would neither have been *convenient* for *me,* nor profitable for those *plain Folks,* whose *Edification* I have all along aimed at" ([London, 1691] Sig. A2 verso).

On the Continent, of course, belief in apparitions was attacked and ridiculed at some length. In his *Monde Enchanté* Balthazar Bekker attempted to demonstrate that "il est constant par les lumieres de la Raison & de la Nature, qu' excepté l'Ame de l'homme, de pareils Esprits ne sont point en être" ([Amsterdam, 1694] II, 12). And in his Quixotic *L'Histoire des Imaginations extravagantes de Monsieur Oufle* (1710), Laurent Bordelon spoofed apparitions in particular.

Although witch persecutions gradually disappeared in England during the course of the eighteenth century, belief in apparitions was in Defoe's day still general. Not that England had not had its share of skeptics. Even as early as 1584 Reginald Scot maintained that apparitions were mere illusions. Thomas Hobbes continued this incredulity; and more recently the attack had been waged by John Toland in his *Letters to Serena* (1704) and John Trenchard in his *Natural History of Superstition* (1709). But these men were in a minority. Many of the most eminent attackers of witchcraft distinctly affirmed their belief in apparitions. So, for example, did John Webster, in 1677, and so did Francis Hutchinson in his *Historical Essay concerning Witchcraft*: "the sober Belief of good and bad Spirits is an essential Part of every good Christian's Faith . . ." (2d ed. [1720], Sig. A3 verso).

Realizing that the credulity of previous writers like Henry More and Richard Boulton had prejudiced his case, Defoe discounted the apparitions effected by fraud or imagination. Here the writer on apparitions was able to bring a comic element to a subject all too frequently macabre; the Protestant was able to add an element of polemic satire as he inveighed against Catholic deception. The Protestant writers found ready at hand a veritable treasure of saints legends, mediaeval and modern. In 1570, for example, Ludvig Lavater, in his *De Spectris,* devoted several chapters to Romish impostures, with almost an entire chapter on the Jetzer fraud. To his volume Samuel Harsnett gave the title *A Declaration of Egregious*

Popish Impostures (1603); and a chapter, at least, devoted to Romish cheats became subsequently a standard feature of apparition books. Bekker, who in his *Monde Enchanté* gave the fullest account of world-wide frauds, was following an approved technique.

Defoe, then, in his Chapter XIV, "Of Sham Apparitions, and Apparitions which have been the Effect of Fraud," is playing a popular Protestant game as well as clearing his material and providing some comic relief. Following a roughly chronological and at the same time westwardly sketch, Defoe rapidly surveyed cheats from classical myth and religion, then gave at greater length a contemporary sham from the Greek island of Scyros, freely adapting it from John Ozell's translation of Joseph Pitton de Tournefort's *Voyage into the Levant* ([London, 1718] I, 337–338). Defoe reported with the mock seriousness of a pretended Catholic convert the appearance of Christ to St. Peter at Rome, an apparition taken from a sermon of Richard Smith—a sermon which Defoe reprinted later that same year in his *New Family Instructor* (pp. 122–123). Briefly related stories of angels appearing to St. Francis of Assisi and Ignatius Loyola, and the appearance of Loyola himself to his disciple Leonard Kesel of Cologne, Defoe took piecemeal and almost verbatim from Henry Wharton's polemic *Enthusiasm of the Church of Rome* (1688). The rather fully told story of Jetzer and the monks of Berne, a story which had appeared in book form and been told again and again, Defoe evidently took from the version authenticated and published by Gilbert Burnet in his *Some Letters* ([1708], pp. 30–42).

Finally Defoe went rapidly through the apparition material to be found in the heathen world, drawing upon his voluminous knowledge of travel literature. Two sham apparitions he saved for his last chapter. One, a poltergeist sham played by schoolboys near Dorking, in Surrey, reminds one of the poltergeist fraud investigated by Defoe in his "Vision of the Angelick World" (pp. 291–292) in Essex and found literally to be monkey tricks.[12]

Writers on apparitions were ready to admit the impositions of others; even fervent believers granted that the credulous only too often imposed upon themselves. Although in his *Blow at Modern Sadducism* (1668) Joseph Glanvill pointed out the often neglected fact that one positive experience more than offsets a thousand impostures, he also here reiterated that "*Imagination* . . . is the most *various thing* in all the *world* . . ." (p. 12).

This power of the imagination to shape its fancies no one recognized better than Defoe did. In 1705, in his *Consolidator*, he ridiculed the ill effects which the operation of "Elevators" (the imagination) had upon the minds of the fanciful: ". . . we have some people talking to images of their own forming, and seeing more devils and spectres than ever appeared. From hence we have weaker heads, not able to bear the operation, seeing imperfect visions, as of horses and men without heads or arms, light without fire, hearing voices without sound, and noises without shape, as their own fears or fancies broke the phenomena before the entire formation" (pp. 318–319).

Several years later, in *Farther Adventures of Robinson Crusoe*, the protagonist is noncommittal:

> I have often heard Persons of good Judgment say, That all the Stir people make in the World about Ghosts and Apparitions, is owing to the Strength of Imagination, and the powerful Operation of Fancy in their Minds; that there is no such Thing as a Spirit appearing, or a Ghost walking, *and the like*: That Peoples poring affectionately upon the past Conversation of their deceasd Friends, so realizes it to them, that they are capable of fancying upon some extraordinary Circumstances, that they see them; talk to them, and are answered by them, when, in Truth, there is nothing but Shadow and Vapour in the Thing; and they really know nothing of the Matter.
>
> For my Part, I know not to this hour whether there are any such things as real Apparitions, Spectres, or Walking of People after they are dead, or whether there is any Thing in the Stories they tell us of that Kind, more than the Product of Vapours, sick Minds, and wandering Fancies. . . . (II, 112–113)

Later, in his discussion of the occult in his "Vision of the Angelick World," Defoe had Crusoe omit any discussion of apparitions "because . . . they bear much scandal from the frequent impositions of our fancies and imaginations upon our judgments and understandings . . ." (p. 249). One of the most vivid incidents in the *Journal of the Plague Year* shows a concourse of passers-by strangely fascinated by a deluded man as he points out the motions of an imagined ghost in an adjoining churchyard: "I look'd earnestly every way, and at the very Moment, that this Man directed, but could not see the least Appearance of any thing; but so positive was this poor man, that he gave the People the Vapours in abundance, and sent them away trembling, and frighted; till at length, few People, that knew of it, car'd to go thro' that Passage; and hardly any Body by Night, on any Account whatever" (p. 29).

This appealing mixture of comedy and pathos does not reappear in the hallucinations of *The History and Reality of Apparitions*. Here Defoe uses only two types—the comic and the conscience-stricken. One of the narratives tells how a gentleman was stopped on a bridge by the Devil in the shape of a bear, that is, the servant Gervais later reveals, an ass. Since this story does not involve a proper apparition, Defoe may have built it up from a hint in

Richard Bovet's *Pandemonium,* which relates how Mr. Edmund Ansty's horse was frightened by the Devil in the shape of a *"huge Bear"* with "a pair of very large flaming Eyes."[13] A much more serious type is the apparition induced by the active conscience:

> Conscience, indeed, is a frightful apparition itself, and I make no question but it oftentimes haunts an oppressing criminal into restitution, and is a ghost to him sleeping or waking: nor is it the least testimony of an invisible world that there is such a drummer as that in the soul, that can beat an alarm when he pleases, and so loud, as no other noise can drown it, no music quiet it or make it hush, no power silence it, no mirth allay it, no bribe corrupt it.
> Conscience raises many a devil, that all the magic in the world cannot lay; it shows us many an apparition that no other eyes can see, and sets spectres before us with which the Devil has no acquaintance; conscience makes ghosts walk, and departed souls appear, when the souls themselves know nothing of it. (*HA,* p. 101)

Defoe had already told his favorite story of this type, a story in which accidental circumstances are given a supernatural interpretation by the aroused conscience. It is the narrative of a university student warned from atheism to belief by a voice calling upon him to "Repent!" Defoe may have had the story from George Duckett when he visited him in 1705;[14] but he saved it until 1720, when he used it in his "Visions of the Angelick World" (pp. 296–314). In *The History and Reality of Apparitions* he felt forced to confine himself to a brief reference (p. 7).

In the literature of apparitions one of the most important controversies concerns the possibility of the revenant—the ghost of the dead revisiting the earth to communicate with or appear to the living. For humanity in general this possibility has always been a question of supreme importance, as its authentication would prove an active and personal immortality. For students of literature the problem, oddly enough, has centered around the provenance of the ghost of Hamlet's father and has led to the reprinting of Lavater's *Of Ghostes and Spirites Walking by Nyght,* an event which perhaps demonstrates the superior power of the actual ghost over an imaginary one like that of Banquo, forged in the conscience of Macbeth.

For Protestants the validity of the revenant was strongly compromised by the rejection of the Catholic doctrine of Purgatory. Catholic theory allowed for the revenant; Protestant theology was faced with an embarrassing dilemma, for, according to all but a few factions like the soul-sleepers, the soul upon death immediately wings its way either to Heaven or to Hell. Most Protestant writers who accepted the possibility of apparitions, then, rejected the revenant. Glanvill, however, came more and more to accept it. In his *Blow to Modern Sadducism* he seems to have accepted the

possibility: "*who saith* that *happy* departed *souls* were never employed in any *ministeries* here below?" (p. 87). In his *Essays* (1676)
he was noncommittal. In *Sadducismus Triumphatus*, however, he
quite positively accepted the type; departed souls, he maintained,
"have a Power of appearing in their own personal Shapes to whom
there is Occasion . . ." (Postscript, p. 29). But among learned Protestants Glanvill was in a distinct minority. Richard Baxter admitted the possibility, but did not assert it positively.[15] Increase Mather
indeed wavered on this point. In his *Essay* (1684) he held, "there is
a Gulf fixed" (p. 211), but later, in his *Cases of Conscience* ([1693],
p. 19) he thought the revenant merely "not usual." Others, like
Lavater, Perkins, and Webster, definitely rejected the possibility
of the revenant, although some, like Hall and Hallywell, maintained that the departed continue their affections and concern for
the living.[16]

With this majority opinion Defoe was in complete agreement.
The theory of the revenant he rejected as "perfectly inconsistent
with either reason or revealed religion" (*HA*, p. 123). It is "a notion empty and not to be defended; incongruous, and inconsistent
either with Scripture, the Christian religion, or reason, and founded
only in the bewildered imaginations and dreams of ignorant people, who neither know how or by what rules to judge of such things,
or are capable of right conceptions about them" (pp. 74–75). The
joys of Heaven, Defoe considered, are such that the soul in bliss
would undertake no journey to an alien world which no longer
interested it. And even the soul in Hell would not desire to return
to a world where it had fashioned for itself an eternity of torment
and where no restitution would ameliorate the Eternal Damnation.
So important was this rejection of the ghost for Defoe that he devoted a separate chapter to ridiculing "the many strange inconve-
niences and ill consequences" which would attend the power of departed souls to revisit and take part in the affairs of men:

> How many weeping widows, starving orphans and oppressed families
> have in our age suffered by the loss of money which their fathers and other
> ancestors left for their subsistence and establishment in a certain city cham-
> ber, or put into a certain exchecquer upon the public faith! According to
> this notion, neither the visible nor the invisible world would have been at
> peace: the habited visible world would have been continually haunted
> with ghosts, and we should never have been quiet for the disturbance of
> spirits and apparitions: the invisible world would have been in a contin-
> ued hurry and uneasiness; spirits and unembodied souls asking leave to go
> back again to see their wills rightly performed, and to harrass their exec-
> utors for injuring their orphans; and all the ages of time would have been
> taken up in giving a satisfaction to them in such and such cases. (pp. 98–99)

In the *History and Reality of Apparitions* Defoe never considered, perhaps deliberately, the worldly visitation of a revenant for any journeys other than angry or malicious ones.

Of all the types of apparition, the spirit in transit from this world to the next has always been perhaps the most dramatic and appealing; and the London Society for Psychical Research long ago amassed strong evidence of this particular type. At first Defoe had evidently believed in its possibility. In 1706, when he published the *Apparition of Mrs. Veal,* he gave no indication that the apparition was not to be regarded as the ghost of Mrs. Veal herself. In 1727 in his *History of Apparitions,* however, he devoted two chapters to exhibit as "supremely ridiculous" the idea that such an appearance "must be just in the article of death, just when the person was dying, and the soul departing; as if the soul could stay in its passage, between life and the eternal state, to call at this or that place, and deliver a message. . ." (p. 271). Even though an apparition may actually be seen at such a time, then, it would not involve, Defoe believed, the spirit of the departing.

But if Defoe rejected these types of apparitions, he brought forward evidence and arguments for others: dream visions and apparitions managed by Satan and by a class of intermediate spirits. An important type of apparition for Defoe is the dream vision, or dream apparition: "There may be dreams without apparition, as there may be apparitions without dreams; but apparition in dream may be as really an apparition as if the person who saw it was awake: the difference may be here, that the apparition in a dream is visible to the soul only, for the soul never sleeps; and an apparition to the eyesight is visible in common perspective" (p. 202). Earlier in the "Vision of the Angelick World," Defoe had argued the validity of the dream apparition: "Now every unembodied spirit is an angel of the Lord in some sense; and as angels and spirits may be the same thing in respect of this influence upon us in dream, so it is still; and when any notice for good, or warning against evil, is given us in a dream, I think 'tis no arrogance at all for us to say the angel of the Lord appeared to us in a dream, or to say some good spirit gave me warning of this in a dream;—take this which way you will" (pp. 250–251). As we have seen, these dream visions Defoe had used in a number of his novels: in *Robinson Crusoe,* for example, Crusoe has in a dream a vivid apparition of an angel armed with a spear, sent to warn him of threatened punishment.

Such a belief in nocturnal visitation was in Defoe's day very much the same as it had been in Chaucer's. Most writers on dreams expounded the possibility of the supernaturally inspired dream, as did even Thomas Hobbes: "when God raiseth them supernaturally, to signify his will, they are not improperly termed God's messengers. . . ."[17] Defoe's discussion of this type is not very different from the treatment in Le Loyer's monumental *Histoires des Spectres* (book IV, chs. xxii and xxiii).

In Defoe's day and indeed from the time of Lavater, however, most English theologians and writers on the supernatural thought that apparitions were largely the work of Satan and his evil angels. This belief gained ground especially when most Protestants rejected the possibility of the revenant and when spectral evidence accumulated during the witchcraft trials. But Defoe vigorously opposed the conventional view of their supernatural appearances. Some apparitions, he agreed, are the work of Satan and his cohorts, but far fewer than are popularly imagined. He was not alone in his opposition: writers like N. Orchard, John Wagstaffe, and John Webster thought that witchcraft hunters attributed to Satan overmuch power—a sort of rival omnipotence, a heresy manifest even in clerical circles at Salem. Some, including Webster himself, explained that Satan and his evil angels were acting merely as the executioners of God's vengeance. But this idea also Defoe summarily rejected: " . . . this must at least seem to bring Providence to a necessity of employing him [Satan] for want of other officers, which I think is highly detracting, and dishonouring of the divine Majesty, as if he was obliged to employ the Devil, as we may say, for want of a better" (p. 56). Defoe had a practical as well as a theological reason to oppose such an idea, for if evil angels were sometimes employed on God's missions, then it was obviously quite difficult to distinguish between good and evil angels and to determine how to conduct ourselves toward them.

Similarly, most Anglican and Puritan divines held that angelic appearance had either ceased or greatly decreased since the Bible had rendered direct visitation no longer necessary. Hall, for instance, asserted that "to have the visible apparition of a good Angell, it is a thing so geason and uncouth, that it is enough for all the world to wonder at" (p. 59). Defoe also absolutely rejected the possibility of a Heavenly appearance, except for a miracle. The daily revelation of the Bible had replaced the ministration of angels; and the causes and results of appearances seemed to Defoe to deny their celestial origin: "Is it likely an angel should be sent from heaven to find out the old woman's earthen dish with thirty or forty shillings in it? or an angel should be sent to harass this man for a legacy of perhaps five or ten pounds?" (pp. 35–36). Moreover had Heavenly angels been sent on any mission, he argued, using Scriptural examples as his evidence, their message would have been clear and efficacious rather than cloudy and ineffectual. The apparition which warned George Villers, Defoe maintained, could not have been a Heavenly angel, for "it would have been effectual to have awakened and reformed him" (p. 288). Actually Defoe answered this objection himself: "I might add here what is rational enough to suggest, viz., that Heaven in its infinite wisdom and goodness may have appointed these good spirits to give such notices, yet allowing them to do no more, that the mind of man being duly alarmed at the approaching evil, and believing something very fatal to him is at hand . . . should turn his eyes (at least) a little upward, and call for direction and counsel from that hand, who alone can both direct and deliver" (p. 43). Earlier, in his "Vision of the Angelick World" (p. 255), Defoe had raised and answered this same objection. But in the *History and Reality of Apparitions* he wanted to attribute the inefficacy not to man's willfulness but to the character of the apparition.

If Defoe's ideas concerning the identity of apparitions was unusual, his advice concerning their reception was comparatively conventional. One of the major obligations of the writer on apparitions was to instruct his readers how to conduct themselves in the presence of a spirit; and a proper demeanor depended upon the origin of the specter. Hamlet's first words to the ghost, one will recall, were "Be thou a spirit of health or goblin damned." To assist their readers some of the Catholics had drawn up lists of determining characteristics. Defoe doubtless knew Noel Taillepied's suggestion (ch. XXIV) that good angels inspire awe and reverential fear and that their ideas are in conformity with the word of God. Most Protestant writers adopted these few suggestions; Thomas Tryon, one curious sectarian in whom Defoe was evidently interested, added (pp. 123–124) that good angels are always masculine but never bearded!

It would seem a simple solution to suggest, as Camfield (pp. 84–85) and others did, that good angels come to warn or encourage and that evil angels appear to tempt. But Satan, some pointed out, might disguise his nefarious designs under a cloak of benevolence. As Lavater warned, "Diuels doe sometimes bid men doe those things which are good. . . ."[18] Or Satan might be constrained by God into a mission of good counsel, or appear as a *flagellum dei.* In such uncertainty one could perhaps still best distinguish by the motive and effect of the appearance. Baxter could only say that evil appearances were distinguished by "Lying, Malignity, and Hurtfulness"; and Defoe noted that it was the purpose of devils to hurt, to terrify without amending, as in the frightening of Charles VI of France and Caisho Borough.

Discrimination between good and evil appearances enables the percipient to conduct himself properly toward the apparition. Perhaps Taillepied best stated Defoe's suggested code of etiquette when he suggested the proper greeting: *"If thou art of God, speak; if thou are not of God, begone"* (p. 168). Defoe specifically warned his readers against violence to evil spirits: "I knew one fired a gun at an apparition, and the gun burst in a hundred pieces in his hand, that is, in a great many pieces. Another struck at an apparition with a sword, and broke his sword in pieces, and wounded his hand grievously" (p. 335). On the other hand, one should not be afraid of an evil apparition, for the Devil has no power to hurt without God's permission.

Such advice concerning the proper conduct toward apparitions was naturally followed by injunctions toward a moral life which would invite the intercourse with the blessed angels and discourage Satan from any onslaught. Drage thus admonished, "Our best way is to desire GOD's Protection, and pray to him and keep our selves from wickedness. . . ."[19] Increase and Cotton Mather advised fear of God, keeping close to the Bible, fasting, prayer, and (particularly Cotton Mather) soul and church work. But perhaps Defoe himself best summed up the due preparations toward apparitions: "There's no scorning the terrors of a messenger from the other world, but by a settled, established composure of the soul, founded on the basis of peace within, peace of conscience, peace and innocence, or peace and penitence, which is, in effect, all one . . ." (pp. 316–317).

IV | Defoe, Mrs. Veal, and Mrs. Bargrave

E VEN MORE INTERESTING than the beliefs and evidences of Defoe's *Essay on the History and Reality of Apparitions* (1727) is the ghost story widely recognized as the gem of the eighteenth century genre—*A True Relation of the Apparition of one Mrs. Veal, the Next Day after her Death, to one Mrs. Bargrave at Canterbury, the 8th of September, 1705* (published 1706).[1] *The Apparition of Mrs. Veal* especially demands reconsideration because Defoe bibliographers have never provided any convincing evidence that Defoe wrote it and because three recently discovered versions of the story, all of them earlier than Defoe's, are not available to throw light upon it. Anterior to Defoe's version are four accounts dated 1705: E. B.'s letter of September 13; Lucy Lukyn's letter to her aunt, dated October 9; Stephen Gray's report to John Flamsteed, of November 15, embodying an account written by an "ingenious Gentleman"; and the account published in *The Loyal Post* on December 24. To these four must be added three accounts subsequent to *The Apparition of Mrs. Veal* and based upon it and upon interviews with Mrs. Bargrave: some additions and corrections made in his copy in 1714 by an anonymous interviewer; an anonymous account, perhaps by John Spavan, prefixed in 1720 to Spavan's abridgment of Charles Drelincourt's *Christian's Consolations against the Fears of Death*; and the detailed version by the Reverend Mr. Payne, based upon an interview with Mrs. Bargrave in 1722, but unpublished until 1766.[2]

Any reappraisal of *The Apparition of Mrs. Veal* made in the light of these accounts must consider several problems. Did Defoe actually write *The Apparition of Mrs. Veal*? What role did Mrs. Bargrave play in the genesis and transmission of the story? Was she merely the reporter, or was she creator and author as well? Did Defoe interview her? Did he believe her story? Was Defoe taking advantage of sensational material without regard to its veridity; or was he reporting what seemed to him to be a striking manifestation of man's communion with the world of spirits?

Ever since 1790, when George Chalmers listed it in his bibliography of Defoe, biographers and bibliographers have taken it for granted that Defoe wrote *The Apparition of Mrs. Veal*, but they have never provided any evidence that he did so except for a "tradition among the Booksellers," a tradition perhaps eighty-odd years old when Chalmers first recorded it.[3] But as will be demonstrated below with *Duncan Campbell* and *The Dumb Philosopher*, the acceptance of an item in the Defoe canon for a hundred and seventy-five years does not guarantee its authenticity.[4] A number of Chalmers' ascriptions have already been rejected. As a ghost story printed in collections of spiritualistic narratives and as an introduction to Drelincourt, *The Apparition of Mrs. Veal* enjoyed a phenomenal lifetime. But it remained anonymous there until 1840, when it became embodied in the corpus of Defoe's works.[5]

If other sources reveal little evidence that Defoe wrote *The Apparition of Mrs. Veal*, we might turn to the discussion of the story during the eighteenth century. Here only one reference to the authorship or credibility of the story has hitherto been cited. Indeed Sir Charles Firth asserted that no other such reference could be found.[6] But several interesting references occur, especially in the periodicals.

In 1726, in *The Penny London Post*, Mrs. Bargrave's story was mentioned with obvious incredulity in an account of a funeral conducted by a burial society: "We hear, there are two other Societies of the Fair Sex, one at Shoreditch, and another in Cripplegate Parish; at the Head of which last, is Mrs. Veale, mentioned in M. Drelincourt's *Book of the Consolation against the Fear of Death*: This last Society meets every Saturday in the Afternoon to talk about their Spiritual Concerns."[7] This news story concludes with an obvious take-off on the Veal story: it parodies the Saturday afternoon religious séance of Mrs. Bargrave and "Mrs." Veal, properly so denominated as a respectable spinster; and it substitutes the dead Mrs. Veal for Mrs. Bargrave, who had been in London in 1722 and was presumably still living there.[8] The Reads, who published *The Penny London Post*, had in 1718 already disparaged Defoe's facility at fabrication, sneering at " 'the little art he is truly master of, of forging a story, and imposing it on the world for truth.' "[9]

This attitude of disbelief appears also in two essays in *The Universal Spectator*, which was edited by Defoe's son-in-law, Henry Baker. Neither notice was written by Baker himself,[10] but the first appeared in 1732, while he was still in charge of the periodical: "There is an Apparition, as I take it, of one Madam *Veal*, which, because it recommends the Original Author, *Monsieur Drelincourt*, and his elaborate Discourse upon *Death*, to all Readers whatsoever, must therefore be of singular Use to the *Translator* as well as *Editor*: And there are many Others, of which an Account can be given but from Trick and Design, in Order to promote some temporal Interest and Advantage. . . ."[11] This essay on apparitions, incidentally, mentions Defoe as an apparition-writer under his pseudonym Moreton.

The second essay, which appeared in 1734, after Baker had ceased to edit *The Universal Spectator*, may well have been written by the same man. It also is skeptical: "There is scarce a little Town in all *England* but has one of these *old Female Spirits* appertaining to it, who, in her High-Crown Hat, mighty *clean Linnen* and a *red Petticoat*, has been view'd by half the Parish. This Article of *Dress* is of mighty Concern among some *Ghosts*; wherefore a skilful and learned *Apparition-Writer*, in the *Preface* to *Drelincourt on Death*, makes a very *pious Ghost* talk to a *Lady* upon the important Subject of *scowring a Mantua*."[12] Here the "pious *Ghost*" is obviously Mrs. Veal; the lady, Mrs. Bargrave; and the subject, Mrs. Veal's "scowred," or cleaned riding dress. The "skilful and learned *Apparition-Writer*" is evidently the author of *The History and Reality of Apparitions*—Daniel Defoe. This reference, then, a jest at apparitions in general and at Defoe's use of inconsequential detail in particular, gives us our first evidence that Defoe wrote *A True Relation of the Apparition of Mrs. Veal*. We need no longer rely entirely upon a vague tradition among the booksellers more than half a century later.

A tone of disbelief in the entire tale, as has been seen, characterizes the reference in *The Penny London Post* and those in *The Universal Spectator*. This same skeptical tone continues to appear until *The Apparition of Mrs. Veal* becomes regarded as a proverbial lie. In 1749 Henry Fielding made an acid comment in *Tom Jones* concerning stories which were difficult or impossible to swallow: "Such is that memorable Story of the Ghost of *George Villers*, which might with more Propriety have been made a Present of to

Dr. *Drelincourt*, to have kept the Ghost of Mrs. *Veale* Company, at the Head of his Discourse upon Death. . . ."[13]

In 1774 Augustus M. Toplady, an acquaintance of Dr. Johnson, also used the story as a notorious yarn. Only a few years later Toplady was to assert in his sermon "The Existence and the Creed of Devils Considered," "There is nothing absurd in the metaphysical theory of apparitions."[14] But in 1774 he wrote to a friend concerning an epitaph, ". . . pray, let me see the epitaph; which is no more the worse for the misinformation with which it was introduced to your acquaintance, than the intrinsic merits of Mr. Drelincourt's Excellent Treatise on Death, are impaired by the fabulous legend prefixed to it, concerning Mrs. Veal's apparition."[15]

The only evidence hitherto cited concerning the reliability of the Bargrave story is the conversation between Dr. Johnson and Boswell: "BOSWELL. 'I do not know whether there are any well-attested stories of the appearance of ghosts. You know there is a famous story of the appearance of Mrs. Veal, prefixed to "Drelincourt on Death'." JOHNSON. 'I believe, Sir, that is given up. I believe the woman declared upon her death-bed that it was a lie.' "[16] Dr. Johnson's statement is late, as it was made in 1772, and it was not positively asserted. But it must carry a great deal of weight. Johnson was intensely interested in ghosts, and on a point of such importance it is not likely that his memory failed him.

The probability that Mrs. Bargrave made up the entire tale seems stronger when we examine motive, ability, and opportunity. Hitherto we have been misled by the insistence of the reporters that Mrs. Bargrave had no reason to lie, that she would accept no gratuities for telling her story and received no material benefits from it—was in fact forced to seek some seclusion from undesired notoriety. But Mrs. Bargrave had a very compelling motive—revenge. All the accounts mention Mr. Bargrave's cruelty: obviously Mrs. Bargrave spread the details all over town. As we know now, on the day after Mrs. Veal died, Mr. Bargrave came home in a frolicsome mood, evidently drunk, felt his wife's hand, found it hot, and put her outside to cool. In fact he left her there all night. The next day, as Defoe confirms, she was abed all day with a fever. Such treatment, if it did not cause an actual hallucination, might easily have provoked a story told partly out of malice, partly out of a desire for notoriety. As to ability, Mrs. Bargrave was the daughter of a prominent clergyman who had not been backward to defend himself.[17] Moreover, disquieting information recently rediscovered in *The Loyal Post* would seem to suggest that she had the opportunity to concoct her story. Particularly damaging is the report carried there of a recent visit paid by Mrs. Veal to Canterbury: "Mrs Veal had been about the beginning of September last at Canterbury, and paid a Visit to Mrs. Bargrove, and went well from her. . . ." Moreover, on the very night of the séance, "her Husband coming home at Night, in the midst of some Angry Words, told her, now her Friend Mrs. Veal was Dead . . ." (pp. 260, 261). As Mr. Secord suggested,[18] these two pieces of information seem to reveal how Mrs. Bargrave could have obtained both the intimate and recent knowledge of her friend's clothes and affairs which she used to authenticate the apparition and how, knowing that her friend was dead, she was given the opportunity to spend her night in the garden or the wet washhouse creating a dialogue which would obtain for her notice and sympathy, and revenge upon her husband. Thus it seems to be now generally agreed that Mrs. Bargrave was lying.

But our readiness to convict Mrs. Bargrave may be to some extent a prejudice of contemporary skepticism. The very fact that these two recently rediscovered data appear in only one of the eight versions of the story suggests that both data may be inaccurate. The earlier visit is in fact contradicted by the other accounts. According to Lucy Lukyn, Mrs. Bargrave had not seen Mrs. Veal "these 2 years and ½" (p. 3). Defoe agreed that "Mrs. *Bargrave* had not seen her in two Years and a half" (p. 2). Spavan reiterated the same information; and Payne later said that Mrs. Bargrave "had neither seen nor heard from her for a year and half" (p. 525). Since the Luykn letter is independent of the later, published accounts, it seems obvious that Mrs. Bargrave stated early and continued to insist that the ghostly visit was the first in years; and the testimony that Mrs. Veal usually had a travelling companion and that she customarily visited her Uncle Watson in Canterbury increases the probability that Mrs. Bargrave would not have risked detection and exposure by trying to conceal a previous visit, for had such a visit been demonstrated, her credibility would have collapsed. Too much seems to be made of the scowered silk gown and other personal data as veridical evidence for there to have been a fleshly visit a week earlier. Had Mrs. Veal paid such a visit the Watsons at least would have heard of it and would not have been a whit impressed by the fact that Mrs. Bargrave knew of their niece's renovated dress. On the contrary, as E. B.'s letter indicates, Margaret Watson knew of the dress from a visit to Dover: "Mr. Watson's Daughter who had been at Dover lately Says She had such a Gown" (p. 156).

Although her story came later to be regarded as fabulous, in 1705 and 1706 Mrs. Bargrave certainly managed to convince both neighbors and visiting experts that she was telling the truth. In gaining credence she encountered formidable opposition. Her story was obviously embarrassing, for it blazoned abroad her husband's cruelty and Mr. Veal's undutifulness: from the accounts of E. B. and the Gentleman it seems obvious that at least for a time Mrs. Bargrave dramatized her visitant as a ghostly voice demanding that her brother use money which she had left to erect a tombstone over the graves of her parents and herself. Opposition developed at once in Mr. Bargrave. Only two days after Mrs. Bargrave began to tell her story, E. B. wrote that "her Husband abuses her & reflects on her for discoursing wth y[e] Devil" (p. 157). By the time Stephen Gray made his report to Flamsteed, on November 15, Mrs. Bargrave was not only being embarrassed by "stories Raised by her Husband and the Beans his campanions," but "Mr. Veal her Brother at Dover and his Relations and friends that live here at Canterbury being willing to have it forgotten Do all they Can to stifle it" (p. 158). This opposition had fully developed by the time Defoe wrote his account: ". . . since this Relation, she is Calumniated by some People, that are Friends to the Brother of Mrs. *Veal* who Appeared; who think the Relation of this Appearance to be a Reflection, and endeavour what they can to Blast Mrs. *Bargrave*'s Reputation, and to Laugh the Story out of Countenance." Mr. Veal now "does all he can to Null or Quash the Story," Defoe reiterated (pp. 1, 2).

The major charge against Mrs. Bargrave raised by the opposition, a charge unfortunately revived recently,[19] was that she was prone to see ghosts. Since, as was then commonly known, many apparitions are hallucinations forged by the morbid imagination of the melancholy, Defoe's narrator ascertained that Mrs. Bargrave was of a "Chearful Disposition" and that there was "not the least sign of Dejection in her Face" (p. 1). To Flamsteed's request for a report concerning her possible proneness to hallucinations, Gray responded, ". . . as to your fourth Query Whether she have Reported the houses wherein she has formerly lived to be Haunted and on what occation she did it she told me these were only stories Raised by her Husband and the Beans his companions that there was noe other Grounds for such Reports then this, that one Evening as she and her Husband were Walking in the Garden they saw a Woman makeing her Escape over the Wall upon which she said she thought it to be an Apparition, but they afterwards found it to be an ill Woman that was want to use that house . . ." (p. 158). After making further inquiries to elucidate this incident, Gray clarified:

> its Reported of Mrs. Bargrave that she is wont to Report the Houses where-in she has lived to be Haunted as you have heard how far this is true you

have heard in part already but I have Received a Full information of this chatter then Mrs Veal's Modesty would permitt her to give me though Consonant Enough to what she told me. Mr Bargrave one day Rid a Hunting with some Gentlemen and when they had done towards night went to a Publick House about 9 miles from Canterbury where he Got Drunk and lay there not only that night but some days after his Wife hearing where he was went after him to see if she could get him home (for she is very Carefull of him notwithstanding his severity to her) it hapened she Came at a time when her Husband was in the Companie of a Hore they were it seems together in the House of Eas Mrs Bargrave when she Came in asked for her Husband they told her he was without in the Garden wither she went the Hore it seems saw her and for fear of being Discovered Fled Imediatly and before she was got over the Wall Mrs Bargrave saw her and when her Husband Came to her told him that she had seen somewhat getting over the wall which she thought was an Apparition which he seemd willing to belive being Glad of the opertunety of soe Pretty a Delution to Conceal his Rogery and this Mr B. has been heard to Relate him self longe before the Aparition of Mrs Veal to Mrs Bargrave. . . ." (pp. 161–162)

The other, less interesting "ghost" was, as Mrs. Bargrave explained, merely a servant so elusive that she once jestingly so called her. ". . . She says she used these Expressions only jocously for she did not then believe there were Apparitions" (p. 158). Despite Mr. Bargrave and the Beans this accusation against Mrs. Bargrave never became widely current: of the eight extant versions of the story, only Gray mentions it, and then only to dismiss it as "chatter." There seems to be no reason, then, to suppose that Defoe ever heard it. If he did, he evidently also considered it "chatter."

In face of this opposition Mrs. Bargrave adhered consistently to her story. According to *The Loyal Post*, she gave to all—"Dr Boyce and other Eminent Persons, both Clergy and Layety"—"the same Relation, not varying in a Tittle" (p. 261). *The Loyal Post* was in a position to compare accounts: "There are many Persons in Town that have Letters giving an account of a remarkable Passage that happned lately in the City of Canterbury. Several Letters thereof from Persons of Good Credit have reached our hands, besides Relations we have had by Word of Mouth . . ." (p. 260). Defoe's narrator also stressed Mrs. Bargrave's consistency: "Mrs. *Bargrave* never varies in her Story, which puzzles those who doubt of the Truth, or are unwilling to believe it" (p. 7). In 1722, finally, Payne remarked, ". . . Mrs. Bargrave never deviated from her account, nor has time, and the general curiosity which stories of such consequence must raise, ever produced any thing to discredit it . . ." (p. 531).

Surely these reporters meant to underscore Mrs. Bargrave's factual consistency, not any rote presentation. Defoe's narrator seems to suggest a spontaneous, not a routine presentation: "All the time I sat with Mrs. *Bargrave*, which was some Hours, she recollected fresh sayings of Mrs. *Veal*" (p. 7). Perhaps the only direct evidence that Mrs. Bargrave ever changed her story came in 1720, from Spavan, who commented merely, ". . . 'twas a ridiculous Weakness that made some Persons take considerable Pains to persuade Mrs. Bargrave to conceal what the *Apparition* said against the crying Enormities of *Party-Zeal*" (pp. xix–xx).

With her reputation for honesty and her consistent presentation, Mrs. Bargrave gained and retained local belief. After all, she was the daughter of John Lodowick, a clergyman "of good parts and right for the Church, and a sober man."[20] E. B. called Mrs. Bargrave "a very good & discreet Woman," and added, "all people speak well of her" (pp. 155, 156). Acting upon instructions from John Flamsteed, Stephen Gray, later a Fellow of the Royal Society and already a contributor to its *Philosophical Transactions*, investigated Mrs. Bargrave's reputation and character and reported favorably, "Sir I have taken the account I have had of Mrs Bargraves character from Persons that are Esteemed Qualified in all things as you Direct from those that have known her Conversation both when she lived at Dover and here in Canterbury as well of the Clergie as others and all give her the Character of a Religious Discreet Witty and well accomplished Gentlewoman[.] She was bred up in the Church of England her father who was Mr. Lodowick was in his life time Minister of the Church at Dover and she is seen often to frequent the Divine Servise of the Church . . . I cannot finde but she is a serious Person not given to any thing of levety . . ." (p. 158). "Both Mrs Bargrove and the Deceased," *The Loyal Post* agreed, "were Persons of Reputation . . ." (p. 261). Defoe convincingly presented Mrs. Bargrave as *"a Woman of much Honesty and Virtue, and her whole Life a Course as it were of Piety."* For this certification he had the assurance of his narrator, Mrs. Bargrave's neighbor, a woman *"of so discerning a Spirit, as not to be put upon by any Fallacy."* Of Mrs. Bargrave she asserted, ". . . she is my Intimate Friend, and I can avouch for her Reputation, for these last fifteen or sixteen years, on my own Knowledge; and I can confirm the Good Character she had from her Youth, to the time of my Acquaintance." Defoe's final words reiterate this confidence: "Mrs. *Bargrave's* Authority and Sincerity alone, would have been undoubted in any other Case" (Sig.[A1] verso, pp. 1, 9).

The clergy and other experts were similarly convinced of Mrs. Bargrave's reliability. According to E. B., "my Lady Coventry's Chaplain & other of ye Clergy have been wth her and I dont find any disbelieve her" (p. 156). Gray registered his own conviction: ". . . upon the whole Consideration of all Circumstances I Cannot say those that doe not believe Mrs Bargraves Relation to be true are altogether without Reason yet I think the Arguments for the truth of it are of much Greater validety then those against it and am Inclined to believe that Mrs Bargrave did Realy Converse with the Apparition of her Deceased friend . . ." (p. 162).

Further questions need to be considered. Did Defoe interview Mrs. Bargrave? Did he believe her story? Some scholars have sent him to Canterbury for an interview. According to Paul Dottin, for example, ". . . au début de l'année 1706, il se rendit à Canterbury pour mener une enquête sur une historie de fantômes qui lui avait été signalée par un de ses vieux amis du Kent. Vite, voilà De Foe en quête, interviewant les gens, notant avec minutie les plus petits détails, reconstituant peu à peu l' histoire de la dégageant des bavardages. Rentré à Londres, il met en oeuvre ses notes et rédige un récit qui obtient un succès extraordinaire."[21]

True, Defoe reached London on November 6, 1705, and in 1714 Mrs. Bargrave's anonymous interviewer assumed that " 'The editor, no doubt, learned all particulars by word of mouth from Mrs. Bargrave' " (p. 98). But in the absence of any evidence for such a visit, one must assume, instead, that Defoe, like John Flamsteed, relied for his information not upon an interview with Mrs. Bargrave but upon a report emanating from Canterbury. As Sir Walter Scott pointed out in his memoir of Defoe, Defoe made an impressive case for each link in the provenance of his third-hand account, but he knew that each link weakened appreciably its reliability. The attestation of a first-hand report would have been far more convincing. Defoe probably did not claim the authority of a personal interview because he could not conscientiously do so. On this point, moreover, one need not rely upon merely a probable assumption: Defoe and the anonymous 1714 interviewer have given us the testimony of Mrs. Bargrave herself. She evidently did not claim to have entertained at Canterbury an interviewer from London. According to Defoe, "She says, *she had a Gentleman who came thirty Miles to her to hear the Relation* . . ." (p. 9). Now in 1706 Canterbury was about fifty miles from the southeast fringe of London, even as the crow flies, and Defoe was evidently then living in a northern suburb of London (Moore, *Defoe*, p. 47). Moreover, according to her 1714 interviewer, she asserted that she did not know the "editor" of Defoe's version of the story (p. 98). In *The Apparition of Mrs. Veal*, then, Defoe evidently relied for his material upon an account originating in Canterbury and transmitted, as he stated, by a gentleman of Maidstone, perhaps the Mr. Tongue to whom that very spring Defoe directed that twenty-five copies of his *Remarks on the Letter to the Author of the State Memorial* should be sent for distribution there.[22] In addition to this account Defoe may have read the version published on December 24 in *The Loyal*

Post, but no evidence of borrowing seems apparent. Thus Defoe may have relied upon one basic source for this material.

Did Defoe believe Mrs. Bargrave's story? As has been seen, Mrs. Bargrave, despite strong opposition, succeeded in convincing her neighbors, the local clergy, and the other experts that she was telling the truth. Moreover, in London Defoe would evidently have heard favorable reports of her—if the eight extant versions, all of them favorable to her, provide any trustworthy index of her reputation there. Some scholars have recently insisted on Defoe's artistry in *The Apparition of Mrs. Veal* at the expense of his spiritual integrity. If he were to be considered here merely as a venal journalist, the question of his belief would, as the late Mr. Secord insisted, remain relatively unimportant. "Was he not like the journalists of today who exploit popular interest in King Tut's curse and Friday the 13th?" he asked (p. 649). The answer should be a resounding "No!" The work of G. A. Starr and J. Paul Hunter has recently demonstrated the importance of spiritual themes and forms in Defoe's fiction. If any conviction concerning Defoe's mind and purpose emerges from a study of Defoe and the supernatural, it is that he would not have prostituted his pen to make what he believed to be a lie into an account demonstrating the communion between the world of spirits and the mundane world. It seems highly probable that Defoe did believe Mrs. Bargrave's story—until possibly he met her in London some years later or until he changed his mind about the possibility of the ghost, or revenant. When he wrote *The Apparition of Mrs. Veal*, he believed in the possibility of the revenant. On March 29, 1705, only a few months before Mrs. Veal died, he answered, as secretary of the Scandalous Club, the inquiry of a correspondent concerning ghosts: ". . . the Society must agree to the General part of the Question, That *there may be such a thing as we call* a *Spirit*, an *Apparition*, a *Phantome*, a *Spectre*, a *Ghost*, or what you please to call it" (*Review*, II, 43).

The most important aspects of *The Apparition of Mrs. Veal* for our examination, then, are not the qualities of its style, but the evidences which the narrator provided for the veridity of the apparition—for the reality of the supernatural—and the underlying themes.

In addition to indicating other manifestations of Mrs. Veal's unsubstantiality, Defoe developed three main evidences of veridity: Mrs. Veal's dress, her bequests, and the confirmation furnished by the neighbor and the servant. One of the most impressive evidences is the scowered silk dress. This is also the first piece of evidence which Mrs. Bargrave herself developed. In E. B.'s account Mrs. Veal entered "wth a Wrapping Gown & held it together wth her hand to across, an handsome suit of Night Cloaths & hood & Silk handk. tyed about her neck" (p. 155). Far more vivid is the description of Mrs. Veal's clothing in *The Loyal Post*, where she is "attired in such a Dress as she usually wore; in a Coloured Riding Gown wrapt about her, a Yellow Gause Handkerchief about her Neck, a Night-dress on her Head with Scarlet bridle-strings" (p. 260). But only with Defoe's account do the details of the dress become progressively vivid as the significance of the dress becomes more obvious. Ignoring the vividly colored accessories, which are of no veridical importance, Defoe concentrated, as the Gentleman had done, upon the gown: Mrs. Veal arrived in "a Riding Habit." When it was handled by Mrs. Bargrave it was more precisely designated as "a Scower'd Silk, and newly made up." Finally, Mrs. Bargrave described to the Watsons "what Gown she had on, and how striped And that Mrs. *Veal* told her it was Scowred. Then Mrs. *Watson* cry'd out, *you have seen her indeed, for none knew but* Mrs. *Veal and my self, that the Gown was Scowr'd*" (pp. 2, 5, 6). The increasing detail as the data become more obviously functional and the dramatic cry of conviction seem to be marks of Defoe's superior dramatic perception and craftsmanship.

The evidence of the gown could be attested by Mrs. Watson on the Monday following Mrs. Veal's death and the Saturday séance, but the evidence provided by the bequests and the contents of Mrs. Veal's cabinet carried the narrative beyond this immediate scope of time. Miss Lukyn mentioned only that Mrs. Veal "desired Mrs. B. if she should dye to tell her Bro: y^t she would have Mrs. Marg^{tt} Watson have a suit of mourning, if not her best gown and petticoat and severall other things she had in a Cabinett" (p. 3). Though the bequests were only hinted at in *The Loyal Post*, they were developed in Gray's account. According to the "ingenious Gentleman," the apparition told Mrs. Bargrave "of somethings she had in her Cabinet and of a Sute of Cloths which she would have given to her Cosen Mrs Margret Watson with some other things which Mrs B will relate to noen but Mrs Veals Brother" (p. 160). One of the "Cheif Objections" of the skeptical to Mrs. Bargrave's story, according to Gray, was that "Mrs Bargrave mentions some things in the Cabenet that Mr Veal when he opened it Cold not find there though he opened it in the Preasance of several persons whom he called as Wittnesses" (p. 161).

As veridical evidence Defoe also advanced the bequests: Mrs. Veal insisted that Mrs. Bargrave write her brother that "*she would have him give Rings to such and such; and that there was a Purse of Gold in her Cabinet, and that she would have Two Broad Pieces given to her Cousin Watson*" (p. 4). Moreover, in Defoe's account the active opposition is both heard and confuted on this point:

> "Mr. *Veal* says he ask'd his Sister on her Death Bed, whether she had a mind to dispose of any thing, and she said, No. Now what the things Mrs. *Veals* Apparition would have disposed of, were so Trifling, and nothing of Justice aimed at in their disposal, that the design of it appears to me to be only in order to make Mrs. *Bargrave*, so to demonstrate the Truth of her Appearance, as to satisfie the World of the Reality thereof, as to what she had seen and heard: and to secure her Reputation among the Reasonable and understanding part of Mankind. And then again, Mr. *Veal* owns that there was a Purse of Gold; but it was not found in her Cabinet, but in a Comb-Box. This looks improbable, for that Mrs. *Watson* own'd that Mrs. *Veal* was so very careful of the Key of her Cabinet, that she would trust no Body with it. And if so, no doubt she would not trust her Gold out of it." (pp. 7–8)

Concerning the bequests, Payne added a note in 1722, that a secret communicated by the apparition to Mrs. Bargrave and transmitted to Mr. Veal, "though at present it put him into a great passion, yet obliged him to pay the legacies"(p. 530).

The final piece of evidence, one that almost establishes the veridity of the apparition, is the witness of the neighbor and the servant. According to Gray's "ingenious Gentleman," just after Mrs. Veal left her, Mrs. Bargrave, "before she went into her own house stept into a neighbours whoe asked her what made her look soe Cheirfull Mrs Bargrave Replied that she had had 2 hours Conversation with an old friend of hers which was come to Renew her friendship." Moreover, ". . . the next neighbours maid as she was at work in the yard heard Somebody talking very Pleasantly with Mrs Bargrave and when she came in told her Mrs soe who said Mrs Bargraves Husband does not use to be soe pleasant with her upon which the Maid said noe that it was both Womens voices she heard but was not near enough to Distinguish their words" (p. 161). In Defoe's account the evidence is even stronger, admissable, indeed, by the standards of modern parapsychological investigation had the two witnesses been identified: "A Servant in a Neighbours Yard adjoining to Mrs. *Bargraves* House, heard her talking to some body, an hour of the Time Mrs. *Veal* was with her. Mrs. *Bargrave* went out to her next Neighbours the very Moment she parted with Mrs. *Veal*, and told what Ravishing Conversation she had with an Old Friend, and told the whole of it" (p. 7). In 1722, in her interview with the Reverend Mr. Payne, Mrs. Bargrave still insisted upon this same evidence: "Mrs. Bargrave at that instant [immediately after the séance] told a neighbour of Mrs. Veal's visit, and the matter of their conversation; and a neighbour's servant from a yard near her window heard some of their discourse, and being asked by her mistress, if Mr. Bargrave was talking with his wife, made answer, that he never talked of any thing so good" (p. 529). The early and continued insistence upon this evidence should caution us not to be dead certain that Mrs. Bargrave was lying. She may have been telling the truth: she may have experienced a feverish hallucination, or she may have entertained a spiritual visitant.

These evidences for the veridity of the apparition furnished some of the other reporters merely sensational material. Defoe used them to warrant the concern of the world of spirits for the world of mortals. But even more important to him as material than these evidences was the subject of the intercourse between these worlds, especially the Christian's consolation for the fear of death and the theme of undying friendship.

The theme of Christian consolation Defoe did not obtrude into the Bargrave story. In E. B.'s account of the séance, to the implication that Mr. Bargrave's cruelty still persisted, "Mrs. V. reply'd She must be patient & She would be delivered in a little time" (p. 155). In Lucy Lukyn's account as in Defoe's "somebodys consolations agt ye fears of death" was used to introduce the theme of heavenly consolation: "Says Mrs. Veal, ye things of the other World are not as we here think them. She sayes, you know yt book tells us so, and upon yt they had a great deal of very heavenly talk" (pp. 3–4). Obviously Miss Lukyn was not interested, as Defoe was, in detailing the very heavenly talk. Nor was the reporter of the account in *The Loyal Post*: he recorded merely that Mrs. Veal was "Exhorting her to bear all things as well as she could, for it would not be long Ere she should be delivered out of all her troubles" (p. 260). Here, as elsewhere, the narrative of the Gentleman is closest of all to Defoe's account: "Mrs Veal there upon undertook to Comfort her by giveing her hope that in a little time it wold be other wais and then fell into some Religious Discourses and Exhortations." Mrs. Veal commended Drelincourt as "an excelent Book and full of truth [.] Mrs. B. Answered she preferred it to any she had seen on that subject yes said Mrs Veal but death and Eternety are much other things then the World takes them to be" (p. 159).

This theme of heavenly consolation is of paramount importance in Defoe's account. It is introduced along with the discussion of Drelincourt:

> Then Mrs. *Veal* reminded Mrs. *Bargrave* of the many Friendly Offices she did her in former Days, and much of the Conversation they had with each other in the time of their Adversity; what Books they Read, and what Com-

> fort in particular they received from *Drelincourt's Book of Death*, which was the best she said on that Subject, was ever Wrote. She also mentioned Dr. *Sherlock*, and two *Dutch* Books which were Translated, Wrote upon Death, and several others: But *Drelincourt* she said, had the clearest Notions of Death, and of the Future State, of any who have handled that Subject. . . . Says Mrs. *Veal*, Dear Mrs. *Bargrave, If the Eyes of our Faith were as open as the Eyes of our Body, we should see numbers of Angels about us for our Guard: The Notions we have of Heaven now, are nothing like what it is, as* Drelincourt *says. Therefore be comforted under your Afflictions, and believe that the Almighty has a particular regard to you; and that your Afflictions are Marks of Gods Favour: And when they have done the business they were sent for, they shall be removed from you.* And Believe me my Dear Friend, believe what I say to you, *One Minute of future Happiness will infinitely reward you for all your Sufferings.* (pp. 3–4)

The other theme basic to the story is that of undying friendship. All the accounts give some attention to this part of the consolation, at least casting Mrs. Bargrave and Mrs. Veal in the role of friends. According to E. B., for example, "She & Mrs. V. were very great Lovers," and Mrs. Veal encouraged Mrs. Bargrave under her afflictions: "And as they had lov'd well, they should love better wⁿ they met in H'n. . ." (p. 155).

This theme of consolatory friendship Defoe carefully prepared in introducing his cast of characters. Mrs. Veal "would often say, Mrs. *Bargrave you are not only the Best, but the only Friend I have in the World; and no circumstances of life, shall ever dissolve my Friendship.*" "And so like two Christian Friends, they comforted each other under their Sorrow" (p. 2). In Defoe's account the theme is elaborated through discussion of Norris. Nowhere else in the early versions of the story is Norris mentioned except by the Gentleman, who used him, as Defoe did, to develop the theme of friendship as a consolation.[24] The theme Defoe presented with a wealth of detail. After mention of friendship among the primitive Christians as exhibited in Horneck's *Ascetick*, Defoe continued:

> *There was a Hearty Friendship among them, but where is it now to be found?* Says Mrs. Bargrave, *'tis hard indeed to find a true Friend in these days.* Says Mrs. Veal, Mr. *Norris* has a fine Coppy of Verses, call'd *Friendship in Perfection*, which I wonderfully admire, have you seen the Book says Mrs. *Veal?* No, says Mrs. *Bargrave, but I have the Verses of my own writing out. Have you,* says Mrs. *Veal, then fetch them*; which she did from above Stairs, and offer'd them to Mrs. *Veal* to read, who refused, and wav'd the thing, saying, *holding down her Head would make it ake,* and then desired Mrs. *Bargrave* to read them to her, which she did. As they were admiring Friendship, Mrs. *Veal* said, Dear Mrs. *Bargrave,* I shall love you for ever. . . . (p. 4)

At the close Defoe's narrator returns to insist that the apparition's "two great Errands were to comfort Mrs. *Bargrave* in her Affliction, and to ask her Forgiveness for her Breach of Friendship, and with a Pious Discourse to encourage her" (p. 8). Only Gray and Defoe, then, adequately developed the theme of the consolation of friendship.

Later, in his *History of Apparitions*, Defoe denied not only the possibility of the ghost and the spirit in transit from this world to the next but maintained specifically that the soul in Heaven is unconcerned with the woes of those left behind in mundane cares. In 1706, however, this assumption of friendly or saintly concern, unceasing at death, underlies the theme of friendship and consolation, the discussions of Drelincourt and Norris. It is with the announcement of this theme of spiritual consolation that Mrs. Veal explains her journey: "*I had so great a Mind to see you before I took my Journy. . . . My Dear Friend, I am come to renew our Old Friendship again . . .*" (p. 3).

Only Defoe, moreover, pointed up the general theme or moral. In most apparition stories, as in Bovet's *Pandemonium* or Defoe's *History of Apparitions*, the points are usually made at the end of the narrative, if at all.[25] In *The Apparition of Mrs. Veal* Defoe furnished also a Preface to authenticate the story and to point the moral of the narrative:

> *The use which we ought to make of it is, to consider, That there is a Life to come after this, and a Just God, who will retribute to every one according to the Deeds done in the Body; and therefore, to reflect upon our Past course of Life we have led in the World, That our Time is Short and Uncertain, and that if we would escape the Punishment of the Ungodly, and receive the Reward of the Righteous, which is the laying hold of Eternal Life, we ought for the time to come, to turn to God by a speedy Repentance, ceasing to do Evil and Learning to do Well: To seek after God Early, if happily he may be found of us, and lead such Lives for the future, as may be well pleasing in his sight.* (Sig. [A1] verso)

Some of our distrust of Defoe's spiritual motives in writing *The Apparition of Mrs. Veal* probably emanates from our persistent suspicion that there must be some truth in the old tradition that Defoe wrote the story to advertise Drelincourt. In 1722, evidently, Payne remarked, "One thing has much contributed to sink the credit of the story with many who have known it no otherwise, and that is, its being published in a new edition of Drelincourt's Treatise . . ." (p. 531). The legend of meretricious composition was advanced by Chalmers along with his attribution to Defoe: "The tradition among the Booksellers is, That when *Drelincourt's Consolations against the Fears of Death* first appeared, the book would not sell. DeFoe said he would make it sell, and he made *the Apparition* recommended Drelincourt's Book on Death, as the best on that subject ever written."[26] In 1799 in his edition of Boswell's *Johnson*, Edmond Malone positively asserted that Defoe fabricated

The Apparition of Mrs. Veal: "This fiction is known to have been invented by Daniel Defoe, and was added to Drelincourt's book, to make it sell."[27] Malone's statement was further developed by Sir Walter Scott and William Hazlitt. Adding considerable imaginary detail, they asserted that Defoe invented the whole tale in order to help sell Drelincourt. Thus Malone elaborated upon Chalmers, and Scott upon Malone.

This legend of composition was completely demolished in 1895 by George Aitken. Printing the account of an interview of Mrs. Bargrave which had taken place in 1714, Aitken demonstrated the fact that far from being a fiction of Defoe, the pamphlet relates a supernatural event actually reported by Mrs. Bargrave of Canterbury. Chalmers may have been partly right about Defoe's motivation. That Defoe depended upon his pen primarily for his livelihood should not, however, mislead us into the conviction that he was unconcerned about the truth or the effect of what he wrote concerning the spiritual world. Dr. Johnson, who is generally regarded as his moral and spiritual superior, once maintained, "No man but a blockhead ever wrote, except for money." It must have been Defoe himself, rather than his Canterbury narrator, who remarked at the close of the report, "*Drelincourt's Book of Death* is, since this happened, Bought up strangely" (p. 7). But as we now know, the discussion of Drelincourt was originally reported, or invented, by Mrs. Bargrave. Probably Defoe also contributed to dramatizing the discussion of Drelincourt. In the narrative of the Gentleman as well as that of Defoe the importance of Norris in the discussion of friendship is accentuated by Mrs. Bargrave's trip upstairs to get the verses of her own writing out. Probably Mrs. Bargrave herself, no mean dramatist, was responsible for this touch of suspense. But Defoe used the same device to bring Drelincourt vividly into the picture. In some of the other accounts it is introduced by accident. Miss Lukyn, for example, related, ". . . there lay a book in ye Room where they were wch had like to have thrown down [.] Mrs. Veal, askt her w^t book it was. She told her it was somebodys consolations ag^t ye fears of death (but I have forgot ye mans name y^t writt it)" (pp. 3–4). That Miss Lukyn got this part of her story straight seems demonstrated by the Reverend Mr. Payne's account in 1722: "Mrs. Bargrave, moved with the discourse, chanced by a turn of her chair to throw down from a shelf Drelincourt's treatise of the Christian's Defence against the Fears of Death, which gave the first hint to tell her there was Drelincourt they had so often read together" (p. 526). In *The Loyal Post* the subject arises casually: ". . . she says, that to her thinking she took up a book, and told her, that they two had passed away many Hours with that Good Book" (p. 260). Only in Defoe's account is it dramatically introduced—by another special trip upstairs to fetch the book.

But Bragg, the publisher, rather than Defoe, probably added the Advertisement at the close of the narrative: "Drelincourt's Book of the Consolations against the Fears of Death. *has been four times Printed already* in English, *of which many Thousands have been Sold, and not without great Applause: And its bearing so great a Character in this Relation, the Impression is near Sold off*" (p. 9). The claim of the Advertisement that "this Relation" has already had an effect on sales of Drelincourt probably refers to the Bargrave story in its various versions rather than to Defoe's account. The Advertisement was evidently a part of the original issue. But Bragg was at this time rapidly approaching a break with Defoe; and it was he who would soon advertise Drelincourt even more blatantly and profit from the process. By September 30, 1706, having severed relationships with Defoe, Bragg evidently reached an agreement with the publishers of Drelincourt to sell them the narrative to use as a preface (Dottin, III, 812). For the third (the second separate) edition, moreover, Bragg provided an advertisement of Drelincourt on the title page itself, adding to the original title the puff "Which *APPARITION* recommends the Perusal of *DRELIN-COURT*'s Book of *Consolations against the Fears of Death.*" The discussion of Drelincourt, then, Defoe made more functional, meaningful, and dramatic than had any previous reporter; but the "tradition among the Booksellers" that he wrote *The Apparition of Mrs. Veal* to help sell Drelincourt remains unsubstantiated.

Although the emphasis in any study of *The Apparition of Mrs. Veal* should be placed upon the evidences and the themes, its stylistic qualities need not be ignored. Accepting Defoe's account of the provenance of his material does not obligate us to accept literally the assertion of the Preface that the account came to Defoe "as it is here Worded." Doubtless for his pertinent facts Defoe adhered with scrupulous fidelity to his source. In the dramatic treatment of his themes and in his commentary, however, he must have felt considerably freer to select, arrange, and even heighten the drama and tension of his material. From Mrs. Bargrave's complaint to her 1714 interviewer, we know that Defoe, or his source, made some omissions and other alterations in the story. In her judgment, " 'all things contained in it, however, were true, as regards the event itself, or points of importance; but one or two circumstances relating to the affair were not described with perfect accuracy by the editor' " (p. 98). For example Mrs. Bargrave had her interviewer insert in his copy of Defoe's account the addition "Something was also mentioned in this conversation of the former times when the Dissenters were persecuted by King Charles the Second. At which, says Mrs. Veal: 'People should not persecute one another whilst they are all upon the road to Eternity' " (p. 98). Of all the stylistic distinctions in Defoe's treatment of Mrs. Bargrave's story, the most obvious is his dramatic style, especially his use of dialogue. All of the five early accounts of the story employ some direct discourse. There is a minimum in *The Loyal Post*, about 1 per cent of the central narrative, and in Miss Lukyn's where it amounts to somewhat above 3 per cent. In the narrative of the Gentleman it is considerable, amounting to 12 per cent; and in E. B.'s account it is about 16 per cent. In Defoe's version, however, about 37 per cent of the narrative is placed in direct discourse, distinguished by italic type. There is all the difference in the world between the comparatively colorless summary of *The Loyal Post* and the vivid, dramatic presentation of Defoe.

Another contribution which Defoe made to the effectiveness of the narrative, commentators have suggested, is that of withholding until the proper psychological moment the dramatic revelation that Mrs. Bargrave's visitor is actually a ghost. Lucy Lukyn introduced her account as "a long story of an Apparition y^t appeared to One Mrs. Bargrove here at Canterbury at noon day" (p. 3). In the narrative of the Gentleman the full information about her death is given in the second sentence: "Mrs Veal died friday September 7th at Dover but visited Mrs Bargrave on Saturday the 8th" (p. 159). Defoe delayed to the end of the visit the precise information: "Mrs. *Veal* Dyed the 7th of *September* at 12 a Clock at Noon, of her Fits, and had not above four hours Senses before her Death, in which time she received the Sacrament" (p. 5). One difficulty about evaluating the effectiveness of this "flashback" is that we already know that Mrs. Veal is dead and that the visitor must then be a ghost. Although Bragg rather than Defoe may have provided the title page containing the precise information, the second sentence of the narrative informs the reader that "Mrs. *Bargrave* is the Person to whom Mrs. *Veal* Appeared after her Death" (p. 1). The flashback still has the impact of the expected shock. However in E. B.'s account the revelation that Mrs. Veal is a ghost is similarly delayed until the same point in the story, and there is not even a prior hint of her death. E. B. introduced her story merely as the "Relation" of "an extr. Thing in ye Town" (p. 155). Thus here again we encounter the possibility that we have been giving to Defoe credit for a dramatic touch originally embodied in the narrative by Mrs. Bargrave herself.

V | Defoe as Prophet

ALTHOUGH in his other occult works Defoe was earnestly endeavoring to exhibit God's continuing care for man and the Devil's persistent assaults, he five times, between late 1710 and early 1715, donned the specious garb of prophet. The first of his five prophecies, printed at Newcastle, has evidently not survived. Those which are extant and can be identified are *The British Visions, or Isaac Bickerstaff's Twelve Prophecies for the Year 1711; The Highland Visions, or the Scots New Prophecy, Declaring in Twelve Visions what Strange Things shall Come to Pass in the Year 1712; The Second-Sighted Highlander, or Predictions and Foretold Events, Especially about the Peace, By the Famous Scots Highlander* (1713); and *The Second-Sighted Highlander, Being Four Visions of the Eclypse* (1715).

In *The Review* for April 26, 1711, Defoe ironically suggested that *The British Visions* deserved "just as much regard for *John Partridge, Poor Robin,* or *Willy Lilly* us'd to do, in the Day of their Predictions" (VIII, 53). Such almanacs were still numerous and popular; indeed the entire library of many eighteenth century families probably consisted of the Bible and a copy of a current almanac.[1] Although he did not normally advertise them in his *Review*, on November 13, 1705, Defoe listed twenty-five almanacs as ready for sale;[2] and in addition to these at least eighteen other eighteenth century almanacs were published either that year or at least before 1711 in London, Oxford, Cambridge, Scotland, Dublin, or elsewhere in Great Britain.[3] From such almanacs eighteenth century British readers still expected a yearly budget of predictions, political as well as meteorological, for the astrologer could, according to the credulity of the ignorant, predict the human effects of meteorological phenomena.

Some of these almanacs, like *Dove, The Ladies Diary,* and John Wing's *Olympia Domata,* lacked political predictions, but others were studded with them. Almost all of these predictions were so vague or general that some sequent event could later be pointed to as having satisfied them. Thus Moore in his prediction for April of 1708 could safely foresee "some one of the Long Robe removed by Death or falls under some disgrace, and an old doting Courtier bewitch'd by a young Female."[4] Or for March of 1708 Job Gadbury could forecast, "Poor *Jupiter* is Retrograde, and in his Detriment, and opposed by the *Sun.* This should indicate," Gadbury predicted with some assurance, "as if some great Clergy-man, or Lawyer, falls under the Frowns of his Prince, for being too diligent in contriving how to censure, if not to oppose the Actions of their Superiours; but by the means of some great Woman he is got into Favour again."[5] Sometimes these almanac-makers shared concerns which actuated Defoe. Thus for August of 1708 John Partridge, who was more specific in his predictions than some, feared the prospect of plague and prayed that "God preserve the City of *London* from some feverish Distemper"; and in his prediction for October of 1708 Gadbury forsaw "Many grave and sober Consultations for Peace; and many labour for reconciling of Differences. Blessed are the Peace-makers."[6]

A more immediate inspiration for Defoe's prophecies was Jonathan Swift's *Predictions for the Year 1708, by Isaac Bickerstaff, Esq.* and its flock of sequels and imitations. Far from preventing *"the People of* England *from being further impos'd on by vulgar Almanack-makers,"* as his title page announced, Swift probably only drew further attention to them. Doubtless he stunned and momentarily silenced Partridge himself, but that veteran astrologer, who had weathered such attacks before, was aging and really drawing toward the death sportively predicted for him by Swift, Steele, and others. In several ways Swift set Defoe a precedent. Swift did not rely, for example, upon the vague predictions of the almanacs. "Then, for their Observations and Predictions, they are such as will equally suit any Age, or Country in the World. *This Month a certain great Person will be threatened with Death, or Sickness."*[7] Instead, Bickerstaff claimed to have noted down precise trial predictions which have proved "true in every Article, except one or two, very minute" (II, 143). He then ventured to predict not only the imminent demise of Partridge, but several more notable casualties, including "the Death of the *Dauphine*, which will happen on the 7th [of May], after a short Fit of Sickness, and grievous Torments with the Strangury" (II, 146).

In his prophecies, however, Defoe was only carrying copy to Newcastle. Ever since 1704 he had, as Mr. Review, been expected to furnish not only the news, but a forecast of things to come. When on September 4, 1708, Mr. Review interviews his "Mad Man" concerning the fate of the besieged Lisle, the latter ultimately replies, "*What, do you want a mad Prophet?* . . . I do not pretend to that Gift" (V, 273). But Mr. Review frequently complied with a forecast of military probabilities and political contingencies. Sometimes he was notably inaccurate. "We cannot suppose," he wrote on January 1, 1708, "all the Colonies on the Continent [North America] should league together. . ." (IV, 556). Even when he was eminently successful in his predictions, however, he normally claimed no more credit than does our Drew Pearson:

> I entreat the Reader's Pardon, for advancing so much to the Credit of my former Guesses, *for they were no more*; and I do this not for the Vanity of having more foresight than my Neighbours, but because having a great deal more guess Work before me, I bespeak their favourable Censure of what I shall Suggest may yet be to come, from the Rational Conjectures I made before.
> This way of Writing is something like Judicial Astrology, where tho' all seems to be meer Guess, yet the Calculation of Probabilities may give a Man an Insight further into an Affair, and its Consequences, than every one may think possible; and when what was rationally deduc'd comes to pass, the Man is taken for a Conjuror, with some that know nothing of the Matter, when in Truth, every Man may Conjure as well as he, if he would study the Reasons, and natural Consequences of the Thing." (I, 334)

Earlier, in 1705 after his prognosis had proved surprisingly accurate, he disclaimed supernatural pretensions: "Really, Gentlemen, I am no Prophet, nor the Son of a Prophet, but honestly suggested, the too great Probability of a Miscarriage from the Rational Calculations of Forces . . ." (II, 189). Just about the time his first prophecy appeared, however, he was claiming some proficiency in his predictions in the *Review*:

> Ye will not allow the Author of this Paper to be a Prophet, nor since Prophecying is of late grown so Enthusiastick, do I desire that Title ——But sure you may allow a Body some Skill that Way, or at least I deserve it as much, as some that more eagerly Claim it——Since they have positively Predicted what never came to pass, and all that I have Predicted yet, has actually been fulfill'd.——
> Did I not tell you of the King of *Sweden*, That if he push'd foward his Designs upon *Muscovy*, he should be Defeated. and should not

easily find his Way Home again, *Review*, Vol. Nᵒ . . .

Did I not tell you of the *Danes*, in so many Words, that if they Attack'd *Schonen*, they should not prosper, they should be beaten? *Review* Vol. VI. *p*. . . . .

Did I not tell you of the Plague, when it first brake out in *Poland*, That it should spread into *Germany*, and Visit all *Europe*? And has it not already gone a great Way to make it good, even enough to give us great Reason to tremble at what is to come? *Review* Vol. VI, p. . .

Did I not long since in plain Words near 8 Years ago, Predict to you, That God would Eminently shew his Displeasure and just Vengeance on those Scandalous Wretches, who Insulted the Memory of King *William, by Drinking the Horse's Health that threw his down?* And have not 13 of those unaccountable Creatures been sent into Eternity, by Falls from their Horses? *Review* Vol. VI. *pag*. . . . . (VII, 481–482)

The first of Defoe's prophecies has apparently disappeared, leaving behind only a tantalizing trace in a letter which his Newcastle printer, Joseph Button, wrote to him towards the end of December 1710: "Yours of the 23 Inst recd, but had Sent you before 400 Pa[   ] prophecies. I knew there were Severall Errata's in't but did [not?] think it worth while to amend; however when I've sold these [   ] I've already done, & do more, shall both correct and print [   ] addenda's."[8] From this discussion of corrections and addenda, as well as the large number of copies forwarded to Defoe, it would seem that Button was discussing an early prophecy by Defoe. Although a considerable tear in the letter prevents full identification of the title given there, it seems quite likely, from his second venture, when he came to "do Bickerstaff," that his first was to "do Partridge," and that the title was something like *Partridge's Prophecies for the Year 1711*. At least as early as 1703 Partridge evidently began to issue supplementary prophecies with such titles in order to increase sales of and profit from his almanacs. *Mr. Partridge's Most Strange and Wonderful Prophecy, or Predictions for the Year 1704*, reprinted at Edinburgh, was doubtless followed by others, as well as by *The Right and True Predictions of Dr. Partridge's Prophecy for the Year 1712* and *Dr. Partridge's Most Strange and Wonderful Prophecy for the Year 1713*.

In publishing his second prophecy, *The British Visions*, Defoe made elaborate arrangements to mislead credulous purchasers into believing the predictions to have been supernaturally inspired— the gift of second sight. The project he evidently planned with the Newcastle printer Joseph Button on his way to Edinburgh late in 1710 and perhaps wrote there and in Newcastle early in 1711 on his way "up" to London. When in *The Review* he later dated *The British Visions* as the product of 1710, he could have truthfully so dated only the original, uncompleted manuscript. On April 21, 1711, for example, he maintained, ". . . I have had one of the Books by me near six Months" (VIII, 47). "This Thing was Written in *October*," he commented a few days later, "or thereabouts" (VIII, 55). On April 26, 1711, he asserted, ". . . I saw it in *Scotland* in *November* last" (VIII, 53). "I saw it in Manuscript in *November* last," he clarified, "and in Print at Newcastle some short Time after" (VIII, 54). Evidently Defoe forgot that in the Preface, as Bickerstaff, he opened *The British Visions*, "In the Year 1711 . . . I . . . am moved. . . ."[9]

In February the prophecy may have been typeset and a proof copy or two struck off and perhaps even sold; but if so, printing was otherwise held up until Defoe could incorporate as a striking prediction some important event in the early year. In his "Advertisement" in *The Review* for May 5, 1711, he asserted, "The Book was printed in Newcastle at a Publick Printing-House" by Joseph Button, the publisher J. Saywell, and two workmen, there named, all of them ready to "certifie that it was Printed and Finished, the same that it is now, without any Alteration, the latter end of *January* last or the beginning of Fe—ry" (VIII, 72). From his use of the word "alteration" here and elsewhere in regard to *The British Visions*, Defoe evidently meant specifically some change in the text, not the insertion or omission of material, though he doubtless was willing to allow his readers to interpret the word more generally. Meanwhile in *The Newcastle Gazette* Button and Saywell probably proceeded to advertise the prophecy as "in the press," though no copy of this periodical from 1711 survives so to testify. "The whole Country thereabouts are Witnesses," Mr. Review asserted, "that in *February* and the beginning of *March*, they were cried and publickly sold in the Streets there, and Mr. *Baker*, the Publisher here offers to make Oath, that he had them offer'd to him to sell here, at least two months before the Death of the *Dauphin*" (VIII, 72). "The whole country" as witnesses would be tantamount to no witnesses at all, and if any copies were sold early in February, they must have been proof copies lacking the striking predictions. Probably Defoe had made publishing arrangements with Baker several months before the pamphlet appeared.

When news arrived in London that the Dauphin had unexpectedly died, on April 14, 1711 (N. S.), Defoe hurriedly included this event and dispatched final copy to Button with orders to print immediately and rush the copies to J. Baker in London. From the numerous uncorrected errors of the compositor, the slippage of three lines in alignment, and the evident failure of the pressmen to cut proper friskets—the inked furniture has left numerous smudges on the margins—it seems obvious that this was indeed a rush job. In *The Review* for April 21 (O. S.), probably before the first copies arrived from Newcastle, Defoe began "puffing" the prophecy, including long quotations. His failure here to designate page numbers, as he later did, suggests that at that time no printed copy had reached London. He interrupted his discussion with a "Note"—*"That since I wrote the above, I am told the Book is in Town, and the Publisher of this Paper desires me to say he has it to Sell"* (VIII, 46). Only in the next issue, for April 24, did Baker actually advertise the pamphlet, as published "yesterday."[10]

Such rapid exploitation of the Dauphin's death was an achievement, and the dating of *The Review* in Old Style (a difference of eleven days) makes it seem now more impressive; but had Defoe waited a few days longer, he could have taken advantage also of the death, on April 17 (N. S.), of the Emperor Joseph of Austria. Determined not to be outdone, Defoe quickly inserted this prediction also, preparing his readers in *The Review* of April 21 with a "Letter . . . out of the North": *". . . in the Original Manuscript . . . it was also expressly said, the Emperor should die in the Month of* April; *but the Publishers fearing they might be brought into some Danger, refus'd to Print that Paragraph—"* (VIII, 47–48). Then in the first London printing of *The British Visions* Defoe began his Prophecy IV, for April:

> Note, *In this place in the Original Manuscript, the following Paragraph was Inserted* [!]. *which the Printer in the* North *declin'd to put in, for fear of giving offense:*
> The Words are these,
> "The House of *Austria* feels a Blow this Month, which Changes the Measures of *Europe*; the Emperor resigns to Fate; and the Choise both of a new Emperor, and the new King of *Spain*, takes up the Consultations of all the Courts in Christendom." (p. 7)

This first London printing was already on sale by April 26, for Defoe quoted from it in *The Review* for that date. But in making this insertion of an additional prophecy, Defoe in his haste forgot that he was failing to remove from his prediction for the same month an incongruity concerning the Emperor's subsequent activity: "The Emperor retreats from Vienna for fear of the *Turks* and *Hungarians,* and goes to *Prague* . . ." (p. 8). When the first London printing was exhausted, Defoe removed this incongrous prediction from the second.

In addition to the three editions mentioned above—the "Newcastle" and the two Baker printings—there were possibly piratical reprints. On April 28 Baker advertised in *The Review*, ". . . There have been several Pyrated Copies Printed and Publish'd, of a little Book, Entitled, *British Visions, or Twelve new Prophecies,* particularly one by *Edward Midwinter,* Printer, who is now Prosecuted at Law, and will be made an Example of for the same: These are to Advertise all that have Occasion to buy the said Book, that the only True and Original Printed Copy, Printed at *Newcastle* and Reprinted here, is sold by *J. Baker* at the *Black-Boy* in *Pater-Noster-Row"* (VIII, 60). A piratical edition would doubtless have taken away some sales from Baker and Defoe, but such a charge of piracy as Baker made would have furnished Defoe a convenient explanation for the "omissions" in the Newcastle edition: "The Pyrate Printers," he charged, ". . . have Printed it so many Ways, and with so many false Additions and Abbreviations . . . for a Peny or a Half-peny . . ." (VIII, 54). Perhaps Midwinter bought from Baker the unsold stock of the Newcastle printing, with the assurance of some free advertising. With disarming disingenuousness Defoe replied in the same issue to charges of misrepresentation: "If I were to Print the Book for them, I would put in the Stabbing Mr. *Harley,* the filling the Lottery, and every Remarkable Thing that has happned [*sic*] since the Time of the Book; for why should not the People be Cheated that desire it?" (VIII, 54).

Defoe's elaborate preparations for publication were followed up by elaborate exploitations in *The Review.* To this prophecy Defoe devoted the issues for April 21, April 26, May 17, and September 11, 1711; and in the number for May 5 he gave the last page to an "Advertisement about the late PROPHECY." In these issues Defoe not only replied to the charge of hoax, exploited the alleged "predictions," worked up interest in those which were still to be realized, but also built up the persona of the Highland seer, warned of the approaching plague, and pleaded for peace, foreign and domestic.

In *The British Visions* the persona is "I *Isaac Bickerstaff,* Elder, having the 2d sight."[11] "The Author of this Book, who calls himself by the late so much borrow'd Name of *Isaac Bickerstaff,"* Mr. Review commented, "is said to be above 100 Years Old . . ." (VIII, 45). Even in the first notice in *The Review* for April 21, however, Defoe felt compelled to denominate his seer as "this North Country Prophet, for they say he came out of the Hills in *Scotland"* (VIII, 47). This persona he gradually developed in the subsequent prophecies.

Defoe began at once to exploit the successful "predictions." Not only did he make capital of the alleged predictions of the death of the Dauphin and the illness of the Pope, but having written the greater part of his pamphlet probably no earlier than February and completed it in April, he was naturally able to admire the accuracy of the "predictions" for the early months. On April 26, for example, he quoted some of his predictions and commented upon their fulfillment:

> 2. Another Thing he says, whether it be Verify'd in the Measures of *France* let any one Judge, I am sure, if it is not spoken with a Spirit of Prophecy, it is spoken with a great deal of Judgment and Spirit, in respect to Public Affairs—The Words are these. *Prophecy, p. 5.*
> France *Consults how to support* Spain, *Embroil* the Emperor, *bring Home the* Swede, *restore* Bavaria, *doze* Savoy, *fright the* Dutch, *and divide the* English, *and he will, in some Measure, accomplish them all*—I leave it to all Men to Judge, whether this is not exactly true.
> . . . .
> 4. Again—*The Confederates Attempt Vigorously to Succor King* Charles *in* Spain, *but O THE SUCCESS!* Proph. p. 5.
> O the Truth of this, both in what has been, and may be fear'd.
> 5. —*Now the* Swedes *prepare to break out of* Pomeren—*The Armies of* France *and* Spain *are in the Field first; much Blood shall be shed in* Spain *before the end of* February, *and* Philip *shall fight three Battles in* Spain, *in two of which he will be Victor.*
> The Action of *Bruhega* and *Villa Viciosa* answer for this, and may very well be the two first; and as this Thing was written in *October,* or thereabouts, when no Account could be had of these Battles, I think it seems so exact, as it is very Unaccountably strange; I leave it to other Men to pass their Judgment. (VIII, 55)

Having predicted the death of Marshall Boufflers for April—"*Boufflers* lies now in the *Bed* of *Honour*" (p. 11)—Defoe was able on September 11 to point with amazemnt to the death of the Marshal on August 22, 1711. An early death for Boufflers was probably inevitable because his conduct in battle was brave to the point of extreme personal risk, but Defoe was scattering his shots. *The British Visions* contains also a number of unrealized predictions in the Bickerstaffian manner: the demises of Philip of Spain and Louis XIV of France in May, of the Duke of Bavaria and the Elector of Cologne in April, and in the same month the prediction, omitted from the later, London editions, "The King of P———a [Polonia] demits his Crown in Favour of his Son, and submits to go the way of all Princes" (p. 11).[12]

When Button wrote to Defoe about the prophecies, he warned, "When you do Bickerstaff I wou'd not ha' you fright all people as you say you will; perhaps the Governmt may call us in question for intimidateing her Majesties good subjects—"[13] Button was probably expostulating with Defoe about the way he was proposing to use the plague, which was for Defoe evidently a genuine fascination as well as a sensational appeal. In *The British Visions* the plague figures prominently and inevitably reminds the reader of the *Jour-*

nal of the Plague Year in the beginning, spread, devastations, and subsiding of the disease. In May "Now *Europe* begins to Tremble, the Poeple [*sic*] find an Employment different from the War, the Living having Work enough to Bury their Dead" (p. 12). In June the plague threatens England: "Shall *Britain* be free! flatter not your selves with Epectations [*sic*] of it, many Plagues visit this Nation, and whole parties of Men suffer the Infection; all sorts of Men shall die, some politickly, some really; the Grave makes no Distinction of *Whig* or *Tory*, High or Low *Church*. Three Bishops go off the Stage First, Dukes, Earls, Barons and Privy-Counsellors follow; a great Rot falls among the Court-Sheep, and the Murrain upon the Stallions of this *Sodomitish* City. The Infection spares none . . ." (p. 14). August will evidently be the critical month: "if the real Plague spreads near us, it is the same Month, GOD preserve our populous Towns from such a stroke, the Desolation of, *Dantzick,* where they tell us a Fifth part of the People perish'd, will be a Flea-bite to what we must suffer, but the Prophet tells you, *If you escape this Year, you should not flatter your selves about the next*" (p. 17). Only in October will the plague in Europe remit.

The plague as an inevitable accompaniment of war and famine was a theme in *The Review* from October 22, 1709, until almost the final issue, though Defoe was noticeably silent on this matter in 1710. On October 29, 1709, for example, he warned, ". . . without Pretense to Impulses, Agitations, or Prophecies, I am still bold to say, we are under very comfortable Views of missing the Infection here this Season—But if the War in the *North*, which some say is begun, and most People agree is determin'd, should break out— I cannot but, with more Assurance than usual, foretell you, it shall visit a great Part of *Europe*, and US among the rest" (VI, 353).

But the plague is but one of the devastating followers of war, and war and peace forms the major theme of all the prophecies. As Defoe explained the method and purpose of *The British Visions* in *The Review* for May 17, 1711: "The considering Reader of the Book may evidently see there are two strains in it—*One* the Predictor, who ventures to say Things of great Consequence—*The Other* the Writer or Methodizer, for Publication, which seems, in a Preface particularly, to cover or colour the Substance, with an Air of Banter, Ridicule, and I know not what—Borrows a *Name* formerly Jested with in the World; pretends to the *great Age* of a Person who is really *no Body*; talks of a second Sight, and such kind of Stuff, perfectly wild and wide from the main Design." But, he explained, this fiction was adopted "2. To cover the serious part a little from the Eye of every Reader, that it might not have so solemn an Aspect till it went a greater Length; or 3. To suit the Thing to the loose Humour of the Age, who sometimes must have a light loose Way taken with them, to Introduce more serious Things to their Reading—Or 4. Meerly to make the Book vulgar, and make the Publication of it easie to the Booksellers. . ." (VIII, 94).

This serious purpose places Defoe's prophecies with *The Review* and with the numerous pamphlets advocating peace which he was publishing during the same year. In much of his work during these years Defoe emphasized the waste and horror of war and the need for peace. Doubtless he wished to assist his patron Harley to secure public approval of his peace negotiations, but Defoe's concern seems also a personal conviction. This theme unifies *The British Visions*, for it is with military preparations that the predictions begin, with war that they progress, and with preparation for the resumption of war that they conclude. Nothing is accomplished: "This Year is a Year rather of Blood than of Victory, no *Bleinhim* [sic], no *Pultowa*: No Decisive Battle happens any where on this side *Hungary*, yet more Men killed than would be in many such Battles" (p. 13). Even in December Europe seems no closer to ending its madness: "Now the World enters into Council, Parliaments, Assemblies of Estates, Regencies, Divans, Grand Councils of War, meetings of Generals and Mareschals, take up all the Nations of *Europe*; nothing of Peace is heard among them, but *carrying on the War with vigour* is the Word, Taxes for raising Money, and Money for raising Men, filling of Magazines, refitting of Navies, and recruiting Armies is the Language of all this part of the World." "Would the great Men of *Europe* bring all their Accounts together," the prophet recommends, "would they cast up their Accounts, and bring the Ballance of the whole to one foot of Profit and Loss, the Madness of Mankind would appear monstrous, and be seen in its own proper Colours. A Million of Lives have been lost this Year by War, Pestilence and Famine. Vast Treasures exhausted beyond the possibility of Account, Countries wasted, Cities ruined, Villages burnt, Frontiers plundred, yet the Nations of *Europe* prepare to carry on the furious Quarrel, as if not thing [sic] but the Destruction of Mankind was in their Design" (pp. 21–22).

The British Visions is thus a plea for peace. Like many contemporary issues of the *Review*, it is also a plea for national unity. As Defoe wrote in his *Review* for April 14, 1711, a few days before he sent final copy of his prophecy to Newcastle, "When our Breaches at Home grew wide, Tumult Reign'd, . . . Parties prevail'd and Feuds grew high, what was the Consequence? *France* reviv'd, Entertain'd new Hopes, broke off his Negotiations of Peace, talk'd high, and resolv'd for offensive War—" (VIII, 33). The very first prediction, for January, disparages party strife: "The Councils of this Nation shal, produce great Strife, Faction and *M*alecontent stirs, with *H*eats and *A*nimosities among the several Parties that are among us, to the great Encouragement of our Enemies, and to the great Discouragement of good Men; yet the Calmness and Prudence of some shall lessen, or at least protract the Danger for a while; Disputes of Ecclesiastick Affairs shall embroil this Island, and those *P*eople who regard neither God nor Devil shall make the greatest stir about Religion, every Church (however safe) cries out they are in danger. . ." (pp. 5–6).

In his *Highland Visions* Defoe followed in 1712 the same pretense of supernatural vision which he had so successfully exploited the previous year, but his preparations were this time not quite so elaborate. Since the earliest advertisement in *The Review* and the first "puff" there both appeared on April 3, 1712, one can assume that Defoe again waited for some striking event to occur early in the year. He decided to use the death of the Dauphiness, on February 12, ingeniously inserted it in his prepared prophecy for July, and sent final copy along to his printer, Joseph Button, in Newcastle. Meantime he gave the new prophecy advance publicity in London as if it had been published and available in the north for some time. The same type of advertising which Defoe had given *The British Visions* the previous year he also provided for *The Highland Visions. The Review* for April 3, 1712, was almost entirely devoted to it; it furnished material largely for the issues of May 31, August 12, August 23, and November 25. On April 3, 1712, Mr. Review reminded his readers of the successful predictions in *The British Visions* and commented at length upon those in the new pamphlet. From *The Highland Visions* he singled out especially the July prediction (having arranged a disarmingly incorrect month for this "forecast") *"The Dutchess of* Burgundy *seems to be pointed at by Death, and a great* French *General also."* "If this was Printed in *January*," commented Mr. Review disingenuously, "and the Dutchess of *Burgundy,* that is, the *Dauphiness,* and the Mareschal *Catinate* dyed both in March [they did not]—Then something must be in our *Highlander* more than I understand" (VIII, 646).[14] Concerning the ineffectual peace negotiations of February and March, he added, "This to be said near three Months ago, has something very strange in it, nay, if it had been said but a Month ago; and the Book has been publish'd here, I believe a Month it is surprizing . . ." (VIII, 646). As soon as the supply "from North *Britain*" was exhausted, Baker reprinted the prophecy, but without introducing additional successful predictions and without advertising against piracies.

In 1712 a major change in *The Highland Visions* is the change in persona. Before Defoe could issue his 1712 predictions, Richard Steele, who had with Swift's blessing appropriated the pseudonym

Bickerstaff for his *Tatler*, published his playful and delightful *Bickerstaff's Predictions for the Year, 1712, by Isaac Bickerstaff, Esq. in a Letter to the Author of the Oxford Almanack*. From what Mr. Review had already suggested, however, it seems probable that Defoe would have changed the mask even if he had not been anticipated in 1712 by Steele. In the Preface, signed *"The* Highlander," the new persona explains,

> This is but the second Time that the Author hereof hath undertaken to appear in this publick Manner, although he has for many Years been known to have strangely foretold several Things, which have precisely come to pass. . . .
> He was perswaded the last Year to give Leave to a Friend to Publish his Prophetick Observations, who did it with an inexcusable Weakness, turning much of it into Jest and Ridicule; and setting the Imaginary and Threadbare Name of Isaac Bickerstaff to it: This made the more serious Part of it suspected by Wiser People, and made the Whole look more like something Prophane and Romantick than a Prediction of Wonderful Judgments to befal the World.[15]

During the remainder of the year Mr. Review constantly reminded his readers of the "Highlander." On August 12 he claimed to have kept up a correspondence with him for some time, and he printed a letter from him concerning the plague (IX, 8). On the other hand, on November 25, 1712, "my *Highlander"* became "that Inhabitant of *Terra Incognita"* (IX, 65). The mask slipped so often that Defoe sometimes hardly bothered to hide behind it.

In *The Highland Visions* the seer not only pointed to the accuracy of his last year's predictions concerning the spread of the plague to Denmark, but made the plague even more the tenor of his warning. In April and May the plague, he predicted, would spread into several Northern states of the German Empire. "If *Hamburgh* escapes not the month of *May*," he specified, *"Britain* escapes not this Year, and if both escape this Year, let them take it for a Reprieve from Heaven till the next, to move them to Repentance before the Sword is drawn, and before the Destroyer lands among them" (p. 10). The August prediction was especially alarming. "About this Time let *London, Edinburgh*, and *Yarm*. [outh] enquire narrowly into some Ships, who, in spight of *Quarantines*, will set on Shores some Diseased People, and several die of strange and violent Fevers; yet the great *Terror* begins not yet." "I will hope *Great Britain, Holland* and *France* shall Escape this Year, but dare not expect any longer Sparing; yet Men Repent not . . . ," the seer warned in his September prediction (p. 13).

These alarming predictions Defoe followed up in *The Review*, concentrating in 1712 upon the threat of plague far more than he had done during the previous year and reverting to the theme so often that he evidently made himself a jest thereby among his witty readers. In the issue for August 12, 1712, the Highland seer warned:

> *I Notice the Account you send of the new Distemper among you, the same is begun in this Country, tho' it touches many, it kills none; you ask my Thoughts; they are briefly, assure your self, the Plague WILL visit Britain, but Heaven, I hope, spares her this Summer also; I think I could name the Time exactly, but I refrain—The present Distemper is sent before it, to put you in Mind of its Approach; let it be observ'd neither those WHO HAVE this Distemper, or those THAT ESCAPE, without being touch'd, will be the particular Objects of the Great Visitation; I have a sad View of the Misery of that Day, too great to express; besides, the Age care for no bad News, they do not love to be affrighted. (IX, 8)*

"I had not said any Thing more to it, than I did from my *Highland Prophecy*," Mr. Review commented, "if I had not found all the notices which have been taken of it, and the Thing itself also, turn'd into Ridicule and Banter, by the People of this Age. . ." (IX, 13).

But in *The Highland Visions* Defoe's major theme is again that of war and peace. In many issues of the *Review* of late winter and early spring in 1712 he discussed aspects of peace negotiations, especially the lack of cooperation given by the Allies; and on February 23, 1712, he suggested that peace was necessary if only to demonstrate to them England's determination and unity (VIII, 580). This same lack of cooperation the seer exhibits. In January "THE Councils of *Europe* having been long busie upon the great Dispute about Peace, begin now to see it not so certain as some People imagined; and therefore with great Diligence apply themselves to make preparations for War . . ." (p. 4). Peace negotiations are at first hampered especially because of the adamant position of the Emperor, and in March the divisive tactics of the French begin to be successful. In the prophecy for April "PEACE surprizes the World now rather by the various Shapes it appears in, than the Means it is procured by: The Nations seem rather to drive one another to Peace, than approve of it . . ." (p. 7). In May an uncertain war opens. "NOW they begin the Campaigns; some Fight and some Treat, and some both Treat and Fight; and some who talk as big as any, neither Fight nor Treat: the War goes on Awkwardly and Heavily, as if they fought with an Ill Will: *French Cunning* prevails in many *Courts*, and they have Peace in Effect, when they have War in Appearance: Thus the War now rather Impoverishes than Destroys, and there is likely to be more Money than Blood lost this Campaign" (pp. 8–9). Although October brings at least a halt in hostilities, "We find the Conclusions at Utrecht unable to put a final End to Jealousies and War; and tho' we have now the Appearance of Peace, they all stand with Sword in Hand, as if ready to break out into a New War" (p. 14).

Just as disappointing as peace efforts abroad will be civil dissentions, especially those concerning the peace treaty:

> The Parties in *England* carry on a furious War, and fight many Battles, which, tho' without Blood, have very fatal Effects upon the Nation: Things look dark, and the People begin to see the Circumstances their own Folly has brought them to: National Divisions threaten the Nation's Peace, Trade lost, Credit sunk, and the People uneasy.
>
> The Queen exhorts to Peace: What *People* but those would let her perswade in vain? (p. 9)

In 1713, in publishing his *Second-Sighted Highlander, or Predictions and Foretold Events, especially about the Peace,* Defoe again took advantage of the demise of a prominent foreign nobleman, this year of Frederick I, King of Prussia, who died on February 25, 1713 (N. S.). On February 28 (O. S.) *The Review* carried the first advertisement of the new prophecy, and here also Mr. Review announced, "I Was presented this very Day, by the Publisher, with my old *Scots Highlander's* new Visions for this Year coming, 1713." ". . . it has been publish'd already above a Month ago, tho' I never had one till upon this Occasion," Mr. Review equivocated. "You will be equally surprised with me now, when I shall tell you, That he has now as exactly foretold the death of the King of *Prussia;* who, this very last Post says, dy'd at *Berlin* . . ." (IX, 127). In the brief interval between reception of the news and publication of the prophecy Defoe hardly had adequate time to get his copy to Newcastle and printed copies back to London. But though he kept up the old pretense of earlier publication he did not maintain that his new prophecy had been published in the North: both advertisements and title page announced merely that it was printed for and sold by J. Baker in London.

In the persona of the Highlander there was no change. Here the publisher added a note, probably supplied by Defoe, to explain that the Highlander, whom *"having oblig'd us to conceal his Name, we call the* Highlander with the Second Sight, *hath been very backward this Year to give us his Notions of Events."*[16] According to this note, the seer "was resolv'd to foretell you no more" (p. 4). In this prophecy for the first time he "explains" his occult power of second sight: "Moving Air describes in (to others invisible) small and exactly shap'd Clouds, the very Faces, Shapes, Names and Distinctions of such Persons, Nations, Towns, Cities, and People of whom those Mists, Meteors, and other Clouds represent the Actions: Darkness it self forms the Posture of things by which *WE* see, and every Cloud is fill'd with Hieroglyphicks for the Assistance of this uncouth Attainment called *SECOND SIGHT"* (p. 5). This explanation, however, may have been intended less as a defense of super-natural pretensions than as a preparation for a more dramatic and vivid prophetic style. In *The British Visions* and *The Highland Visions* there was little attempt outside the introductory sections to be personal and dramatic. In *The Second-Sighted Highlander* for 1713, on the other hand, each of the ten visions is given a picturesque setting.

The Second-Sighted Highlander for 1713 devoted comparatively little attention to the spread of the plague, although in his vision for May the seer perceives that in the clouds "the legible Part spells *Hamburgh, Hungary, Constantinople, Italy, Bremen, Pomeren*; if the *Plague* visits not most of these *Parts* this year, my *Second Sight* must fail more than I think it shall; let other nearer *Parts* prepare for it" (p. 13). The overriding concern was, instead, peace. On the title page the word "PEACE" looms largest of all, and in the visions attention is centered upon it. The first vision disappoints: "The bright little Body of Cloud which represented Peace moved on, but stopp'd before the Place design'd for its Rest; so no Peace seems to be yet ripe enough to be declared in *Europe*, whether General or Separate" (p. 6). In March, "the *French* and Imperialists begin the War as if they had cast off Thoughts of Peace" (p. 9). In May "The first publick Steps toward a General Peace are taken" (p. 13), the seer predicted, his second sight failing to warn him that peace would have already been attained in April. In June, "*Utrecht* is now the Scene of War: There the Fate of Kingdoms seems to be absolutely decided, neither Side make any considerable Advantage of the War in the Field, yet some small Advances are made in the Treaties, and the several Pretensions of the *Princes* are so great, and the Interests so inconsistent with one another, that they come yet to no Conclusion, the Breach has been too wide to be soon closed" (p. 15). Prospects for peace fluctuate, but in August hopes become stronger, and in September the vision is even more optimistic: "I see here the Year closing without a perfect Conclusion of the *Peace*, but the Expense of a fruitless War on both Sides seems to incline all Parties, even *France* it self, to a greater readiness to comply" (p. 20). The seer continues, "I see indeed great Probability that it shall be finally compleated in the Months of *September* and *October*, but some Accidents may still intervene to prevent it" (p. 20). The final vision, in October, is encouraging: ". . . I see Hopes that the End of the Year closes with *Peace* . . . the *Peace* as entertain'd by the *British* Sovereign, appears made for our selves, and such of our Allies as stand with us; the rest complain loudly, and talk high, but see a Necessity of Complying, and putting an End to the War which now every Body think [sic] better of than they did before" (p. 21).

Here again in 1713, however, peace at home is as important as peace abroad. As Mr. Review commented on February 28, 1713, concerning this prophecy, ". . . this Consequence may be drawn from it in short, (viz.) It is the greatest Folly in the World for People to rage at one another, and at the Instruments of publick Transactions on one side, and on the other" (IX, 127). As in his previous prophecies, Defoe in *The Second-Sighted Highlander* of 1713 defended the efforts of those who were framing the peace and disparages those who were making political capital out of their difficulties. Thus in August the Highlander foresees "strong siding against Great Ones, quarrelling the Peace, impeaching the Integrity and Design of those who have brought it to this Length, as what has been a Ruin to the Measures formerly taken both at Home and Abroad; great and formal Accusations of Ill Practices against the publick Welfare involve several Great Persons on either Side, and these again embark Parties to their several Interests, the Heats rouze both Sides to terrible Attacks upon each other, and Rabble decides the Controversie at last . . ." (p. 18).

Especially is the seer concerned in his visions for unity in the nation over the succession of the House of Hanover: "*WE*, who in this Island have upon our Hands a Matter of the last Moment respecting a Succession of our Monarchs, cannot be without Concern in such an Affair, and if some Attempts are made to its Prejudice, they may be expected about the Months of *June* or *July*; let the *People* of *Britain* take heed of pulling down with their own Hands their Securities: None can hurt them but themselves" (p. 14). More specifically, attempts in favor of the Pretender are foreseen (as Defoe had warned in his *Review* for February 21, 1713): "Great Talk and private Attempts about *March*, to make Way for the *Pretender*, but the Fruit is not ripe, and some who pretend to pull it before it is come to Perfection, make much of its Fall to the Ground in the shaking. . ." (p. 10).

In his concluding vision of *The Second-Sighted Highlander* for 1713 the seer promises to include in his next year's visions, predictions of securing the peace and safeguarding the succession of the Throne (p. 22). But no prophecy for the year 1714 seems to be extant. Perhaps the illness and death of Queen Anne early in the year made Defoe hesitant to publish a prediction for that year; or more probably, his own illness and other difficulties gave him no proper opportunity. Moreover he now lacked *The Review* as an effective advertising medium.

In 1715, however, a meteorological event was imminent on which he decided to capitalize. For April 22, 1715, the astronomers predicted a total solar eclipse such as London had evidently not witnessed since the year 1140.[17] A number of astronomers published charts showing the path of the eclipse. Edmund Halley issued as an engraved broadsheet *A Description of the Passage of the Shadow of the Moon over England, in the Total Eclipse of the Sun.* John Flamsteed, royal astronomer, published *Mr Flamsteed's Figure of the Eclipse of the Sun that will happen April 22nd 1715, Showing how it will appear at London*; and using his computations, William Whiston published *A Calculation of the Great Eclipse of the Sun April 22nd 1715 from Mr Flamsteed's Tables.* These predictions were intended not only to inform but to allay groundless fears. Halley, for example, published his chart so "that the suddain dark-ness, wherin the Starrs will be visible about the Sun, may give no surprize to the People, who would, if unadvertized, be apt to look upon it as Ominous, and to Interpret it as portending evill to our Sovereign Lord King George and his Government."[18] Some prophets, however, evidently took advantage of the superstitions of the ignorant, with pamphlets like *The Black Day, or a Prophet of Doomsday, Exemplified in the Great and Terrible Eclipse which will Happen on . . . the 22d of April 1715.*

Also taking advantage of the popular interest and concern, though not to exacerbate Fears, Defoe published what was evidently his last prophecy, *The Second-Sighted Highlander, Being Four Visions of the Eclypse.* Later it may have cost Defoe a twinge of conscience to have the persona of his *Journal of the Plague Year* write, "The Apprehensions of the People, were likewise strangely encreas'd by the Error of the Times; in which, I think, the People, from what Principle I cannot imagine, were more adicted to Prophesies, and Astrological Conjurations, Dreams, and old Wives Tales, than ever they were before or since: Whether this unhappy Temper was originally raised by the Follies of some People who got Money by it; that is to say, by printing Predictions, and Prognostications, I know not; but certain it is, Books frighted them terribly; such as *Lilly's* Almanack, *Gadbury's* Astrological Predictions; Poor *Robin's* Almanack and the like . . ." (p. 25). To profit from the excitement, J. Baker evidently published Defoe's last prophecy just two days before the eclipse itself—on April 20.[19]

One of the most striking aspects of this prophecy is the comparative modesty of its supernatural claims. A "Conclusion," supposedly appended by the publisher, asserts that many of the predictions "have been written some Months ago," but that "every one is at Liberty to take the above Account either for a real Prediction, or for a fictitious Fabulous Ramble of Fancy."[20] "As to the Visions here mentioned," the Conclusion reiterates, "the Reader is left at full Liberty to put as little weight on them as he pleases; the main End and Design of the whole being to prevent Atheistical Influence of those, who take our Eyes so effectually from them. . ." (p. 45).

In view of this change, other differences, and the Highlander's failure to refer to his previous predictions, this prophecy can be claimed for Defoe with less assurance than its predecessors. But Defoe probably wrote it, and all the bibliographers have followed Trent in assigning it to him.[21] Since Baker continued to be Defoe's principal publisher for some time, one can assume that only with Defoe's permission would he have issued such a prophecy capitalizing upon the earlier successes, and Defoe was hardly in a position to hand along his prophetical cloak to a new wearer. The main motifs and materials are similar to those of the earlier prophesies, and there are some striking parallels with Defoe's other works. The discussion of the natural consequences of the eclipse, along with providential warnings, (p. 43) anticipates similar meteorological explanations in *A System of Magick*. Moreover the rather unusual citation from "the ancient Prophetick Discovery of the *Second-Sighted Cowil*"—"*Pushes from* Pomeran *into* Sluce"—reiterates Defoe's earlier discussion of this same prediction (from Samuel Colvil's *Whigs Supplication*) in *The Review* for February 22, 1706 (IV, 21–22).

As has been suggested, *The Second-Sighted Highlander* for 1715 differs from the earlier prophecies in several respects. Most noticeably of all, Defoe here arranged his prophecy geographically rather than chronologically, having his vision of things to come review successively France, Sweden, Great Britain, and the Empire of Germany. Perhaps he was here modifying the traditional section of the almanac which was devoted to predictions for the four seasons rather than the separate months and which customarily commented upon the significance of the eclipses and other striking meterological phenomena.

The persona of the Highland seer, on the other hand, is retained, though Scotland was hardly the proper locale for this vision. The total eclipse was nowhere visible there. In this prophecy for the first time the Highlander identifies himself, as "I *Archibald Mac Donald* of *Inverlocky*" (p. 3). Here in 1715, moreover, the technique of concentrating upon one vision involving four parts of Europe rather than diffusing the prophecy through ten or twelve separate visions allows Defoe to dramatize at some length:

> Led by this Ray of supernatural Light it was, that, at Midnight that *first* Day of the Month of *January*, rising from my Bed of Feathers, soft and refreshing to me as Pillows of Down, and standing on the highest Pinnacle of the Mountain *Aphlec*, in one of the floating Islands of the miraculous *Lough-loman*, I was mov'd to regard the Aspect of celestial Nature.

The *Dancers*, those *Igni Fatui* of the *Northern* Regions, those Lights found in the Abyss of Darkness, shone brightly with their dazling and unsteady Rays, leaving Nature it self, and all the wise Discoverers of her most secret Parts, at a Loss; and in the Dark, to know from whence they proceed. The Stars shone portentous, and with Aspect malignant, boding Evil to the doz'd World, gave Notice to me, that I might suddenly expect an extraordinary Vision of things to come; I had repeated Warnings from secret Foreknowledge, that something dreadful attended.

Expecting, with some Affliction, what should offer to an extended Sight, there appeared a vast globular, but dark Body, passing swiftly in a circular Motion; no Appearance at first offering to my Sight, of its being so much as capable of a reflex Light, till passing by me in a parallel Position, I discern'd it to be the Body of the Moon, some time after its Conjunction with the Sun, called by Men the *Change*. (pp. 6–7)

This dramatic introduction prepares us for a prophetic view of the consequences of "the most effectual and central Conjunction that had been visible to those Parts of the World, for 800 Years past" (p. 7).

Even though he does not attempt to capitalize this time so much upon his predictions, the seer again scatters his shots to anticipate a possible sequel the following year. This time he foresees dangers threatening or death attending the kings of Spain and Italy, the Pope, the doges of Genoa and Venice, the Grand Duke of Tuscany, the Grand Seignior, and the King of Prussia. Again he returns to the threat of plague: ". . . the Contagion which visits *Europe*, passes not lightly here, entring by the Rhine, traverses a third Part of the Kingdom, and passes either into *Italy* or *Spain*, making great Devastation" (p. 17). England, however, will be spared: "I see not indeed a general Plague, at least not yet. . ." (p. 35).

Again in 1715 the Highlander concentrates upon the need for domestic concord. In passing he genuflects to the ghost of Queen Anne. He sees "aspiring a pleasant Clowd, enlighten'd with seraph-ick Flame, and surrounding a crowned Appearance, shapeless, but amiable, noting the remov'd Person exalted and accepted, and declar'd innocent of the Mischiefs design'd to the Countries committed to the Rule of her Scepter, tho' politically abused, and made to skreen the Crimes of Men, as if they had been her own" (p. 26). In George I he sees a strong ruler able to unify Britain and put an end to party strife: ". . . there appears the Sovereign, vested not only with Power enough to quell, but with Temper, Wisdom, and Council, to calm the Tempests of Men's Minds on either Side" (p. 28). When factions turn their contentions to supplanting one another in the King's favor, they alarm him "to suppress contending Parties, by a strong Arm; taking the Reins of Government into his own Hands" (p. 30). "Here the exalted Sight obtain'd a vision, portending the Destruction of all Party-Administrations in the Days yet to come," and all evils "appeared at one Blast, by the sagatious Breath of a wise Governour, dissipated, disjoined, separated, and entirely dispersed" (p. 32).

Because of the inept planning, timing, and inadequate support of the Pretender, the seer is able to predict his failure with some assurance: ". . . the Fate determined for the Nation, is happily superceded; the Minds of Men much agitated, and some Signs tending to Blood; but discovered to be no other, in the Issue, than the Blood of Criminals, shed in due Regard to the Safety of the Publick, and, perhaps, in crushing Rebellion and Treason" (pp. 25–26). ". . . I see a great Flash of *Fire*, the *Noise* loud, but the End Smoke, the intelligent *Soul* sees in this, a fruitless Attempt, *Qui fatez mille traca*, a mighty Noise, threatning Invasion, War, and Depredation upon Great Britain; the pretending Enemy making such stir, loud Boasts, and Cloathing himself with infinite Plumes of Feathers, Trophies of his own *Imagination*, mov'd along with a swift Pace towards this Island; but I see him . . . vanish into Smoke, noisome and contemptible, his Cloud vanish'd in a Blast, his Feathers are pluck'd off, and blown up into the Air, and the weak Creature dies contemptible" (pp. 36–37).

Evidently *The Second-Sighted Highlander* for 1715 was Defoe's last prophecy. Having waited a decent interval into 1716, Joseph Addison, in his *Freeholder* No. 27, for March 23, 1716, wrote a mock vision taking off the Highland seer, on whose account Mr. Review had admitted that at least one gentleman had accused him of *"Dealing with the Devil"* (IX, 7). Addison's vision was that of

> a *Highland* Seer, who is famous among the mountains, and known by the name of *Second-sighted Sawney*. Had he been able to write, we might probably have seen this vision sooner in print; for it happened to him very early in the late hard winter; and is transmitted to me by a student at *Glasgow*, who took the whole relation from him. . . .
>
> *Sawney* was descended of an ancient family, very much renowned for their skill in prognosticks. Most of his ancestors were second-sighted, and his mother but narrowly escaped being burnt for a witch.[22]

Part Two

The Spurious:
The Illusory Defoe

VI | Dorothy Dingley: A Laid Ghost

N°o matter how fully documented and illustrated any exposition of Defoe's ideas concerning the supernatural may be, these ideas will be misunderstood and their sincerity doubted as long as we continue to attribute to Defoe spurious books and pamphlets which employ the occult for meretricious or adventitious purposes. One of these spurious attributions, a ghost story employing the ritual of exorcism, has already been dropped from the Defoe canon. Once firmly established as Defoe's, "A Remarkable Passage of an Apparition" was included in collected editions of Defoe from 1840 through George Aitken's edition of 1895 and 1899 and G. Maynardier's of 1903 and 1908, though not all who read it there notice Maynadier's admission that it "was probably not his." In 1869 William Lee pontificated, "There can be no more doubt that this was written by Defoe, than that he wrote the Apparition of Mrs. Veal..." (I, 323). Even as late as 1931 Thomas Wright devoted two pages to the story in his *Life of Daniel Defoe* as "certainly from his pen."[1] Thus many remember and associate with Defoe the story of the Launceston boy haunted by the ghost of Dorothy Dingley—until the local parson—schoolmaster, John Ruddle, was brought in by the boy's parents to cure their supposedly love-sick or lazy son. Moved by the boy's story, Parson Ruddle, one recalls, went to the field where the ghost frequently intercepted the lad, met the ghost and "spoke to it with a loud voice, in some such sentences as the way of these dealings directed me." "I was not in the least terrified," Ruddle asseverated, "and therefore persisted until it spake again, and gave me satisfaction." The same evening, he continued, "it quietly vanished, and neither doth appear since, nor ever will more to any man's disturbance."[2] Those who know the story will look in vain for reference to it in twentieth century bibliographies of Defoe. It is no longer an official part of the Defoe canon. In 1907 William P. Trent quietly dropped it, in a footnote, from the approved list: "From the communications of Alfred F. Robbins to *Notes and Queries* . . . ," he admitted, "it would seem that Dr. Ruddle rather than Defoe wrote 'A Remarkable Passage'; and certainly all stylistic tests point away from Defoe."[3] For an addition to the Defoe canon no further proof was in the past generally required than the *ipse dixit* of the then recognized Defoe bibliographer—Chalmers, Wilson, Hazlitt, Lee, Trent, or Hutchins. But for a journalist to remove an item from the canon is no mean achievement; the late Sir Alfred, one feels, deserved his knighthood.

The story first appeared in 1720 in *Mr. Campbell's Packet for the Entertainment of Gentlemen and Ladies*, dated 1665 there and assigned to Mr. Ruddle, who names himself in the process of his narrative. How William Bond, author of *The History of the Life and Adventures of Mr. Duncan Campbell* and editor of *Mr. Campbell's Packet*, got hold of the story, does not appear. It was subsequently issued separately by the publisher, Edmund Curll, for sixpence, as "A Surprizing Account of the Apparition of a young Woman, who appear'd to the Rev. Mr. *Ruddle* of *Launceston* in *Cornwall*, and of his Conversation with her. Attested by Himself."[4] Though this part of its history has evidently never been noticed, the narrative quickly became a favorite in collections of ghost stories. It was included in 1752 in *A View of the Invisible World, or General History of Apparitions*, in effect a late edition of Defoe's *History and Reality of Apparitions* (1727), with a score of new stories. Subsequently it appeared in *Life after Death* (1758), which opens with this story; in *Visits from the World of Spirits* (1791), a very late revision of Defoe's *History of Apparitions*; and in John Tregortha's *News from the Invisible World* (1813).

Then in 1817 the Reverend John Ruddle's manuscript account was printed by Charles Sanloe Gilbert in his *Historical Survey of the County of Cornwall*, evidently in complete ignorance of its popular existence in collections of ghost stories. The new account was practically identical with the one already widely published, but it identified some of the characters involved, including the haunted lad, Sam Bligh. Given a new lease on life by being thus authenticated and accepted in the county histories, the story began to appear in collections of local stories as well as in general ghost collections. It was included, for example, in Fortesque Hitchins's *History of Cornwall* (1824), where the ghost, Dorothy Dingley, was somehow renamed Dorothy Dudley. From Hitchins, John Mason Neale took the account for his *Unseen World* (1847). It appeared also in T. M. Jarvis's *Accredited Ghost Stories* (1823), where it is accorded the climatic position; in "Horace Welby's" (John Timbs's) *Signs before Death, and Authenticated Apparitions* (1825); in *The Spectre, or News from the Invisible World* (1836); in Clarence S. Day's *Remarkable Apparitions, and Ghost-Stories* (New York, 1848); and probably in a score of similar collections.

Not until 1840 was the story ascribed to Defoe, and then perhaps by accident. George Chalmers, in 1790, had attributed only *Duncan Campbell* itself to Defoe; but the editor of the 1840 edition of Defoe, in reprinting from the second, or corrected edition of that biography, included also the attached pieces from *Mr. Campbell's Packet*, despite the fact that neither Chalmers nor Walter Wilson had claimed for Defoe anything from the appended pamphlet. Finding the ghost story in an edition of Defoe puzzled Mrs. Anna Elizabeth Bray, who had originally come upon the story in Gilbert and had used it as the basis for her novel *Trelawny of Trelawne* (1837):

> Soon after the publication of "Trelawny," my much esteemed friend, the Rev. F. V. J. Arundell, informed me, that, whilst engaged in his antiquarian researches in Cornwall, he found among some old and original papers the manuscript account in Dr. Ruddell's own handwriting, of his encounter with the ghost in question. This he lent Gilbert, who inserted it in his "History of Cornwall;" and there I first saw it. . . .
> . . . He assured me there could be no mistake as to the genuineness of the ghost document he had found, as he had compared the manuscript with Ruddell's handwriting in other papers, and saw it was one and the same.

In a note appended to the novel, Mrs. Bray added, "I am informed a field near Launceston, exactly agreeing with Dr. Ruddell's account, as given in Gilbert's History of Cornwall, is still pointed out by tradition, as the scene of the boy's encounter with the spirit, and where it was laid to rest by the good Doctor."[5]

Although in defending Defoe's authorship, William Lee was in 1866 forced to impugn the authenticity of Mrs. Bray's account,[6] the only weak link there seems to be the subsequent disappearance of the Ruddle manuscript of the story. The Reverend Francis Vyvan Jago-Arundell, a native of Launceston, was still living when Mrs. Bray published her note, and during the years 1805–1815 he had been preparing a history of Cornwall. In 1810 he had published a note in *The Gentlemen's Magazine* asking for help in locating John Anstis's manuscript history of Launceston, and some of the plates which he intended to incorporate in his work seem to have been engraved, and a prospectus seems actually to have been published.[7] His sending materials along to one of his speedier, more successful rivals seems quite probable, especially since he had for some years turned his attention to the Near East.

The elaborations which the tale received at the hands of the Cornish poet Robert Stephen Hawker, on the other hand, prejudiced some scholars from accepting Mrs. Bray's Account. In May of 1867 Hawker published in *All the Year Round* "The Botathen Ghost," his version of the Dingley story, based, he alleged, upon Ruddle's "Diurnal," which had fallen by chance into his hands. His story he claimed to have based upon this diary, pretending to quote from it even where his account obviously paraphrased the already published version. Hawker's story is couched in archaic language unlike Ruddle's and interspersed with highly colored descriptions which suggest the Cornish poet rather than the schoolmaster-priest. In the latter part of his narrative, moreover, or his "lewd engraftment," to use a Richardsonian phrase, Hawker added a sequel wherein Ruddle seeks, obtains, and successfully employs permission from the Bishop of Exeter to exorcise the ghost of Dorothy Dingley: "January 7, 1665. At my own house, I find, by my books, what is expedient to be done; and then, Apage, Sathanas!"[8] Not only the Launceston journalist Alfred Robbins, but Hawker's biographer Sabine Baring-Gould accused Hawker of fabricating the diary.[9] From the biographies of the Cornish poet, a critical reader could surmise as much for himself. There it is clear that Solomon's pentacle, which Ruddle is alleged to have inscribed for the ghost, was one of Hawker's favorite seals; that he feared and protected himself against the Evil Eye and thought himself the peculiar object of other diabolical activity; and that he hoped for a revival of the exorcism which the Bishop of Exeter reluctantly grants Dr. Ruddle: "Exorcism duly performed," Hawker wrote Claude Hawker, "would make strange discoveries in these assemblies of the people. There are words and signs which would throttle many a loud bully, and cast him on the ground foaming."[10] Doubtless Hawker must have been reminded of the Dingley ghost when he preached his Visitation sermon at Launceston in June of 1866, and later, in November of that same year, he may have read William Lee's account of the ghost story in *Notes and Queries*. As Hawker's son-in-law and biographer, C. E. Byles, admitted, "This habit of hoaxing became so ingrained in his nature that perhaps, as he grew older, he was hardly able himself to distinguish between jest and earnest, fact and fancy, belief and simulated belief."[11] Moreover Hawker was writing a ghost story for a popular magazine, not writing a local history.

Perhaps the final touch to Hawker's engraftment was the version printed by his biographer the Reverend Sabine Baring-Gould, who not only acquired and reproduced (*mirable dictu*) "Parson Rudall's" portrait, but confused the two best-known ghost stories ever credited to Daniel Defoe: "It must be noted that Defoe in his printed account . . . changes Dorothy Dingley into Mrs. Veale"!¹²

But still other ghosts must be laid at Hawker's door. In 1893 Thomas Firminger Thisolton Dyer, perhaps inspired by Hawker, added, "Local tradition still tells us that 'Madam Dudley's ghost did use to walk in Cumnor Park, and that it walked so obstinately, that it took no less than nine parsons from Oxford "to lay her." That they at last laid her in a pond, called "Madam Dudley's Pond," and, moreover, wonderful to relate, the water in that pond was never known to freeze afterward.' "¹³ Perhaps credit for such inventiveness should go not to Dyer, but to some local wag bored by continued inquiries concerning the now famous local ghost. But no such excuse can be made for the Reverend Montagu Summers, who with customary carelessness included Hawker's account of the exorcism as a main historical exhibit in his *History of Witchcraft and Demonology*.¹⁴

Sir Alfred Farthing Robbins, the historian and journalist who finally convinced Defoe bibliographers that Ruddle had written the story of Dorothy Dingley's ghost, published five studies of the story, all of them before he was knighted for distinguished journalism. In the first, printed in his *Launceston: Past and Present* (1884), he quoted in extenso the pontifications of William Lee, assigning the story to Defoe, and added information concerning Ruddle, citing "a manuscript account of the tradition, written in the early years of this century by George Farthing, great-uncle of the present Author, and read by Mr. E. Robbins before the Launceston Working Men's Club in 1864, but now unfortunately missing" (p. 218n).

His second study, "Defoe's 'Remarkable Passage of an Apparition,' " was the lead article in *Notes and Queries* for September 21, 1895. Commenting there upon George A. Aitken's inclusion of the story in his recent edition of Defoe, Robbins gave entire credit for the story to Ruddle, cleared up some of the errors in earlier accounts of the story, and supplied considerable information concerning the author, calling attention to the parish registers still extant, partly in his hand, and quoting Ruddle's verses to the memory of his first wife and his letter, "from the Bishop's registry at Exeter," to his "Cosen Cooke."¹⁵

His third study came in response to an article which his previous note had inspired. In *The Speaker* for October 12, 1895, Sir Arthur Quiller-Couch, maintaining that the story "is one of the best ghost-stories in the language," asked, "May not the son [William Ruddle] have taken Defoe's narrative (itself constructed out of his father's copious notes) and added a correction or two from his own local knowledge? And may not this MS. of *William* Ruddle's (the son) have been the one discovered by Mr. Jago Arundall . . . ?"[16] Recognizing that this suggestion would have permitted Defoe bibliographers to reclaim the story for Defoe, Mr. Robbins replied in the very next issue of *The Speaker,* for October 19, 1895. In "Dorothy Dingley and Daniel Defoe" he reiterated, on external and internal evidence, his claim for Ruddle's authorship.

These articles Mr. Robbins quickly followed up with another contribution to *Notes and Queries,* for November 2, 1895. There he demonstrated the reliability of the Reverend Mr. Arundell and publicized new evidence of Ruddle's authorship: "investigation has been made at Launceston which has yielded the most striking result. Mr. O. B. Peter, A. R. I. B. A. [co-author of *Histories of Launceston and Dunheved*], has published in the *Launceston Weekly News* a copy of the story which is in the possession of a lady of the town. This is identical, almost in every word, with the tale as printed by Defoe. . . ." According to Mr. Peter, "The age of the paper and the characters of the script establish its genuineness." This version of the Dingley story was signed "John Ruddle" and documented with almost disturbingly complete data concerning its provenance:

> This is a copy of w[t] I found written by my father and signed John Ruddle. Taken by me William Ruddle.
> The readers may observe y[t] I borrowed y[e] remarkable passage of y[e] grandson of John Ruddle who had it from his Uncle William Ruddle. I think I'm exact in its transcription. I well know the sd John Ruddle to have had (and I daresay deserved) the character of a Learned and eminent Divine, and I also well knew his son y[e] sayd William Ruddle, a Divine whose character was so bright y[t] I have no room to add to its Lustre, and I hereby certify y[t] I copied this from y[e] very handwriting of the sayd William Ruddle. *Quinto die Februarii Anno Dni:* 1730. JAMES WAKEHAM.[17]

Finally, in *The Cornish Magazine,* in 1898, at the invitation of the editor, Sir Arthur Quiller-Couch, Mr. Robbins gave a full demonstration of Ruddle's authorship and supplied photographs of the locales involved in the story of Dorothy Dingley's ghost. The only comment from Defoe scholars subsequently has been the quiet admission of Mr. Trent. Doubtless he thought that the less said about the Dingley ghost, the better. But one wonders how many other ghosts still walk in the Defoe canon.

VII | Duncan Campbell, Daniel Defoe, and William Bond

THE MOST INTERESTING—and damaging—group of occult materials which has been attributed to Daniel Defoe is that which dramatizes another deaf and dumb seer, the fortune-teller Duncan Campbell. The group consists of six pieces: *The History of the Life and Adventures of Mr. Duncan Campbell* (1720), *Mr. Campbell's Packet, for the Entertainment of Gentlemen and Ladies* (1720), *A Spy upon the Conjuror* (1724), *The Dumb Projector* (1725), *The Friendly Daemon, or the Generous Apparition* (1726), and *Secret Memoirs of the Late Mr. Duncan Campbel* (1732). Of these the first and by far the most important is *The History of the Life and Adventures of Mr. Duncan Campbell*. It has been assigned to Defoe ever since George Chalmers, giving no evidence, attributed it to him in 1790, and it has been reprinted in every extensive edition of his works.[1] Less interesting in itself, but no less significant in the derogatory implications its authorship would cast upon Defoe's character and integrity is *The Friendly Daemon*. All six of the Campbell items have at one time or another been fathered upon Defoe, and these two are still reprinted as his and are currently given to him in John Robert Moore's *Checklist of the Writings of Daniel Defoe*. There appears to be no evidence, however, that he had a hand in a single one of them.

In order to establish the authorship of these two works, it will be necessary to consider the picture which the whole group presents of the life and supernatural pretensions of the seer, to compare the occult ideas and the style which the two works exhibit with those of the established works of Defoe, and finally to provide a picture of the character, life, and writings of the real author of *Duncan Campbell*—William Bond.

A deaf and dumb fortune-teller and quack doctor, Duncan Campbell, or Campbel, was a picturesque figure in London from about 1710 until his death in 1730. In *The Tatler* and *The Spectator* Addison and Steele gave him considerable attention. Addison was the less sympathetic, but even he regarded Campbell as a rarity not to be missed. The imaginary opera which his projector arranges in the *Spectator* for April 5, 1711, for the convenient display of all of London's wonders, opens with Alexander's "consulting the Oracle of *Delphes,* in which the dumb Conjuror, who has been visited by so many Persons of Quality of late Years, is to be introduced as telling him his Fortune."[2] In his *Spectator* for March 11, 1712, Addison had a fashionable and gullible young lady confide to her journal, "Waked by Miss *Kitty.* . . .Went in our Mobbs to the Dumb Man, according to Appointment. Told me, that my Lover's Name began with a *G. Mem.* The Conjuror was within a Letter of Mr. *Froth*'s Name. &c. (III, 184).

In his *Spectator* for October 9, 1712, Addison glanced at the Highlands ancestry and gifts of second sight which the seer boasted. There a Moorfields correspondent, "Titus Trophonius," recommends himself as an interpreter of dreams, as he could claim Highland ancestry through his wife: "My great Uncle by my Wife's side was a *Scotch* Highlander, and second-sighted." The conclusion of the letter seems pointedly skeptical: " '*N. B.* I am not dumb' " (IV, 293, 294). In the *Spectator* for June 28, 1714, Eustace Budgell acknowledged the seer's amazing popularity: "EVERY one has heard of the famous Conjuror, who, according to the Opinion of the Vulgar, has studied himself *dumb*; for which Reason, as it is believed, he delivers out all his Oracles in Writing. Be that as it will, the blind *Tiresias* was not more famous in *Greece,* than this dumb Artist has been for some Years last past in the Cities of *London* and *Westminster*" (IV, 512). In an accompanying letter, signed "Cornelius Agrippa," and probably written by Addison (IV, 512, n. 1), the seer renounces his affection of dumbness:

From my Cell, June 24, 1714

SIR,

'*BEING* informed that you have lately got the Use of your Tongue, I have some Thoughts of following your Example, that I may be a *Fortune-teller* properly speaking. I am grown weary of my Taciturnity, and having served my Country many Years under the Title of the dumb Doctor, I shall now Prophesie by Word of Mouth, and (as Mr. *Lee* says of the Magpie, who you know was a great Fortune-teller among the Ancients) *chatter* Futurity. I have hitherto chosen to receive Questions and return Answers in Writing, that I might avoid the Tediousness and Trouble of Debates; my Querists being generally of a Humour to think, that they have never Predictions enough for their Mony. In short, Sir, my Case has been something like that of those discreet Animals the Monkeys, who, as the *Indians* tell us, can speak if they wou'd, but purposely avoid it that they may not be made to Work. I have hitherto gained a Livelyhood by holding my Tongue, but shall now open my Mouth in order to fill it. If I appear a little Wordbound in my first Solutions and Responses, I hope it will not be imputed to any want of Foresight, but to the long Disuse of Speech. I doubt not by this Invention to have all my former Customers over again, for if I have promised any of them Lovers or Husbands, Riches or good Luck, it is my Design to confirm to them *vivâ voce* what I have already given them under my Hand. If you will honour me with a Visit, I will compliment you with the first opening of my Mouth, and if you please you may make an entertaining Dialogue out of the Conversation of two Dumb Men. Excuse this Trouble, worthy Sir, from one who has been a long time

> *Your Silent Admirer,*
> Cornelius Agrippa.' (IV, 512–513)

Finally, in his *Spectator* for November 12, 1714, Thomas Tickell hit at the practice of astrology, with which Campbell then evidently did not wish to be publicly associated. To a request from "Charissa," desiring "to be eased in some Scruples relating to the Skill of Astrologers" Mr. Spectator noted, *"referred to the Dumb Man for an Answer"* (V, 115).

Less barbed were Steele's notices. The first appeared in the *Tatler* for May 12, 1709. Writing from White's Chocolate House, Mr. Bickerstaff commented:

A gentleman here this evening was giving me an account of a dumb fortune-teller, who outdoes Mr. Partridge, myself, or the unborn-doctor, for predictions. All his visitants come to him full of expectations, and pay his own rate for the interpretations they put upon his shrugs and nods. There is a fine rich City widow stole thither the other day (though it is not six weeks since her husband's departure from her company to rest) and, with her trusty maid, demanded of him, whether she should marry again, by holding up two fingers, like horns on her forehead. The wizard held up both his hands forked. The relict desired to know, whether he meant by his holding up both hands, to represent that she had one husband before, and that she should have another? Or that he intimated, she should have two more? The cunning-man looked a little sour; upon which Betty jogged her mistress, who gave the other guinea; and he made her understand, she should positively have two more; but shaked his head, and hinted, that they should not live long with her. The widow sighed, and gave him the other half-guinea.[3]

Most flattering of all, however, was Steele's *Spectator* for September 3, 1712, so flattering indeed that it was later incorporated in *Duncan Campbell*:

Mr. SPECTATOR,

'ABOUT two Years ago I was called upon by the younger Part of a Country Family, by my Mother's Side related to me, to visit Mr. *Campbell* the dumb Man; for they told me That was chiefly what brought them to Town, having heard Wonders of him in *Essex*. I, who always wanted Faith in Matters of that Kind, was not easily prevailed on to go; but least they should take it ill, I went with 'em; when, to my Surprize, *Mr. Campbell* related all their past Life, (in short, had he not been prevented, such a Discovery wou'd have come out, as would have ruin'd the next Design of their coming to Town, *viz.* buying Wedding Cloaths.) Our Names—tho' he never heard of us before—and endeavour'd to conceal— were as familiar to him as to ourselves. To be sure, Mr. SPECTATOR, he is a very learned and wise Man. Being impatient to know my Fortune, having paid my Respects in a Family *Jacobus*, he told me (after his Manner) among several other things, that in a Year and nine Months I should fall ill of a new Feaver, be given over by my Physicians, but shou'd with much Difficulty recover: That the first Time I took the Air afterwards, I shou'd be address'd to by a young Gentleman of a plentiful Fortune, good Sense, and a generous Spirit. *Mr.* SPECTATOR, he is the purest Man in the World, for all he said is come to pass, and I am the happiest She in *Kent*. I have been in quest of Mr. *Campbell* these three Months, and can't find him out: Now hearing you are a dumb Man too, I thought you might correspond, and be able to tell me something; for I think my self highly obliged to make his Fortune as he has mine. 'Tis very possible your Worship, who has Spies all over this Town, can inform me how to send to him: If you can, I beseech you be as speedy as possible, and you will highly oblige

Your constant Reader and Admirer,
Dulcibella Thankley.'

Ordered, That the Inspector I employ about Wonders, enquire at the *Golden Lion,* opposite to the *Half-Moon* Tavern in *Drury-Lane,* into the Merit of this silent Sage, and report accordingly. (IV, 181–182)

The results of these notices doubtless made Campbell appreciate such publicity. In 1717, in order to reclaim his old customers and attract new ones he evidently agreed with the notorious publisher Edmund Curll, who cared more about profits than principles, to publish a biography. Curll began to build up publicity in March 8, 1717, by announcing a forthcoming biography of the seer by "J. B."[4] For some time, progress on the project seems to have been impreceptible. As a matter of fact, Campbell seems to have been absent from London during a considerable part of the year, perhaps most of it. On January 4, 1718, he announced his return in the columns of the *Weekly-Journal, or Saturday's Post*:

Madam,

THE Uneasiness you seem'd to express at my Absence, your Desire to have the first Notice of my Return, and whether my Intentions were to continue the Business for which you account me so justly wonderful, makes me acquaint you, that I am now come to my House over against Short's

Gardens in Drury-Lane, where I shall at all Times be ready to perform plainly what the World has so long experienced of me, what by Thousands here in Town I am known to have done from my Childhood, and what your Ladyship shall not fail to have your Satisfaction in, by

Madam,

Your most Humble,

Most Devoted Servant,

D. CAMPBELL (p. 333)

Somewhat later this same month Campbell and William Bond began to focus publicity upon the seer in the columns and advertisements of Bond's *Weekly Medley*. The opening advertisement came in the lead article of the issue for January 31–February 7, 1719. Here every woman who attends the masquerades is advised that she

should go to one that could really tell Fortunes with good Success, before she should venture to enter in. Mr. *Campbell* lives pretty near at Hand, who, tho' he may be *dumb*, is able to *tell* them how far it may be fortunate or unfortunate for them on such or such an Evening to go to that Diversion, better than any *cunning* Man *living* that has his *Tongue* never so much at *command*. I would therefore advise most Ladies, who are at so much Cost for their Habits, to lay out as they may with much more Prudence and Benefit One Piece of Gold more to see him for so much previous wholesome Advice; or if they are so silly as not to follow my Counsel, they would be at least so wise to themselves as only to personate the *Mutes*, and learn to be *dumb*, during the Time of Entertainment, to every Sollicitation that tends toward Love or carrying on a Society with any Man beyond the Threshold of the Door. However, it will be better for them to seek the Advice of this skilful *Gentleman*, who, as I am informed, has very opportunely for the Season taken Lodgings so very near the Haymarket, as the back-side of the Ship-Tavern, Chairing-Cross.[5]

The very next number brought a follow-up in a letter from "Clarinda" to "The Busy Body" confirming from her own experience the marvelous skill of Campbell:

. . . upon my having recourse to him, Mr. Campbell the Dumb Gentleman, to whom I was directed, and whom I am ever bound to Love more than my own dear Father; he told me every particular Incident beforehand, and predicted to me the happy Day at the Year's End. I was incredulous in these Things as Mrs. Any-Body and therefore bethinking myself that the best way of Fathoming the Depth of his Occult Science, was, first and formost, What was the Name of the Person to be my Husband? As soon as he had wrote down the very self-same Syllables, which I was in doubtful Pain to see. No Transport could surely be equal to mine! The Joy I was affected with at that critical Juncture left me scarce room to be so much amaz'd as I should have been otherwise at the Skill and Penetration of Mr. Campbell, whom I ever since call by the Name of my good Love-prophet. . . . And as I wish all my Sex Felicity, so I can't help directing all under my amorous Circumstances to Mr. Campbell, who lives at present at the back of the Ship Tavern. . . . (p. 176)

This pair of commendations was followed ten weeks later, in the issue for April 18–25, 1719, with *"A Letter from one Sister to another, concerning the Happiness of her Friend, who consulted Mr.* Campbell *the Dumb Gentleman, at the* Ship-Tavern, Chairing-Cross," which reinforces the earlier recommendations:

> Well, but said I to her, My Kitty, (for I had the Medley I sent you then in my Hand) this Paper, which put me in Mind of the Masquerade, tells me too, that Ladies who go there, would do wisest, If they would first consulted one Mr. Campbell a Dumb man, who sees into Peoples Fortunes—for otherwise there's a danger of being lost, . . . Well, said she, If I can't go to the Masquerade, I will go to him this Minute, and you must and shall go with me—I told her he must be a Conjuror—but the fear of the Conjuror was not as great as her longing for a Husband—We went—The first thing he did, after we were seated, he presently shew'd us he could do wonders, he welcom'd us by our Names; a Thing! an amazing Thing! which he practices to all Strangers whatsoever. Then she proposed the Question, What would be her Lot, if she went to the next Masquerade? He told her, she would certainly be the Lady of a certain Baronet, that she lov'd. . . . (p. "232" [238])

So indeed it proved.

Less than two months after these preparations there appeared, in the issue for June 13–20, 1719, Campbell's first avowed advertisement:

> Mr. Campbell, the Dumb Gentleman, famous for many Years for writing Persons Names on Sight of them, and foretelling them the past Affairs of their Life, and their future Fortune, is for the Conveniency of Persons of Distinction, (who have always done him the Honour to consult him,) is removed to the back-side of the Ship-Tavern in Spring-Gardens, where he will devote his Time entirely to Satisfaction of such Persons as shall please to consult him. N. B. The Life of the said Mr. Campbell, containing an Account of his Birth and Family, and of what he hath done in his Way to the Satisfaction of Persons of all Ranks and distinction; with a philosophical dissertation on the Gift of a second Sightedness is now in the Press, and will speedily be published. (p. 288)

This advertisement was replaced in the number for August 29–September 5, 1719, by a similar one promising the book, "written by a Scotch Gentleman," in October.[6] This altered advertisement was allowed to run into October; then the issue for October 10–17 announced a further delay to permit publication by subscription. The detailed list of chapters, which corresponds closely with that of the published book, shows that the book was by this time pretty well planned and probably written, except that from the final chapter as originally planned there was later omitted a narrative, "How being address'd to by the French Prophets for Help, he baffled them, and proved them wicked and vile Impostors" (p. 390). This long advertisement was during the nine ensuing weeks sometimes carried, sometimes omitted, until the issue for December 12–

19 announced a further delay and a change of address for the conjuror.[7] Meantime Campbell had not been altogether neglected in the paper. In the number for December 5–12, 1719, a "correspondent" who signed herself Eusebia and suspiciously dated her letter "Exeter-Court in the Strand, Tuesday 2d December 1719," where Bond was evidently then living with Campbell, adverts to the previous numbers discussing masquerades and Campbell, evidently in order to publicize his recent removal.[8]

Finally on April 30, 1720, there appeared *The History of the Life and Adventures of Mr. Duncan Campbell, a Gentleman, who, tho' Deaf and Dumb, writes down any Stranger's Name at first Sight; with their future Contingencies of Fortune. Now Living in Exeter Court over-against the Savoy in the Strand*. The book was designed to appeal by its narratives to a wide, general public; by its learned disquisitions to establish the authority and legitimacy of Campbell's occult powers; and thus to advertise the seer so that new customers would flock to his publicized doors. Discussions of sign language, guardian angels, second sight, and natural magic are delayed so that interest of the reader can be aroused in the story of Duncan Campbell, and these discussions are carefully interspersed or even shunted off into an appendix so that they will not detract from the more personal and dramatic materials.

The biography gives a romantic picture of the ancestry, birth, childhood, and practice of the seer, and paints an attractive portrait of his personality. According to the story, the seer was the grandson of a Campbell who fled from Civil War in Scotland to the Shetland Islands. There the father, Archibald Campbell, marooned one night on the famous eerie Ness of Brassah, was rescued by a Dutch boat which he loaded with seabirds and eggs for a Dutch market. On their return trip, however, they were blown away from Holland around to the North Cape. There Campbell wooed and married a Lapland lady, who died soon after their son, Duncan, was born. After the father's return to Scotland and his remarriage, Duncan, a deaf mute, was taught "finger talk," or sign language. After both father and step-mother died, he was sent by an uncle to London, at the age of twelve, and here the boy drifted into the profession of fortune-telling. After a period of success, he lived for a while the life of a man about town, gradually giving up his profession as beneath the dignity of a gentleman. He sought a commission in the army, went to Holland to be ready for his post, and became separated from his friends. Eventually he managed to return to England. There he resumed his practice as fortune-teller, married a well-to-do widow, and now continues to amaze London by his display of supernatural powers. Interwoven stories demonstrate these marvelous gifts. Though a professional, Campbell is pictured as extremely sensitive and conscientious. He dispenses more moral advice than get-rich-quick instructions. He refuses to accept fees to exert powers which he cannot or will not exercise. His door is always open to the unfortunate consultant who has no fee.

Sold to regular customers for five shillings, the biography bid fair for an immediate success. On Wednesday, May 4, 1720, the *Daily Post* announced, "Last Monday, Mr. Campbell, the Deaf and Dumb Gentleman (introduced by Colonel Carr) Kiss'd the King's Hand, and presented to his Majesty *The History of his Life and Adventures*, which was by his Majesty most graciously receiv'd." That same week, on May 9, *The Daily Post* printed a commendatory letter purportedly from "The Oxford Club" signed by an evidently fictitious W. Langley as Secretary. A few days later, on May 12, the *London Post* announced further that Campbell had been introduced by Lord Stanhope to the Prince and Princess and had presented to them his book, "which their Royal Highnesses very favourably receiv'd."[9]

On June 18, to boost sales of the biography, William Bond, with a few of Campbell's other admirers, published *Mr. Campbell's Packet, for the Entertainment of Gentlemen and Ladies*, a brief pamphlet of praise for him and for each other.[10] It consisted mainly of verses by some of the literary group which evidently met frequently at Campbell's house: "H. Stanhope," or William Bond, whose "Parallel" was the only considerable piece in verse; Martha Fowke (later Mrs. Sansom, collaborator the same year with Bond in *The Epistles of Clio and Strephon*);G[eorge] S[ewell], who had evidently helped Bond occasionally with his continuation of *The Spectator*; and J[ohn] Philips, a Curll man who had published some dramatic pieces about 1717. The pamphlet was eked out by the addition of the ghost story of Dorothy Dingley, a story which, as has been seen above, used to be attributed to Defoe.

So popular did the fortune-teller's story promise to become that even before the first edition was exhausted, the sanguine publisher, Edmund Curll, ordered a second. A page for page reprint of the first, uncorrected edition, it was duly advertised as "The Second Edition corrected."[11] In this second edition there were few alterations of any consequence. Campbell had evidently already protested against the Price engraving of his portrait by Hill, for Price had made him appear portly; and this engraving had already been replaced by a slimmer version, by Van der Gucht, though the unflattering engraving was later economically used in *The Secret Memoirs* when the dead seer could no longer protest. The Epistle Dedicatory was now dated April 7, 1720. But the most important change was that *Mr. Campbell's Packet* was incorporated as part of the volume, though it was not reprinted for the book, noticed in the title page, or anticipated in the catch-word on [A4] verso. In the newspapers it was, however, advertised as part of the new edition; Curll had evidently ordered an adequate supply of the *Packet* intending to add it to his second edition of the biography.

These are the only two English editions of *Duncan Campbell* to appear in the eighteenth century. "Editions" subsequent to these are merely reissues of the unsold sheets of the first and second editions. On June 20, 1728, reissued sheets of both of the 1720 editions appeared with a new title: *The Supernatural Philosopher, or the Mysteries of Magick, in all its Branches, clearly Unfolded.* Here for the first time the author was named: William Bond, Esq., of Bury St. Edmunds, Suffolk. One other feature of the 1728 issue is that in at least one state it carried the recommendation of Sir Richard Steele: "*I must confess, I think this remarkable Treatise, is a Work of immense Erudition; full of curious Disquisitions into speculative Philosophy, comprehending a large Fund of Philosophical Learning, and furnished with some Remarks that have escaped the Pens of former Authors, who have wrote in any Faculty whatsoever.*"[12] After Curll disposed of the still unsold sheets, evidently no attempt was made to keep them distinct. Copies of the 1739 "edition," "Sold by the Men who distribute the *Treatise of Husbandry*, and the *Voyages* and *Travels, &c.*" and of the 1748 "edition," "Printed for, and sold by James Fleming, Bookseller in Newcastle upon Tyne; also by the other Booksellers in Town and Country," seem to be made up indiscriminately of sheets from the first and second editions.[13]

Back in 1720, however, Curll had no idea that he had ordered a supply adequate to last beyond mid-century. He doubtless looked forward to publishing the sequel promised at the end of *Duncan Campbell*: "The most diverting of all [the additional adventures], are to be found best to the life in original letters that passed between Mr. Campbell and his correspondents, some select ones of which will be shortly published in a little pocket volume, for the further entertainment of such readers as shall relish this treatise."[14] The promised volume dragged. It was announced in the *British Journal* on December 15, 1722; but not until March 19, 1724, did *A Spy upon the Conjuror* appear. It was written by Mrs. Eliza Haywood, who in her dedication (to Lord Rutland) signed herself "Justicia," but who is designated in some editions as the "reviser."[15] Campbell, who obviously furnished much or most of the material, decided to publish and sell the book himself. It was advertised as sold by Campbell at the Green Hatch in Buckingham Street or at Burton's Coffee House. *The Spy upon the Conjuror* avoids such serious discussions as characterize *Duncan Campbell* and concentrates instead upon the more scandalous, or at least the more romantic aspects of the fortune-teller's career. It provides a considerable series of letters from grateful clients and "many diverting, as well as surprizing Occurrences; which, if they cannot convince your *Judgment*, will certainly entertain your *Fancy*."[16] Some of the incidents from Campbell's personal life reveal an aspect of his personality not fully exploited, but rather concealed in *Duncan Campbell*—especially the scrapes in which he became involved over debts and duels. One of Campbell's friends, "Don Carlos," is allowed to lecture the seer: *"to my certain Knowledge, you have been arrested above twenty Times within these two Years, have now two Suits in* Chancery, *and two or three Judgments against You?"* (pp. 175–176).

By "Justicia," also, was the next venture, which Mrs. Haywood addressed to the same nobleman: *The Dumb Projector: being a Surprizing Account of a Trip to Holland made by Mr. Duncan Campbell, with the Manner of his Reception and Behaviour there. As also the various and diverting Occurrences that happened on his Departure* (1725). The seer may not have entirely approved of this narrative, for there he is made to visit a bawdy house in the company of some prankster friends. But he evidently furnished the basic story himself, and he used it himself in his *Secret Memoirs*, omitting the scene in the bawdy house.

The following year, 1726, Campbell published *The Friendly Daemon, or the Generous Apparition*, ostensibly an exchange of letters between Campbell and his "Friend, Physician, and Philosopher," wherein is narrated the seer's recovery from epileptic fits through means of the loadstone and the powder of sympathy. The formula, it appears, was revealed to Campbell by his good genius, with the admonition that he must keep secret the prescription:

> ... the latter end of the Year —25, ... as I was slumbering one Morning in my Bed, ... my good *Genius*, or Guardian Angel, Cloth'd in a white Surplice like a singing Boy, appear'd before me, holding a Scrowle or Label in his right Hand, whereon the following Words were wrote in large Capitals.
>
> *READ, BELIEVE AND PRACTISE, THE LOADSTONE SHALL BE YOUR CURE, WITH AN ADDITION OF THE POWDER HERE PRESCRIB'D YOU; BUT KEEP THE LAST AS A SECRET, FOR WITH THAT AND THE MAGNET YOU SHALL RELIEVE NUMBERS IN DISTRESS, AND LIVE TO DO GREATER WONDERS THAN YOU HAVE HITHERTO PERFORM'D; THEREFORE BE OF GOOD CHEAR, FOR YOU HAVE A FRIEND UNKNOWN, WHO, IN THE TIME OF TROUBLE, WILL NEVER FAIL YOU.*[17]

This "wonderful Preservative," Campbell assures his readers, ". . . has not only prov'd so great a friend to my self, but has reliev'd others in the like distress, and, as I have found by three or four late Experiments, is as effectual in suppressing Vapours, and removing, or preventing Hysterick Fits in Women, as it is in Epilepsies and Convulsions in our own Sex, either Men or Children" (pp. 11–12). The final leaf of the pamphlet was reserved for a Postscript which appeared in only the first edition:

> The Powder, communicated to Doctor *Campbel* by his *Genius*, together, with the Use of the Loadstone, having wrought many wonderful Cures upon other Patients as well as himself; this Postscript is to acquaint the Publick, that any Person labouring under one or more of the following Calamities, *viz.* Hypochondrical, Hysterical, Epileptical, Convulsive, or any other sort of Fits that either Sex can be subject to, may be reliev'd, after the same manner as aforemention'd; at Doctor *Campbel's* House in *Buckingham-Court*, over against *Old Man's* Coffee-House, at *Chairing-Cross*, where they may be readily furnish'd with his *Pulvis Miraculosis*, and the finest sort of *AEgyptian* Loadstones, ready arm'd and fitted for the purpose, which if apply'd and continu'd according to Directions never fail of Success." (p. 39)

Although no scrap of evidence has been adduced to substantiate assigning this brazen piece of advertising to Daniel Defoe, it is still saddled upon him. As has already been seen and as will be more fully demonstrated later, Defoe was from 1720 to 1726 engaged in a continuing warfare against such quacks as Campbell, who made a profession of preying upon popular trust in fortune-tellers. Attributing it to Defoe would entail the assumption that his search to demonstrate an unseen world was an insincere pose or a half-hearted gesture, or at most that he would callously sell his pen to dupe the ignorant on matters of spiritual concern. Defoe may not have always exhibited scrupulous integrity in financial concerns; but however scholars interpret his behaviour in business or politics, one must surely present strong evidence to justify fathering upon him such shameless charlatanry. The pamphlet purports to be an exchange of letters between Campbell and a correspondent (perhaps fictitious), and there is no reason to reject Campbell's authorship. It was in 1732 again claimed by the seer, for he had ordered it reprinted with his *Secret Memoirs*.

After the fortune-teller died, there appeared, two years later, the sixth and final book in the Campbell series: *Secret Memoirs of the late Mr. Duncan Campbel, the Famous Deaf and Dumb Gentleman, written by Himself.* A sort of apologia pro vita sua, "to give some Reasons in Defence of my Art after My Death," it was published by subscription, evidently by his widow, and supported by a number of influential Campbells: the Duke of Argyll, Sir James Campbell, Daniel Campbell, Esq., John Campbell, Esq., and Dr. Campbell.[18] In this endeavor Campbell claimed to have had no collaborator: ". . . I resolve to let no Person in the World peruse this

Manuscript, till I am beyond the Reach of Envy or of Malice" (p. 33). For his autobiography Campbell selected episodes from his own practice to illustrate his powers in such areas as white witchcraft, omens, predestination, the powder of sympathy, apparitions, genii, second sight, natural magic, and the loadstone. He then ended the book with a series of letters from correspondents; and a second writer provided a brief appendix to vindicate the seer from the charge of shamming deaf and dumb. To a large extent the *Secret Memoirs* was also an attempt to secure for the widow and the two children a livelihood; for with her and his successor, Campbell explained, he has left not only the memoirs, but a goodly supply of talismans, amulets, and charms, into the virtues of which he has so thoroughly instructed his successor that these will work with full potency even after his own demise.

To complete the story of the Campbell pieces and illustrate the lengths to which some bibliographers have gone in making attributions to Defoe, one should note that occasionally he has been credited with *Times Telescope* (1734), a universal and perpetual almanac written by a Duncan Campbell of Holborn and published after both the seer and Defoe were dead. Other late ephemerides have also been occasionally fathered upon Defoe.

Although biographers have done so, one should not rely for authentic information about Duncan Campbell upon the biography, the subsequent narratives published with the cooperation and approval of the seer, or the posthumous *Secret Memoirs*. All these narratives recommend and in effect advertise one another. *Duncan Campbell* advertises what was later published as *The Spy upon the Conjuror*, which in turn commends *Duncan Campbell* and suggests, "if you have not yet read that Book, that you will immediately send for it" (p. 61). *Mr. Campbell's Packet* praises the picture of the seer as presented in the biography. The *Secret Memoirs* uses some of the material from *The Dumb Projector*, reprints *The Friendly Daemon*, and approves *The Spy upon the Conjuror* and *Duncan Campbell* (pp. 21, 212), which Campbell evidently lent to friends who could not easily procure copies. The seer himself evidently furnished written accounts on which all the narratives were based, undertook to publish some of them by subscription, and wrote two of them without assistance, so that one must assume that he at least supervised the production of all six. If Bond had a collaborator in *Duncan Campbell* it was not Defoe, but Duncan Campbell himself.

To authenticate the details of Duncan Campbell's life and career as a fortune-teller as these are portrayed in *Duncan Campbell* and the later works would be a fascinating undertaking for the history of precognition—or quackery. The incidents selected by Campbell and Bond involved largely actors who were dead when the biography was published, or the accounts are so veiled that no checking is possible. There are few incidents in which the actors can be identified; and it would have been odd indeed if from his long career as a professional fortune-teller Campbell could not remember a few consultations in which his predictions had been verified, just as he was able to tell the well-known Mary Wortley Montagu and her friend Maria Skerrett their names.[19]

Some of the incidents in his private life are doubtless authentic. His trip to Holland is verified by the fact that on August 25, 1703, he actually received a pass to visit Holland on the recommendation of Arthur Forbes, probably a brother or half-brother of Lord Forbes, as the biography asserts (*DC*, p. 168).[20] One is inclined to dismiss the possibility of a deaf and dumb officer, but there was certainly room in the Highland regiment of Lord Lorne for another Campbell. In 1694 the Argyllshire Highland Regiment of John Campbell Lord Lorne had included six Campbell captains, including one Duncan Campbell; three Campbell lieutenants; four Campbell ensigns, including another Duncan; and a Campbell as quartermaster. There may have been some foundation for the incident which Campbell relates (*Memoirs*, pp. 34–36) concerning charges brought against him before Justice Botelar as a gipsy and fortune-teller in retaliation for a duel and a subsequent challenge; for according to the *Post-Boy* of March 24–27, 1711, Campbell was "arrested on suspicion of high treason, but was soon discharged."[21]

But almost certainly fictitious are the accounts of Duncan's romantic parentage and birth. These were surely concocted by Campbell and perhaps William Bond to add the highest possible degree of authenticity and credibility to the seer's claims of occult powers. To this end, probably, they arranged that the seer's father should be born in the Shetland Islands, which had been made famous as the home of second sight by John Aubrey in his *Miscellanies* (1696), by Martin Martin in his *Description of the Western Islands of Scotland* (1703), and by John Beaumont, using Martin, in his *Historical Treatise of Spirits* (1705). The account of the Shetlands, which the narrator states that he "received from others," so that he leaves his readers "to their own judgments, whether it ought to be deemed real or fabulous," seems to be taken from Martin.[22]

Demonstrably derivative is much of the Lapland material in the book, and by inference, Campbell's Lapland mother, for the material here is incorporated in the form of several letters purportedly written before the book was published upon which these letters were based. Much of the material in the letters was patently cribbed from Johannes Scheffer's *History of Lapland, containing a Geographical Description, and a Natural History of that Country, with an Account of the Inhabitants, their Original, Religion, Customs, Habits, Marriage, Conjurations, Employments, &c.,* of which an enlarged English edition had been published in 1704 and from which John Beaumont had drawn heavily the following year for his *Treatise of Spirits.* The Lapland material, however, was taken direct from Scheffer. The phraseology is so close in a number of passages that coincidence would seem impossible and the father's letters consequently spurious.[23] The only parts of the Lapland legend which are really original rather than brief abstracts or paraphrases of Scheffer are the wooing of the Lapland lady, a counterpart of Othello's winning of Desdemona, and the manner of Campbell's reaching Lapland. Here one must admire the author's ingenuity and nerve. It seems utterly incredible that the Dutch, who had made the Shetlands their annual fishery for decades, should have been totally ignorant of the seabirds and eggs there, but Bond chose to make these fishermen the intermediary between the Shetlands and Lapland. He covered in one step what a cautious writer would have taken in two: by means of a heavy gale he bypassed Holland altogether and blew the ship past Amsterdam and Zealand beyond the coast of Finland (which Scheffer actually gave a coast on the North Sea) and around to the North Cape!

The next episode in the legend of Duncan Campbell was the account of his learning, though deaf and dumb, to read and to converse with others. This was evidently his first miracle, "that there is now living a deaf and dumb man, and born so, who could, by dint of his own genius teach all others deaf and dumb to read, write, and converse with the talking and hearing part of mankind" (p. 4). One should perhaps remind himself of the popular interest even yet attached to the achievement of Miss Helen Keller. About 1684, when Duncan was four years old, a graduate of the University of Glasgow remembered having heard John Wallis discourse at Oxford concerning teaching a deaf mute. He sent for the "book," and when it arrived, taught Duncan by Wallis's method. This method Bond then reprinted from Dr. Wallis's letter to Mr. Beverley. The trouble with this story is that Dr. Wallis's "Letter to Mr. Thomas Beverly, concerning his Method for Instructing Persons Deaf and Dumb," dated September 30, 1698, was published fourteen years too late and not as a book but as part of the *Philosophical Transactions,* Number CCXLV, for October 1698. It was later incorporated, in a Latin translation, in the third volume of his *Opera Mathematica* (1699). Previously Wallis seems to have published only a brief theoretical account of his theory and experiment, then only begun, in a letter to Robert Boyle dated Oxford, March 14, 1662, but evidently first published July 18, 1670, in the *Philosophical Transactions*, Number LXI. This letter does not even discuss finger talk. But though the story of Duncan's learning by Dr. Wallis's method was evidently fictitious, it was an interesting one, and Dr. Wallis's letter filled most of Chapter III. Also it probably attracted to Campbell deaf mutes who wished instruction.

The circumstances of Duncan's departure for London are likewise suspect. When his parents have been obliterated, Duncan has only one relative left, an unidentified "Mr. Campbell." His spuriousness seems demonstrated by his being designated both as "a distant relation" and a cousin on one page (p. 97) and as cousin and uncle on the next. Relationships may have been involved in a Highland clan, but an uncle was certainly not a "distant relation." Then the narrator arranges for the Duke of Argyll to set out for his seat in Scotland only a few days before Duncan arrives in London, so that the boy can be left to make his own way and the Campbells excused from their failure to assist him. Just when Campbell came to London and began to practice there is not at all clear. According to the narrator of *Duncan Campbell*, the seer seems to be a fairly well established fortune-teller in 1698 (p. 100), though he may have begun from the time of his arrival in London, allegedly in 1694. In his own *Secret Memoirs* Campbell seems to refer to thirty-eight years of practice (p. 2), which would push back the beginning of his career as fortune-teller to 1692. But even in 1700 he seems to have been relatively obscure. None of the extant periodicals for that year seems to have named him,[24] nor was Samuel Pepys then evidently aware of his existence, though Pepys was fascinated by the subject of second sight. Nor does Campbell seem to be noticed, about this time, in Ned Ward's *London Spy* (1698–1700) or in Tom Brown's *Amusements, Serious and Comical* (1700).

But however interesting the life and publicity schemes of Duncan Campbell may have been, and however interesting the demonstration that Campbell had a shaping hand in the whole series and that the biography was deliberately altered to secure romance and guarantee the authenticity of the supernatural gifts, far more important is the question of the part played in the Campbell legend by Daniel Defoe.

Concerning William Bond's authorship of *Duncan Campbell* there exists ample external evidence. As has been seen, the 1728 issue carried his name as author and clearly identified him. Before that time Curll had evidently humored the seer by preserving the fiction that an elderly Scot closely associated with the Campbells had written most of the biography, but the seer had then seen fit to undertake the publication of his own books. After 1728, then, Curll even permitted Bond to advertise his authorship of *Duncan Campbell* in his other books, like *Clio and Strephon* (1732), by Bond and Mrs. Martha Fowke Sansom, which carries a footnote referring to *The Supernatural Philosopher* as by W. Bond, of Bury St. Edmonds (pp. 14–15). In the German translation of *Duncan Campbell* (1742), again, Bond was acknowledged as author.

Concerning Defoe's alleged authorship of, or hand in *Duncan Campbell*, on the other hand, no external or internal evidence has been produced, and a lack of agreement exists about exactly what part or parts he is supposed to have contributed. Some scholars, dodging the problem entirely, merely assure us that we know that Defoe wrote *Duncan Campbell* and completely ignore the evidence for William Bond.[25] The earlier attitude towards an alleged collaboration assumed that Defoe revised Bond's work. In 1923 Paul Dottin, in his "Daniel Defoe et les Sciences Occultes," maintained that "en 1719, Campbell, se voyant délaissé, jugea nécessaire de se rappeler au souvenir des ses concitoyens au moyen d'une publicité bien comprise. . . . Il trouva facilement un éditeur, qui groupa autour de lui quelques écrivains en vogue, dont William Bond, Brown, Mrs. Haywood et De Foe: tous collaborèrent à l'autobiographie de Campbell. La part de De Foe semble assez importante: il fournit de longues dissertations, compilées d'un peu partout, sur la magie et le Monde Invisible, et les introduisit de force dans le carde de l'ouvrage."[26] The next year in *Daniel De Foe et ses Romans*, Dottin was more specific about the collaboration: ". . . ce livre, composé en grande partie par Bond sous la direction de Campbell, avait été soumis à De Foe, qui avait remanié certains passages pour les rendre plus dramatiques, et ajouté des chapitres traitant de la magie et de l'astrologie en général, résumés d'une compilation habile des oeuvres de Glanvil et de Beaumont."[27]

A more recent suggestion, of H. C. Hutchins and John Robert Moore, reversed this theory and made Bond the reviser: "It seems clear," Hutchins wrote, "that Defoe wrote the History; but his work was probably revised by Bond."[28] Moore's view is not entirely clear. In one passage he mentions Defoe's "original version [written] (perhaps as early as 1717)" or "virtually completed by March 1717." But after suggesting that the work was revised by Bond or Mrs. Haywood, he added, "Possibly Bond had nothing to do with this last compilation [*The Supernatural Philosopher*] except as the author of one or more of the poems in *Mr. Campbell's Pacquet*."[29] Mr. Moore forgets that there was nothing new in the 1728 "compilation" except the title page and (in some states) Steele's brief commendation. Now if Defoe's work was revised by Bond or Mrs. Haywood and Bond is eliminated, Moore would seem to suggest Mrs. Haywood as reviser, even though her own biographer suggested Bond: "Some passages, perhaps by a sentiment too exalted or by a description in romantic style suggest the hand of another writer, possibly Mrs. Haywood, but more probably William Bond, in whose name the reprint of 1728 was issued."[30] But all this discussion of two versions is pointless until someone demonstrates that two "versions" ever existed.

Other types of evidence add impressive confirmation to the conviction that Defoe did not write *Duncan Campbell* and that William Bond did. All these proponents of Defoe's authorship credit him with the occult discussions in *Duncan Campbell*. This theory would seem to make embarrassing for Bond Sir Richard Steele's praise for the learning displayed in these disquisitions by the advertised author—Bond. If Defoe wrote them, Steele was evidently unaware of the fact, and Bond was too shameless to point out to Sir Richard the inappropriateness of his praise or fail, by printing Steele's commendation, to take credit for Defoe's work. Moreover these supernatural disquisitions exhibit marked differences from the supernatural ideas expressed in Defoe's *Journal of the Plague Year* (1720) and in his recognized occult works.

One of the main purposes in *Duncan Campbell* was to provide a philosophical and religious explanation of the seer's gifts and practices which would be acceptable to lawyers, philosophers, moralists, divines, and far more important, to the laity from among whom came most of his consultants. In *Duncan Campbell* and the *Secret Memoirs* the seer insisted upon his absolute foresight only for the incidents of death and marriage. These events doubtless loomed large upon the imaginations of his consultants and were the particular aspects of futurity for which the tradition of second sight, which had somehow escaped specific condemnation under British law and church doctrine, had evolved a formula or interpretation. But since church doctrine in general condemned the belief that any but God had knowledge of futurity, the seer claimed, at least for other events, not a knowledge of absolute futurity but of future contingencies. Thus the Introduction to *Duncan Campbell* refers to the seer's predicting "determined truths of future contingencies" (p. 5); and the Appendix, to this "view of contingencies and future events" (p. 234). In his *Secret Memoirs* Campbell was himself quite explicit: "THERE are two Things to which, we may depend on, we are pre-ordained before we ever see Light, which is the Time and Manner of our Death, and Marriage, if fated ever to enter into that State: . . . As to other Incidents, they are greatly

153

left to our own Choice; and nothing can be more absurd, than for People, after having drawn on themselves, by their own Imprudence, some very great Misfortune, cry, *'Twas their Fate, and they could not withstand it"* (p. 77).

Such a view of man's knowledge of futurity is irreconcilable with that of Daniel Defoe. In the *Supplement to the Advice from the Scandal Club* for October 1704, Defoe attacked judicial astrology:

> That there is an Exact Calculation of Nativities, the Society utterly deny; and think they may very modestly Challenge, all our Judicious Astrologers, from the Time or Government of Planets, at the Birth of any Person, to tell when, or in what manner, or what place, that Person shall Dye.
>
> . . . .
>
> That the Planets may have Influence upon Humane Bodies; we will not deny, . . . But that their Times are fixt, or Fate determin'd, from the Influences of those Stars, or pointed out by them, is an Absurdity too gross to be defended. (p. 24)

Writing in his "Vision of the Angelick World," in the very year in which *Duncan Campbell* appeared, Defoe utterly rejected any systematic, professional knowledge of futurity: ". . . this would be breaking into the limits which the wisdom and goodness of God has put to our present state, I mean as to futurity, our ignorance in which is the greatest felicity in human life; and without which necessary blindness man could not support life, for nature is no way able to support a view into futurity; I mean, not into that part of futurity which concerns us in our state of life in this world." Commenting upon a gipsy fortune-teller, Crusoe noted, "The woman was a little honester than her profession intimated, and freely confessed it was all a cheat, and that they know nothing of fortunes . . ." (pp. 275, 276). But Defoe was even more explicit and detailed elsewhere. In his *Journal of the Plague Year*, which appeared the same year as *Duncan Campbell* and "A Vision of the Angelick World," Defoe's persona H. F. is quite indignant concerning the tribe of fortune-tellers, whom he lambasts at considerable length:

> These Terrors and Apprehensions of the People, led them into a Thousand weak, foolish, and wicked Things, which, they wanted not a Sort of People really wicked, to encourage them to; and this was running to Fortune-tellers, Cunning-men, and Astrologers, to know their Fortune, or, as 'tis vulgarly express'd, to have their Fortunes told them, their Nativities calculated, and the like; and this folly, presently made the Town swarm with a wicked Generation of Pretenders to Magick, to the *Black Art, as they call'd it*, and I know not what; Nay, to a Thousand worse Dealings with the Devil, than they were really guilty of. . . .
>
> With what blind, absurd, and ridiculous Stuff, those Oracles of the Devil pleas'd and satisfy'd the People, I really know not; but certain it is,

that innumerable Attendants crouded about their Doors every Day; and if but a grave Fellow in a Velvet Jacket, a Band, and a black Cloak, which was the Habit those Quack Conjurors generally went in, was but seen in the Streets, the People would follow them in Crowds, and ask them Questions, as they went along.

I need not mention, what a horrid Delusion this was, or what it tended to; but there was no Remedy for it, till the Plague it self put an End to it all; and I suppose, clear'd the Town of most of those Calculators themselves. One Mischief was, that if the poor People ask'd these mock Astrologers, whether there would be a Plague, or no? they all agreed in the general to answer, *Yes*, for that kept up their Trade; and had the People not been kept in a Fright about that, the Wizards would presently have been rendred useless, and their Craft had been at an end. . . . (pp. 32–33)

It is with a sense of sardonic justice that H. F. later comments,

One thing I cannot omit here, and indeed I thought it was extra-ordinary, at least, it seemed a remarkable Hand of Divine Justice, *(viz.)* That all the Predictors, Astrologers, Fortune-tellers, and what they call'd cunning-Men, Conjurors, and the like; calculators of Nativities, and dreamers of Dreams, and such People, were gone and vanish'd, not one of them was to be found: I am, verily, perswaded that a great Number of them fell in the heat of the Calamity, having ventured to stay upon the Prospect of getting great Estates; and indeed their Gain was but too great for a time, through the Madness and Folly of the People; but now they were silent, many of them went to their long Home, not able to foretel their own Fate, or to calculate their own Nativities; some have been critical enough to say, that every one of them dy'd; I dare not affirm that; but this I must own, that I never heard of one of them that ever appear'd after the Calamity was over. (p. 217)

The theoretical part of *Duncan Campbell* consists mainly in three discourses explaining Campbell's art as a supernatural triad: "The art of prediction is not attainable any otherwise, than by these three ways; first, it is done by the company of familiar spirits and genii, which are of two sorts; some good and some bad; who tell the gifted person the things of which he informs other people. Secondly, it is performed by the second-sight. . . . Thirdly, it is attained by the diligent study of the lawful part of the art of magic" (pp. 52–53).

The first explanation of Duncan's gift of prophecy, given at considerable length in the account of his childhood, attributes his knowledge of futurity to his good genius. This genius the nine-year-old Duncan describes for the narrator:

He is a little little pretty boy, about as tall as my knee, his face is as white as snow, . . . his hair is like fine silver threads, and shine like the beams of the sun; he wears a loose veil down to his feet, that is as blue as the sky in a clear day, and embroidred with spangles, that look like the brightest stars in the night; he carries a silver bell in one hand, and a book and pencil in the other. . . . . . . the little boy writes down wonderful things in his book, which I write down in mine; . . . then I go home, read over my lesson in my book, and when I have it by heart, I burn the written leaves, according as the little boy bids me, or he would let me have no more." (*DC*, pp. 57–58)

According to Duncan, this good genius "tells me everything that gets me my reputation among the ladies and nobility," coming to him weekly with "several things to predict to me concerning people, that he foreknew would come to me the week following to ask me questions" (p. 55). Much of this picture seems to have been drawn after John Beaumont's description, in his *Treatise of Spirits* (1705), of the good genius in general and his Ariel in particular. According to tradition, Beaumont tells us, the former "was drawn as a Boy, with a Garment of various Colours, sprinkled with Stars. . . ." His own Ariel, a spirit about three feet tall, often "rung a little Bell in my Ear" (pp. 19, 91). It was certainly from Beaumont that Bond and his publisher took the plates, done by Van der Gucht, illustrating good and evil genii.

In her two works on Campbell, Mrs. Haywood added nothing to the story of Duncan's good genius, but in his *Friendly Daemon*, it will be recalled, Campbell himself exploited it to advertise his "patent" medicine. In his *Secret Memoirs* Campbell claimed to have been attended by both a good and an evil genius from the time of his birth. They direct, he thought, all men (p. 6). Though somewhat hesitant on the identification, Campbell was there inclined to equate his good genius with his guardian angel.

The defense and illustration of the good genius is also drawn from John Beaumont's *Treatise of Spirits*. There Beaumont was analyzing by various senses the avenues through which man perceives spiritual forces. In *Duncan Campbell* these materials show that men have good genii. In the ten exempla, all of them taken from Beaumont, only two really illustrate the ministrations of a good genius. One example, that of the poet John Donne, is a phantom of the living; three others are examples of revenants, or ghosts, which Defoe was thoroughly to discredit in his *Essay on the History and Reality of Apparitions*; two are of wizards, without the apparent aid of good genii; and the two remaining hardly illustrate good genii. Doubtless the accumulations of spiritual evidence served to secure credibility in the average eighteenth century reader; but the discussion does not show the sharp perception of the supernatural world which characterizes the occult writings of Defoe.

Concerning the existence of an unseen world and benevolent spirits who sometimes communicate with men, Defoe was, as has been seen above, certainly convinced. But that these spirits operate either at the beck and call of fortune-tellers, or voluntarily provide them with the information which they need in order to stay in business, Defoe rejected as utterly impossible, incredible, and ridiculous. Fantastical would be the assumption that these spirits could be called up, "That the magicians are a most necesary generation of men, that without them the miserable world would be robbed of the assistance of all those beneficent good spirits in the invisible world, which wait to do us good, but cannot apply themselves to exert the good dispositions they are filled with, for want of knowing the condition and circumstances of those distressed creatures which stand in need of their help; and that those magicians being the only men that converse in that invisible world, and hold any correspondence with the spirits that are disposed to help us, they alone can hand that assistance to us, being the only people that can acquaint the good spirits with our condition" (*SM,* p. 395).

Disposing of the possibility that the fortune-teller could invoke his good genius, Defoe considered also the alternative possibility—that the good genius foresees the need and comes voluntarily:

> But here is a second suggestion to help them out, and this is, that they do not go to converse with these good spirits, by a special influence, calling them to their assistance; but the good spirits (thereby showing themselves to be good and beneficent, as has been said) condescend to come volunteer, to help and assist, counsel and direct, in case of the distress of those helpless creatures called men; and that they do this officiously by the assistance of their chosen servants the magicians; who, like the almoners of a great prince, are always laying before their eyes suitable objects for their help and benevolence.
>
> This is a formal story, and might have some weight in it, if it were not that it wanted truth of fact to support it. . . . (pp. 392–393)

But "by what means," Defoe asked, "do those good spirits come to know when the magician has anything to be assisted in, and in what manner do they claim or desire their assistance? Now the difficulty of this question raises a doubt almost unanswerable . . ." (p. 387).

In the explanation of the seer's art, a major emphasis is placed in *Duncan Campbell* upon the gift of second sight—the visualization, often symbolic, of coming events. The gift, the narrator explains, is a necessary aspect of the seer's art: ". . . as we have not pretended to say . . . that he has his genius always at his elbow or his back, to whisper in his ear the names of persons, and such little constant events as these: so . . . we think ourselves bound to give the reader an insight into the particular power and capacity which he has . . . of the second-sight" (p. 133). Those who possess this gift can see, for example, a man's future spouses, in order, at the side of his phantasm, or can determine from the position of a phantom shroud the approximate time of his approaching death. Campbell's alleged Scottish ancestry made this gift especially appropriate.

Instead of a clear explanation of the second sight, however, we are given, with occasional verbal changes, fifteen pages of analysis and anecdotes of the second sight from Martin Martin's *Description of the Western Islands of Scotland*, not direct, though Martin is used elsewhere in *Duncan Campbell*, but by way of John Beaumont's *Treatise of Spirits* (pp. 110–126). Then after a page and a half from Aubrey's *Miscellanies* (1696),[31] which reappears, paraphrased, in the prefatory epistle, the biographer related the gift of second sight and the attendant brownie to the mediation of the guardian angel and attempted to explain by this combination a number of Campbell's successful predictions. In his Appendix, finally, he added a defense of the fortune-teller's art mainly upon the ground, moral and legal, that this method of predicting was forbidden by neither the law nor the Church.

In his *Secret Memoirs* Campbell simplified this faculty: ". . . the Gift of *Second Sight*, as it is vulgarly called, . . . is no other, in Reality, than the Power of discerning incorporeal Beings: How, therefore, should those ministring Spirits, which the Divine Goodness sets over us as Guardians, communicate their Instructions, excite us to good Actions, deter us from bad ones, or give Notice of the extraordinary Events that shall befal us, but by intellectual Remonstrances: . . ." (p. 63).

Early, in *The Consolidator*, Defoe's moon-voyager is patently skeptical of second sight:

> Here, too, I find glasses for the second-sight, as our old women call it. This second-sight has often been pretended to in our regions, and some famous old wives have told us they can see death, the soul, futurity, and the neighbourhood of them, in the countenance. By this wonderful art these good people unfold strange mysteries; as under some irrecoverable disease to foretell death; under hypochondriac melancholy to presage trouble of the mind; in pining youth to predict contagious love; and a hundred other infallibilities, which never fail to be true as soon as ever they come to pass, and are all grounded upon the same infallibility by which a shepherd may always know when any one of his sheep is rotten, viz., when he shakes himself to pieces. (pp. 306–307)

Later, in his prophecies, as has been seen above, Defoe endowed his seer with the gift of second sight to explain his prophetic skill. But he did not in *The Review* undertake any particular explanation or defense of the seer's gift; it seems more of a convention than a conviction. Still later, in *The unFortunate Mistress*, he endowed his heroine Roxana with this same gift, there seriously employed. (See pages 34–35) By the time *Duncan Campbell* was written probably Defoe seriously accepted second sight as a supernatural reality. Had he written the account of second sight in *Duncan Campbell*, he might well have included there original material which he used later in his *System of Magick*, where he included a considerable discussion (pp. 319–328). There Defoe did not pretend to understand second sight, but accepted it as an inexplicable evidence of the communication between visible and invisible worlds: "I meet with many that have examined into this matter of the second-sight, and who have discoursed with the people who are, what shall I call it? I can hardly say, blessed with it; neither do they call it so themselves; and all that I have inquired of about it, seem only to hold up their hands with a kind of astonishment at the thing, but can give no account of it; they wonder at, but do not understand it" (p. 321).

But after giving several examples from his own knowledge, Defoe expressed the conviction that this supernatural endowment could not be a professional stock-in-trade: "I fancy it seems rather, that what business these invisible agents have to do, and what intercourse they carry on with this world, they generally do it themselves, they are not managed by art, or called in to the aid and assistance of the artists. But as they make things visible at pleasure, they want no agents, they do their business their own way; and in a word, they have no magicians among them, none of those they call cunning men, or that consult with the invisible world in behalf of others; it seems they have no occasion of such men, they are not so fanciful, or overrun with vapours, as we are in this part of the world" (p. 328). Especially did Defoe believe that if angelic spirits communicated frequently with any special person, he was morally and spiritually irreproachable, as Campbell certainly was not. Indeed Campbell by his pretension to this gift thoroughly discredited it. As defined in *A New General English Dictionary* (1735), second sight meant "a pretended inspiration or knowledge of things not yet come to pass, as though they really were in action before one's eyes, a privilege that many inhabitants of the western islands of *Scotland* are said to be endowed with; but Mr. *Campbell*, the famous imposter of that nation lately resident in *London*, hath destroyed the whole credit of that pretension."[32]

In his discussion of natural magic, finally, the author of *Duncan Campbell* maintained that "as all magic consists in a spirit, every magician acts by a spirit" (p. 196). Magicians who use these spirits can be classified according to the type with which they deal: some converse with angelic ones; some invoke, openly or tacitly, the Devil and his fiendish spirits; and others, among them Duncan Campbell, employ natural spirits and natural magic. These are "the natural spirits of the elements" (p. 196); and a physician would be using natural magic, we are informed, if he were to administer his medicine with Christian faith! Indeed in *Duncan Campbell* Bond so played upon the senses of the word *natural* that the reader becomes quite confused. The seer who utilizes only natural magic, Bond insists, is innocent of any wrongdoing because he does not employ any diabolical agency and because he purposes and advises only good.

The natural magic which Campbell is supposed to employ Bond only vaguely described. In the Appendix the author suggested that genethliacal divination, or astrology, was "no evil art" (p. 240). On the other hand, in the Epistle Dedicatory, signed by Campbell but perhaps written for him by Bond, the seer disparaged the Cabalists: "These talismans that Paracelsus pretends to owe to the excogitation and invention of honest art seem to me to be of a very diabolical nature, and to owe their rise to being dedicated by the author to the heathern gods" (p. xvi).

Later, as Campbell became less guarded or was forced more and more, because of his epilepsy, to rely upon his nostrums to support his family, natural magic came to be an increasingly important element of his art, and he became, indeed, *Doctor* Campbell. In her *Spy upon the Conjuror* (1724) Mrs. Haywood suggested that Campbell's "perfect Understanding in the Mathematicks" made one expert regard him as "the greatest Artist of his Time" and admitted that "in some Cases he calls Astrology to his Assistance"; he has "a great Number of Books, such as are only fit for those who study it (*Spy*, pp. 24, 126, 24). By 1727 Campbell had become a byword as an astrologer. In his *Second Discourse concerning Miracles*, Thomas Woolston commented concerning Christ's knowledge of the past of the Woman of Samaria: "*Duncan Campbell*, and other *Moorfields* judicial Astrologers, have done greater Feats of Conjuration than *this*, and never were thought to be Omniscient" (p. 54). But the shameless advertisement of the loadstone and powder of sympathy in which Campbell indulged in *The Friendly Daemon* was in the *Secret Memoirs* widened to include various nostrums.

Although the Epistle Dedicatory of *Duncan Campbell* had ridiculed the Cabalists, in his *Secret Memoirs* Campbell recommends the efficacy of "the understanding some Cabalistical Words, Characters, and Figures, made Use of in a proper Time and Place: "The next are these *Talismans*, of which I have already treated. The wearing of a Loadstone may very well come in for a third Place in the Mystic Roll of secret *Recipes* . . ." (p. 82). He advertised the efficacy of certain amulets, sigils, or charms, and "an inferior sort of talisman wherein cabalistic figures were inscribed upon consecrated Parchment" (pp. 94–95), all of which were advertised as prompting good will towards the wearer and some of which held the peculiar power to "excite the Passion of Love in a Person whose Name is thereon written, or engraved" (p. 86). All of these remain in good supply with his wife (p. 97), who could doubtless engrave the name. Concerning the loadstone in particular, earlier recommended in *The Friendly Daemon* by the good genius, Campbell's successor alone understands the true method of "Setting and Arming" it (p. 135). Nor were these the only riches still remaining at Dr. Campbell's shop. From a letter to the seer from a Scottish correspondent, readers learn that just prior to his death Campbell had been supplied with a shipment of coraline from Skye, some of the "*miraculous* Black Bean," twelve vials of Cleft-Rock water, and a box of Eagle Stones, all of which were still available from his wife (pp. 137–141).

Here in the *Secret Memoirs* is Campbell's most patent admission of the compulsion of "natural" spirits: natural magic "is no other than the Knowledge of certain Spells, by which you may attain a kind of Authority over one of the invisible World, and compel a Spirit so rais'd, to reveal whatever you are desirous of knowing: Nor is this to be done by Witchcraft, or making a Contract with the Devil . . ." (pp. 81–82).

The natural magic which Campbell pretended to utilize, Defoe ridiculed in the *Journal of the Plague Year* and in his *System of Magick*. Particularly horrifying in the plague, according to the narrator, was the practice of "wearing Charms, Philters, Exorcisms, Amulets, and I know not what Preparations, to fortify the Body with them against the Plague; as if the Plague was not the Hand of God, but a kind of a Possession of an evil Spirit; and that it was to be kept off with Crossings, Signs of the Zodiac, Papers tied up with so many Knots, and certain Words or Figures written on them, as particularly the word *Abracadabra*, form'd in *Triangle*, or Pyramid . . ." (*JP*, pp. 39–40). Defoe could not bring himself to believe, for example (*SM*, pp. 316–317), that magicians could, as Campbell maintained both in *Duncan Campbell* and in the *Secret Memoirs,* by their natural magic dispel witchcraft. He utterly despised, moreover, the "jugglers, cunning men, gipsyes, and fortune-tellers" (*SM*, p. 372), though he pitied the ignorant people they imposed upon.

Not only is the professional occultism of *Duncan Campbell* and the other Campbell books rejected by Defoe, but the style of *Duncan Campbell* is utterly unlike that of Defoe in his occult works, published in the same decade. Prominent among characteristics of style exhibited there by Defoe are his dramatic dialogue, his use of rather long, highly dramatized episodes, and his occasional employment of playbook style to indicate the speakers. Perhaps the most obvious of these qualities lacking in *Duncan Campbell* is that of highly dramatized episodes. In these Defoe often indicated his speakers in playbook fashion, as he did in *Farther Adventures of Robinson Crusoe* and in *The History of Apparitions*. There are at least three such episodes in each of Defoe's three occult books. Only one occurs in *Duncan Campbell* (pp. 55–57), and here the author used "*My Question*" to introduce his speech, where Defoe habitually employed "*Author*" or "*A.*"

But even more noteworthy in *Duncan Campbell* are qualities of style which do not appear in Defoe's occult works. The most obvious is the long paragraph. Not counting the short page on which each chapter opens, in the first hundred pages of *Duncan Campbell* in the 1840, Oxford edition of Defoe, which reproduces the original paragraphing, twenty-four pages are unbroken by a new paragraph; there are three pairs of unbroken pages; and one example of three such consecutive pages. Later on in the book are two examples of four continuous unbroken pages. In the first hundred pages of *The History of Apparitions*, *The History of the Devil*, and *A System of Magick*, there is not a single unbroken page. Another stylistic peculiarity of *Duncan Campbell* is the catalogue of authorities listed in abbreviated, classical style. Four such catalogues appear there, but not a single one in the occult works of Defoe. Still other characteristics of *Duncan Campbell* which set it apart from the occult works of Defoe are the failure of the author to give supernatural examples from his own experience, as Defoe always did, and the wholesale plagarism, mainly from one source—John Beaumont. When in his *System of Magick* Defoe borrowed four pages from Jeremy Collier's edition of Louis Moréri's *Great Historical, Geographical, Genealogical and Poetical Dictionary*, he indicated by quotation marks that he was not pretending to originality.[33]

With the prose style of William Bond, on the other hand, the style of *Duncan Campbell* presents similarities, especially in the length of paragraphs. In Bond's essays in the *Spectator*, seven pages in the 1753 edition are unbroken pages; and there are three examples of paragraphs two pages in length. In his brief, thirty-seven page *Case Stated, in a Letter to Archibald Hutcheson, Esq.*, four pages are unbroken; and one paragraph runs over two pages. Although Bond seems not to have devoted much attention to the supernatural outside of *Duncan Campbell*, he was always playful, never serious when he did use this material, as in his delightful essay in *The Spectator* for January 3, 1715. Of this playful type is the mock advertisement inserted at the end of *The Spectator* for May 2, 1715: "Just ready for the Press, *Observations* concerning the late Eclipse, wherein the Notions of *Copernicus*, Mr. *Whiston*, Dr. *Haley*, and our own Professors, &c. are refuted, and their Objections against Astrology in General, the Author, and *Ptolemy*, in particular, are fully confounded, and the whole confirmed by most stupendious and never-heard-of Predictions. By *J. P.* Shoemaker, and *Astrological Professor*: Cambridge."[34] The *Plain Dealer* for April 13, 1724, contains a playful complaint from Doctor Faustus the Enchanter and Magician at Lincoln's Inn Fields concerning his imitator and rival at another theater.[35]

Not only does the internal evidence of ideas and style point away from Defoe and suggest that he had nothing to do with the book, but it tends, on the other hand, to confirm Bond's authorship. Additional evidence against Defoe's authorship and for Bond's is provided in the circumstances of publication and in the relationships of author with publisher and with biographee. *Duncan Campbell* was evidently announced as early as March 8, 1717, as by "J. B." and shortly to be published.[36] Just whom Edmund Curll, the publisher, intended to suggest, or conceal by these initials is far from clear, but they certainly would not have suggested Daniel Defoe. One possible identification which might have occurred to an informed reader of the advertisement would be John Beaumont, the foremost authority on the supernatural fields which were to be exploited in *Duncan Campbell*. Beaumont's continuing interest in the supernatural he was to exhibit in 1725 in his *Gleanings of Antiquities*.[37] In *The Weekly Medley*, however, the author was designated merely as a "Scotch Gentleman."

But if the initials were not intended to suggest John Beaumont, they probably were not intended to suggest anyone to the reader, and the fact that they never appeared on the book would seem to bear out this assumption. Never is the Scottish biographer identified, by initials or name. He is created as a "good old" Scot who seems to be conveniently on hand in Scotland in 1683 and again in 1686 and so intimate with the family that he can feel free to enter the house before Duncan's step-mother is awake. About 1694, just about the time the seer arrives in London, our narrator is brought thither, still on such familiar terms with Duncan that he seems always on hand to witness any remarkable exploits. Since the plan evidently called for wholesale thefts from Beaumont, our biographer reminds us on three different occasions that he knows Beaumont personally (pp. 83, 85, 91). Prior to 1728 there was thus evidently an agreement among the subject, author, and publisher to conceal, rather than to reveal, the identity of the biographer. Incidentally it is perhaps this fiction of the young reviser adding to the work of an elderly Scottish biographer which probably suggested that *Duncan Campbell* was the work of collaboration, or that it was revised by a second author. Of course the biography is a work of collaboration, but between biographer and biographee.

In the pattern of advertisement and publication two factors weigh heavily against Defoe's having had a hand in *Duncan Campbell* and for Bond's authorship: relations between the author and the publisher and relations between the author and the biographee. During the time when the biography was being prepared, Defoe, according to William Lee, made the most violent attack ever launched in print against the publisher:

> Hast thou heard, O Mist, thou Writer of strange Things! I say, hast thou ever heard among the Hell of Sodom, crimes of the Sin of CURLICISM? Know then, this is the Sodomy of the Pen; 'tis writing beastly Stories, and then propagating them by Print, and filling the Families, and the Studies of our Youth, with Books which no Christian Government that I have read of, ever permitted. . . .
>
> There is indeed but one Bookseller eminent among us for this Abomination; and from him, the Crime takes the just Denomination of *Curlicism*: The Fellow is a contemptible Wretch a thousand Ways; he is odious in his Person, scandalous in his Fame, he is mark'd by Nature, for he has a bawdy Countenance, and a debauch'd Mein, his Tongue is an Echo of all the beastly Language his Shop is fill'd with, and Filthiness drivels in every Tone of his Voice.[38]

During the very time when he was accusing Curll of literary prostitution, Defoe is supposed to have been guilty of literary prostitution, of penning—or having just finished penning—a glowing biography of a quack expert on the Invisible World for the very same publisher. William Bond, on the other hand, was a Curll man. During 1719 and 1720, for example, he produced for Curll a steady stream of poems and pamphlets. Curll knew him well and identified him under his pen name "H. Stanhope" for readers of the *Curliad*.[39]

Relationships between author and Campbell are even more revealing, for as has been shown, Campbell had a hand in all the books associated with him, certainly in *Duncan Campbell*. Many details of the seer's life in this book could have come only from him; and in his *Secret Memoirs*, one recalls, Campbell sanctioned *Duncan Campbell* as his authorized biography. In the light of Campbell's importance in furnishing the materials of the book and collaborating in writing and publishing it, it is a damaging blow to the theory of Defoe's authorship that Campbell and his authors never mentioned Defoe in any of the six Campbell books and that Defoe never mentioned Campbell in any of his books on the occult. On the other hand, Bond had lived and boarded with the Campbells during much of the time when the biography was being written. As will be seen later, he knew the whole family intimately—and some of Campbell's clients. During this time, also, Campbell, as has been seen, was advertising in Bond's *Weekly Medley*, and Bond was inserting several dramatic eulogies of Campbell even in his leading articles. Moreover, the delay in the publication of the biography is partly explained in Bond's *Weekly Medley* for June 13–20, 1719: "N.B. The Author has been in the Country ever since October, which has prevented its being published, but is now come to Town" (p. 288). This absence fits the known details of the life not of Defoe, but of Bond. His eldest brother, heir to his mother's share of the Jermyn estate, died, childless, in November at Bury St. Edmonds.[40] Bond evidently left London to attend at his bedside and remained at Bury awaiting financial settlements.

There is thus no evidence for Defoe's authorship of *Duncan Campbell* in the book itself or in the circumstances of publication. The only "evidence" so far adduced seems to be the reviews in *The Theatre* and in *Mercurius Politicus*, which Defoe had revived in 1716. In *The Theatre* for May 7 and 10, 1720, the unidentified "Sir John Falstaffe," giving no suggestion that he was familiar with the seer or his biographer, ridiculed the art of fortune-telling, especially the second sight and judicial astrology. Implying that claims for Campbell were preposterous, he decided "to accompany my Reflections over this Author, with reading, at proper Intervals, the Surprizing Adventures of *Robinson Crusoe*, the Travels of *Aaron Hill* Esq; into *Turkey*, the History of the *Empires* in the *Sun* and *Moon Worlds*, Psalmonaazar's History of the Island of *Formosa*, and, that great Promoter of Christian Piety, the *Tale of a Tub*."[41]

In the May issue of *Mercurius Politicus*, giving the impression that he was unfamiliar with the book first-hand, the editor paraphrased the opinion of "Sir John Falstaffe":

> Sir *John Falstaffe*, in his Theatre of *May* 7, is very pleasant upon Mr. *Campbell's Adventures*, he very ingeniously exposes the Follies of that wretched Book, which is sufficient to be taken Notice of here. It is a great Misfortune that there should be so many senseless People in a Nation, as to maintain a number of cheating *Fortune-Tellers*, who live upon the Folly of such deluded Persons. The Author of the *Theatre* will perform a publick Service if he will proceed in endeavoring to discover to the World the Vileness of such scoundrel Books as he names, *viz. Robinson Crusoe, the Travels of* Aaron Hill, *Esq; into* Turkey, Psalmanaagaar's [sic] *History of the Island* of Formosa, and the more scandalous *Tale of a Tub*. These are Works only fit to lead the ignorant into Error, and to waste the Time, and deprave the Taste of such as being more knowing read them only for Diversion. On the 10th the same Writer very wittily Ridicules all vain Prophecies and Predictions, thus pleasantly entertaining, when at the same time he judiciously instructs. . . .

This condemnation of *Duncan Campbell* was not retracted in the following month, though the June issue noticed the publication of *Mr. Campbell's Pacquet*. Two months after the original condemnation and after the appearance of the second edition, however, in the July issue, the original condemnation was reversed:

> The next Book, which I think very well deserves to be recommended to the Publick, is a Book Intituled, *The Life and Surprising Adventures of Mr.* Campbell, the *Deaf and Dumb Gentleman*, the Second Edition whereof is just Published. This Book has had already a very Extraordinary *run*, as the Term is among the Booksellers. This inclined me to look once more into it a little more considerately: For when I gave it an ill word at its first appearance in the World, in the *Mercurius Politicus*, for the Month of *May*, I had only read here and there some Passages very cursorily, and, from not reading farther, misconstrued them to have this evil Tendency, that they would, as they spread themselves Abroad in the Sale, spread likewise a general Contagion of Infections, and pernicious Superstition, among the Minds of those Readers, who were infirm of Judgment, and rank'd in the lower Class of Understanding. And truly I begun to read it regularly, and before I had turn'd over many Pages, I must confess, I resolv'd to do the Publick this Justice, to tax myself, in this my Monthly Account, of having pass'd an over-hasty Judgment in that foregoing Account, which I mention'd just now.
>
> I am farther obliged to acknowledge, by way of small Recompense to that Pleasure, which the Book administer'd to me in the perusal, that beginning it in the Morning, I could not lay it down, till I had read it all through. Enabled by this Means to speak of its more true Character, then I could before, I must take leave still more severely to correct my former Error, by averring, that it is just the reverse of what I then represented it to be. For, instead of infecting People with Superstition, every Part of the Book is artfully formed to root out that pernicious intellectual Canker. Instead of being filled with Falshoods, to cheat and deceive the Unwary, it wholly consists of Facts well attested, and of such, that if they were even not Facts but Fables, would still be very useful, and both instruct and divert the Readers; because every Story is told in an entertaining Way of Discourse, and terminates in an honest and useful Moral. The Additions, I mean the Verses in this new Edition, by several Persons of a distinguish'd Genius in Poetry, more particularly those written by the ingenious Mr. *Stanhope*, are a very good Proof of what I now say; this last Copy of Verses, being almost entirely taken up in this particular Praise of the Book, that it is made purposely to root out many idle Superstitions, and implant salutary Morals in their stead.[42]

Just what inferences concerning the authorship of *Duncan Campbell* could be legitimately drawn from this reversal of opinion by the editors of *Mercurius Politicus* it is difficult to perceive. These reviews, some Defoe scholars would have us believe, constitute a subtle publicity scheme of Defoe to puff his own book. But although in 1718 Defoe was certainly serving as editor and seems to have continued to do so throughout 1719, the issue for January–

February of 1720, which appeared late, was provided with a new subtitle and prefaced by an Introduction wherein a new editor, *"at his very first setting out,"* outlined his new policies. *"This* Monthly Mercury, *it is hop'd,"* he announced, *"is now improv'd, being brought into a more regular Method than it us'd to be before, and containing more Tracts, tho' less Politicks."* Promising a monthly examination of new books, he gave a snide dig at Defoe's practice of quoting in extenso, especially from himself: *"it is not intended to fill up this Monthly Account with entire Pamphlets already printed"* (pp. i, ii, iii).[43]

But the reversal of opinion concerning *Duncan Campbell* is not a deliberately planned publicity scheme of Defoe's successor, but a genuine difference of opinion between him and *his* successor in turn, for there seems to have been a change in editorship not only with the issue for January–February of 1720, but another beginning with the July 1720 issue. In his prefatory remarks to the July number, the editor discussed the consciousness with which he has "taken upon" him the "Stile of Lover of Old *England*" from the title page and outlines his promises to live up to his ideals of style, factuality, and impartiality. "How well I keep up to any of the three Qualifications of an Historian I have mentioned, I must leave to the Reader's Judgment" (pp. 3–4). Perhaps more important is the ambitious plan announced for the book review section: "I design in the Progress of these Papers, to render this Part of the Performance, as agreeable to the World as it is possible for the future. Whatever the *Mercury Gallant* . . . tells us of the New Polite Authors of that Kingdom . . . whatever the like kind is to be found in the *Bibliotheque Choisi* of Mr. *Le Clerc* . . . shall hereafter be presented to my Readers . . ." (pp. 49–50). Promising to cover also "what passes from Time to Time, that is New and Rare in the Royal Society," he begs this month "to be excused, having neither Materials, nor, if I had Materials, Leisure enough for so accurate an Undertaking" (p. 50).[44]

But the natural tendency is to assign anonymous books to those who are well known, not the unknown. Ignored in the published and even the unpublished Bond genealogies, today William Bond exists only as a brief, uninformative biography in *DNB* and as a name in Pope's *Dunciad*:

Three wicked imps of her own Grubstreet Choir
She [Dulness] deck'd like Congreve, Addison, and Prior;
Mears, Warner, Wilkins run: Delusive thought!
Breval, Besaleel, Bond, the Varlets caught.   (II, 115–118)

Lo Bond and Foxton, ev'ry nameless name,
All crowd, who foremost shall be damn'd to Fame?   (III, 151–152)

He also appears in a footnote by Scriblerus: "He likewise affirms (Key, p. 10) *Bond* to be one who writ a Satire on our Poet; but where is such a Satire to be found? where was such a Writer ever heard of?" Finally, he is included, under his favorite alias, in the "Testimonies of Authors" as "one who takes the name of H. *Stanhope*, the maker of certain verses to Duncan Campbell."[45] "I am quite willing to believe that William Bond was a very remarkable man, wrote R. Straus in his biography of Edmund Curll, "particularly if he was also Henry Stanhope."[46] Perhaps a view of his character, friends, life, and writings will make his personality more real and his authorship of *Duncan Campbell* more acceptable.

In his *Secret Memoirs* Campbell himself was quite severe with the character of his biographer:

> Would I have entered into Measures to beguile my Consulters, I have had frequent Opportunities by the Means of Mr. B——d, a Man of good Family, the more the Pity, he should so far degenerate, he pretends to great Learning, but that I am not a Judge of . . . has Pretensions to Honour and good Nature, tho' never Man had less of either, in Reality; for he looks on all Mankind as his Property, deceives the Men for Interest, and abuses the Women for Diversion; I never knew him to do a generous Thing by the one Sex, nor give any of the other a good Word, excepting one [Martha Fowke?], who by the most vile Actions has drawn on her the Contempt of every-body besides. . . . He essayed all his Arts to set me against my Wife, and even while he was at Bed and Board with us, receiving all the Civilities we could treat him with, was still discontented, because he found it more difficult than ordinary to break that perfect Harmony between us: Failing in that, he insinuated himself into my Son's good Graces, and made him guilty of a Behaviour towards me, which required my utmost Indulgence to forgive.
>
> ·
>
> Nor was I less troubled at the Misfortunes to which Mr. *Rogers*, a Baker, was reduced by the Artifices of this general Deceiver, who so far intoxicated him, by telling him, *He was a Wit, and should join with him in writing a Weekly Paper* [*The Weekly Medley*, 1718–1720], that he neglected his Business, spent all his Time and Money among Printers, Publishers, and Paper Merchants, put his Wife into *Bedlam*. . . . Mr. *Hughs*, a Nonjuring Clergyman, and exceeded by few, in good Sense and Learning, could not defend himself from giving into a Project he proposed to him; in which having spent all he had, and reduced himself to great Miseries, in the End broke his Heart.[47]

According to Campbell, Bond was responsible also for the ruin of the Custom House officials, Loggin and Rotherham, as will be seen. "Never was a greater *Crocadile*," he summarized (p. 29).

This unfavorable portrait of Bond is probably explained in part by Bond's unflattering picture of the seer in *Mr. Campbell's Packet*, by his claiming credit in 1728 for the biography and thus spoiling the legend of the elderly Scottish biographer-friend, and probably by Bond's private exposures of the fortune-teller after the two parted company. The portrait is perhaps best corrected by an examination of Bond's relationships with a few of his considerable circle of friends. Among these should be placed those writers for whom Duncan Campbell's house "for some Years, has been the general Rendezvous" (p. 131): Anthony Hammond, Philip Horneck, the John Philips who contributed to *Mr. Campbell's Packet*, Mrs. Centlivre, Mrs. Eliza Haywood, Martha Fowke, "and other celebrated Wits." To this list must be added George Sewell, Richardson Pack, Aaron Hill, and perhaps William Congreve, Richard Savage, and Sir Richard Steele. Especially important to Bond were Martha Fowke, Major Pack, and Aaron Hill.

Martha Fowke Sansom was for a time an admired poetess with a number of distinguished friends and admirers among the literary lights of her day: David Mallet, George Dyer, Aaron Hill, George Sewell, Richard Savage, James Thomson, and William Bond.[48] If one can accept as accurate the footnote inappropriately obtruded into Bond's *Verses Sacred to the Memory of Henrietta late Duchess of Grafton*, to annotate the hyperbolical line "This is a new Foulke, and that a Gaunt," Martha Fowke derived *"her Genealogy, by a Male Line, from Geoffrey Plantaganet, Earl of Anjou, Son of Foulke, King of Jerusalem, who marry'd Melisinda, Daughter of Baldwin, the Brother, and Successor of Godfrey of Bulloigne, who first conquer'd the Holy Land, and was crown'd there."*[49] Martha's brother, though he did not attain such military prowess, eventually became a Lieutenant General. According to her account in *Clio, or a Secret History of the Life and Amours of the late Celebrated Mrs. S—N—M* (1752), Bond was evidently brought to her attention by a relative. At the old Lord Stafford's, Mrs. Sansom related, "There were some Company who had known the World and Courts. Among the rest, a Relation of my *Strephon's*, formerly a Maid to King *James's* Queen; she used to furnish my lonely Hours with Books, I found one wrote by Mr. *Bond* [doubtless a bound presentation copy of his *Spectator*]; some Things in it pleased my Humour, and I wrote in an empty Leaf my Thoughts of it; which he very obligingly answered. Thus began the Letters you have honoured with your Praises" (p. 147).

If one is to believe the picture of this friendship as given in *Epistles of Clio and Strephon*, retitled in 1732 *The Platonic Lovers*, it became perhaps more than Platonic on the part of Strephon, and remained entirely spiritual for Clio. It is difficult, however, in *Clio* not to cast Bond in the role of the lover who precedes "Hillarius"— Aaron Hill: "Never did two Lovers live a more harmonious Life" (p. 155). "Had he been free, I own I should have preferred him openly, as my Heart did in private in all Things. I consulted with him [about marrying Mr. Sansom], and found his poor Heart torn between Love and Friendship, he knew not what to advise" (p. 157). "We parted with a thousand Tears on both Sides. Never was Sorrow more sincere, I devoted myself to it, till my Health languished, and Love took Pity on me. I retired into the Country to mourn, which I did sincerely, and was long ere I could receive any Consolation . . ." (p. 160).

Some friends of Bond viewed otherwise this friendship between him and Martha Fowke. Eliza Haywood, who was possibly jealous of Martha for attracting Richard Savage, suggested that Martha had driven Bond to drink: "one of them [*the* Bards] who had exchang'd *Apollo* for *Bacchus*, by his enervate Lays, and incoherent Metaphors, sufficiently testifies to the judging World, of what pernicious Consequence to a Follower of the Muses" drink is.[50] Martha, she accused of an incestuous relationship with her own father. Now as any reader of *Clio* will soon perceive, relationships in the Fowke family were hardly ideal. Martha adored her father and as a teenager wrote his love letters for him! She bitterly resented Mrs. Haywood's attack upon her father: "the Scorpion *Haywood* will bear her Sting even" to the grave (p. 47). I hear she even violates the Dead," Martha commented. ". . . How much worse is this female Fiend than the Villain that stabbed my Father's busom, who darts the Poison of her Pen in his very Dust . . ." (p. 48).

Another friend, Major Richardson Pack, a miscellaneous writer who rated a biography in Cibber's *Lives of the Poets*, served with both the Captains Fowke, father and brother, in Colonel Nicholas Lepell's Regiment of Foot. In the army Pack gained the friendship and patronage of the head of the Campbells, the Duke of Argyll, and to him he dedicated several volumes. In the army he also served with Colonel Stanhope, to whom in 1718 he dedicated his *Miscellanies in Verse and Prose*. He was probably the Colonel Stanhope who introduced Duncan Campbell to the Prince of Wales so that the seer could present a copy of his biography. In 1720 Pack bought the site and premises of Bury Abbey, and many of his poems written in Suffolk show an intimacy with Bond's distinguished cousins there. Bond's regard for Pack can be seen in his "Muse's Choice, or the Progress of Wit. An Elegiac Epistle to Major Pack; occasioned by his Miscellanies in Verse and Prose."[51]

To the friendship of Aaron Hill, Bond seems to have been deeply indebted. During 1724 and 1725 they wrote *The Plain Dealer* together; and in 1733 Hill was planning help for Bond financially. In a letter of August 31, 1733, Hill explained his project of forming an Academical Theatre and offered to help Bond secure the post of licencee worth £400 yearly. He offered him also half the profits of six nights of his adaptation of Voltaire's *Zara*, which was to be the opening piece. Two years later *Zara* was performed for Bond's benefit in Sir Richard Steele's Great Music Room; but the project materialized too late to help Bond: he died during the short run of the play.[52]

William Bond, as Duncan Campbell admitted, came of a good family.[53] If our genealogical reconstructions are not faulty, the poet's grandfather Sir Thomas Bond, Comptroller of the Household to Queen Henrietta Maria, was created baronet in 1658 and subsequently purchased from his sister Mary's husband, Sir Thomas Crymes, the seat of Peckham, in Surrey. There he built a fine house and gardens visited and admired by John Evelyn and, long after the Bonds had sold them, by Daniel Defoe.[54] Among Sir Thomas's brothers might be mentioned William, with whom the poet is sometimes confused. This William Bond married Mary Gage, daughter of Sir Edward Gage, and died in 1696, leaving two daughters, but evidently no son.[55] Sir Thomas Bond married Marie, or Mary, a Catholic like himself, daughter of Charles Peliott, Baron de la Garde. Lady Bond's sister, Mlle. de la Garde, plays an interesting role in Grammont's *Memoirs*, where she is described as a "little dark-skinned brunette" who is continually meddling in the affairs of her companions and is used to convince Miss Stewart that the Duke of Richmond is dying of love for her. Before and after Mlle. de la Garde's marriage, in 1669, to Gabriel Silvius, she was a dresser to the Queen. After she died, in 1673, Sir Gabriel married Anne Howard, Dryden's niece and, in 1713, an executor of his estate. After Sir Thomas Bond died, in 1685, Lady Bond lived mostly at Hengrave, Suffolk, until her death in 1696.[56] She was buried in Westminster Abbey.[57]

Sir Thomas and Lady Bond had three children: Henry, Mary Charlotte, and Thomas. Henry, a Catholic and Non-Juror who inherited the title in 1685, served James II as Receiver-General for Ireland, but fled to France with him at the Revolution, when Peckham was sacked by a mob. He sold Peckham and lived most of his life in France. In the first year of the reign of William and Mary he was outlawed for treason, but on June 19, 1698, he was pardoned, allowed to return to England, and in 1707 given back his forfeited estates.[58] With the help of his brother, Thomas, however, he managed to live so luxuriously that by 1712 he was in jail for debt, and John Hervey, first Lord of Bristol, was writing to Lady Bond that he and Sir Robert Davers could not persuade his creditors to agree to his release.[59] Mary Charlotte Bond was brought up in the household of Henrietta Duchess of Orleans and in 1675 married

Sir William Gage, of Hengrave, whose sister had married the poet's great-uncle William Bond aforementioned.[60]

Thomas Bond, the poet's father, in 1682 married advantageously Henrietta Maria, second daughter of Thomas Lord Jermyn. When Jermyn's only son died, unmarried, in 1692, the five daughters became coheirs of their father's estate, but this demise did not appreciably help Thomas Bond; for even when his wife died, December 28, 1698, her share of the estate, £9,000 in 1704 at 4 per cent interest, was earmarked for her eldest surviving son, Thomas. Thus William Bond the writer, youngest son of a younger son, was not destined to inherit title or wealth. William Bond's only overt comment about his father was the hope for his sister Judith for "such an indulgent Husband as your Mother enjoy'd,"[61] but there is evidently a portrait of the essayist's father in the opening number of *The Plain Dealer*. Mrs. Aphra Behn evidently used the father, "one of the *Cavaliers* of the last Century," as the model for Ned Blunt of *The Rover* (p. 1). Blunt is a humorous country gentleman appearing to no advantage in both parts of *The Rover, or the Banish'd Cavaliers*.

Bond's maternal relatives allied him with some important Sussex families. His Aunt Mary, the oldest sister, married Robert Davers, who bought out the interests of the other sisters in the Jermyn estate. Aunt Delarivierre married Sir Symon, third Baronet D'Ewes. Aunt Penelope married Gray James Grove. Aunt Merlina married first, Sir Thomas Spring, and second, Sir William Gage, of Hengrave, where the Hide, "a Celebrated Wood near Hengrove-Hall," doubtless provided many refreshing hours for the poet, for as Major Pack's "Bury Toasts" seems to imply, Bond probably grew up among these cousins, and more remote cousins like the Herveys.[62]

Thomas and Henrietta Maria Bond evidently had seven children. Henry Jermyn I, evidently the eldest son, died August 30, 1693, at the age of six.[63] Thomas, the second son, born about 1688, died childless, in November 1718.[64] A third son, Henry Jermyn II, born after the first child so named died in 1693, evidently became heir to his mother's estate of some £9000. He married Jane Godfrey, had children, and died in 1748. Thomas and Henrietta Bond had also three daughters: Henrietta, evidently the eldest, who was buried at Rushbrook June 14, 1708; Charlotte; and Judith, who lived practically a century, dying unmarried in 1793.[65] The youngest son, who is mentioned, though not by name, in the Jermyn wills, must have been William Bond the poet.[66]

Since his mother's estate was destined for an elder brother and since his father seems to have been a spendthrift, the poet depended mainly upon his mother's relatives. From his familiarity with French authors and references to residence in France, it seems possible that he received some of his education there. His name seems to be missing from all English university lists, and as early as June of 1697 he seems to have accompanied, or followed, his father to Holland, bound, doubtless, for France.[67] His great uncle Henry Lord Dover, one of the most important figures in Grammont's *Memoirs*, at his death in 1708 left the youngest Bond son about a twentieth part of his estate when he came of age or married and provided £30 yearly until that time.[68]

Bond's first identifiable work is his revival of Addison and Steele's *Spectator*, which he continued twice a week from Numbers 636 through 696, from January 3 through August 3, 1715. Most, though not all, of these issues are initialed; and if Bond wrote the two signed "W. B." and those initialed "B.," he contributed at least twenty-nine of the sixty-two numbers. He probably wrote also most, if not all, of the unsigned essays. The collected volume he dedicated to Lord Viscount Gage, who had married his Aunt Charlotte. Only one other writer, T. Willis, wrote as many as seven essays; he was probably Thomas Willis, the Catholic priest or emissary who was in 1714 attacked by the young Protestant J. Battersby, in his *Alarm to Protestants*.[69] Avoiding political subjects, Bond devoted many issues to themes of friendship, love, and marriage, but he wrote also on such subjects as gaming, insolvent debtors, and literary criticism, where he especially praised Milton and Pope. Towards the end of its run *The Spectator* got bogged down with issues made up predominantly or entirely of verse and with Bond's three successive issues debating in formal dialogue the compatibility of Love and Reason. Although Addison and Pope were evidently not much impressed with the continuation,[70] Bond's *Spectator* was for a while an enjoyable paper.

Earlier during this same year of 1715 Bond evidently wrote and published in favor of the Pretender. On September 15, 1718, Mr. Berry informed the Pretender, "I have been chosen to lay before your Majesty the design, first started by Richard Minshull of Borton, then by three others, two of whom are supposed to be the brightest men in the nation for learning and ability. One is William Bond, who with his pen pressed your subjects to their duty when you were in Scotland."[71]

Bond's projected translation of Tasso's *Gerusalamma Liberata* was begun with the publication in early May 1718 of the *Third Book of Tasso's Jerusalem*.[72] The new translation received rather excessive praise from Clio:

> So great thy Reputation and so bright,
> That I shall shine, reflecting by thy Light.[73]

But the public obviously did not share this enthusiasm, for Bond published no more except the translation of Book II, which the thrifty Curll probably resurrected in 1732 to eke out *The Platonic Lovers*. Bond's veneration for Tasso he expressed again when he linked Tasso with Virgil in *Verses Sacred to the Memory of the Duchess of Grafton*. His translations of Tasso are especially interesting for the additional evidence they lend to support his authorship of even the learned discussions in *Duncan Campbell*: although most of the long discourse there (pp. 86–91) concerning Tasso is taken direct from John Beaumont (p. 166, ff.), Bond inserted a characterization of Tasso as "prince of the Italian poets, and scarce inferior to the immortal Virgil himself, and who seems to enjoy the intermingled gifts of the most accurate judgment of this Latin poet, and the more fertile and copious invention and fancy of the Greek one, Homer" (p. 86).

Bond's *Weekly Medley, or the Gentlemen's Recreation*, is perhaps best described by its subtitle, as *Containing an Historical Account of all News, Foreign and Domestick, together with Observations on the Writings and Manners of the Age*. It ran from July 26, 1718, to January 16–23, 1720. Bond evidently left details of management to the former baker Rogers and was absent from London during considerable periods.[74] When he was attacked by *Thursday's Journal* as author of *The Medley*, he denied rather evasively, in the issue for October 10–17, 1719, in a letter "To the Author of the *MEDLEY*,"

> YOU know I never but once gave you any leave by Writing to mention my Name, and that was on the Occasion of a Poem I address'd to the late ingenious Mr. *Addison*. From hence, I suppose, a very impudent Libel last Thursday, against the whole Family of the *BONDS*, came out in Print; in which one Mr. *Bond* is called Author of that Paper, and used very ignominiously. As I have from thence good Reason to suspect this pointed in particular at me, I declare the whole to be scandalous, malicious and false; and inasmuch as Sir Henry Bond is named in so *sawcy* a Manner, I, being one of his nearest Relations, do think my self obliged to desire the *Author* of the *Thursday's Journal* . . . [for an apology or satisfaction].
>   WILLIAM BOND   (p. 389)

The attack in *The Thursday's Journal* evidently came as a reply to some of the attacks in which *The Weekly Medley* engaged early upon it and other papers like Mist's *Weekly Journal* and *The Flying Post*. Especially interesting are two successive attacks upon Mist and Defoe, which open in Number LXIII, for Sept. 26–Oct. 3, 1719:

> To the Author of *Mist's Journal*.
> *Good SIR,*
>   I WILL endeavour to grovel after you for once, and write to you in

your Own Familiar Style, that you may understand me: The Printers will put their Names to Papers that call Names; and Ale-house-Boys, that may have a Property with them, will run about the Town from one Tap to another with Falshood, Scandal and Detraction. It is usual with Persons of a Liberal Education to give them Countenance? Or are you the Person that set up a Publick Writer without a Liberal Education? A Tradesman in the Quill that has a Mind to chaffer Words from the Desk, as you did Goods from the Counter? Return and vend Gold Clocks to adorn the lower part of Womens Legs, but don't pretend to meddle with any thing relating to the Head; for thou can'st not do it without corrupting it with lewd Ideas taken from the Stews, such as throwing up Ladies Petticoats, when they walk the Streets, in print, and shewing the Mob more than their Stockings, which is all that thou ever hadst any Business with. Is this writing Morality? But cries the Trading Pen-Man, There is no such thing as living by Morality. And I answer, Science in itself is not a downright Traffick. If you will write, write as you should, not so much to live by it yourself, as to instruct others how they ought to live. And in order to fit yourself for the Correction of others, correct yourself first: You know *Railing* and *Raillery* are Words as distinct in the Idea as Mob and Gentleman; calling Names is not Satyr, but Billingsgate; it is not copying *Horace* and *Juvenal*, but *Homer*'s *Thersites*; I suppose you have heard those Names, tho' you have little Acquaintance with their Writings; railing and slandering are unchristian Talents; always the Signs of a *desperate* Cause, and a *desperate* Conscience. In the Lieu therefore of copying that part of your way of writing, I give you a Word of wholesome Advice, and that is, that you would leave it off, and cease being a *FOE* to Manners and Morality. (p. 373)

Bond had probably visited London in January, when the first details of the Loggin customs-house revelations appeared in *The Weekly Medley*. Father of a deaf and dumb daughter, Robert Loggin had evidently come to the attention of Bond through Duncan Campbell. "In Hatton Garden," Bond wrote in his biography of Campbell, "there now lives a miracle of wit and good nature, I mean the daughter of Mr. Loggin, who, though born deaf and dumb (and she has a brother who has the same impediments), yet writes her mind down upon any subject with such acuteness as would amaze learned men themselves . . ." (pp. 41–42). *The Medley* for January 17–24, 1719, included information concerning the failure of customs house officials to collect duties on paper and tobacco, information which had evidently been presented to the authorities on November 26, 1716, but which had at that time been ignored. Then in the issue for June 20–27, 1719, probably following Bond's arrival in London, the affair was reopened, and after a great deal of continued publicity, Loggin and J. Rotherham published a pamphlet, *The Present Management of the Customs, being a Detection of Grand Frauds* (1720). It was obviously edited and probably largely written by Bond. Accustomed to thinking the worst of Bond, Campbell accused him in his *Secret Memoirs* of using Loggin and Rotherham for sheer publicity and of being responsible for the jailing of Loggin and beggary of Rotherham (pp. 29–31). Bond of course claimed that it was the duty of the men and of *The Medley* to reveal the scandal. Whatever Bond's actual motive, this publicity probably led to the demise of *The Weekly Medley*.[75]

In 1719, during the time when he was working on *The Weekly Medley* (and his biography of Duncan Campbell) Bond published, under his new pseudonym of H. Stanhope, *Buckingham House*. The poem describes the surroundings, Buckingham House itself, the pictures, and praises the virtues of Sheffield. The poem was by some of the author's friends inordinately admired, especially by Martha Fowke, in *The Epistles of Clio and Strephon*, and by Aaron Hill, who praised it in a letter of 1721: "Going out of the *Park*, by *Buckingham-house gate*, while my eyes glided negligently over the form of the fabrick—it was whispered in my ear, by some unseen divinity—with how much ravishing *softness*, mixed with *fire* and *energy*, has the soul-charming C— [Clio] praised the lines, which *Strephon* writ, on this building!" Perhaps taking the hint from the poem, Sheffield gave the poem an encomium used by Curll to advertise it: "His Grace was pleased, when Mr. Bond presented him with this Poem, to pay him this Compliment, *That it would last much longer than the* Building."[76] The year 1720 saw also the publication of at least two hitherto unidentified pamphlets which Bond may have written—*The Creed of an Independent Whig* and *Priestianity, or a View of the Disparity between the Apostles and the Modern Inferior Clergy*.[77]

By far the most ambitious poetical contribution of 1720 was a joint enterprise with Martha Fowke, *The Epistles of Clio and Strephon, being a Collection of Letters that passed between an English Lady, and an English Gentleman in France, who took an Affection to each other, by reading one another's Occasional Compositions both in Prose and Verse*. This collection, or exchange of letters, tells the story of Clio's growing admiration for the poet Strephon and of his struggle between Platonic and passionate love for her. The poem ends with the celebration of their meeting. Employing the conventional apology for the publication of personal correspondence, Strephon explained in the 1732 issue that copies of the letters "so fell into the Hands of a Gentleman, who published them, and inscrib'd them to a Person of such Worth, as I am proud to be able to call my friend, Sir *Richard Steele*, whose Commendation join'd with that of several other most ingenious Persons, had first, I believe, made them so much and so favourably taken notice of."[78] The second edition of 1729 was reissued in 1732 as *The Platonic Lovers* and dedicated by the poet to his sister Judith.

Another poetical performance of the year 1720 was "The Parallel," the major exhibit in *Mr. Campbell's Packet*, which was certainly edited by Bond himself. This poem, which was highly complimented in *Mercurius Politicus*, reads like a burlesque of Campbell rather than a eulogy, and one wonders whether Bond didn't have his tongue in his cheek when he wrote

> Wizards and jesuits differ but in name,
> Both demon's envoys, and their trade the same;
> Weak wills they lead, and vapour'd minds command,
> And play the game into each others' hand:
> Like spiritual jugglers at the cup and ball,
> Rising by foolish maids, that long to fall.

In the poem Bond went out of his way to attack Pope, whom elsewhere he highly praised:

> Pope, first, descended from a monkish race,
> Cheapens the charms of art, and daubs her face;
> From Gabalis his mushroom fictions rise,
> Lop off his sylphs—and his Belinda dies;
> . . . .
> As wide from these are Addisonian themes,
> As angels' thoughts are from distempered dreams. . . .[79]

This attack upon Pope joined with praise of Addison doubtless gained Bond his inglorious immortality of being included in *The Dunciad*. In 1728, taking advantage of the attack on Pope, the thrifty Edmund Curll reprinted this same "Parallel" as the title piece in his little volume entitled *The Progress of Dulness*, but the initiative was certainly Curll's, and Bond may not even have been consulted. There seems to be no reason to connect Bond with the rest of the volume or with *The Popiad*.

The winter of 1720 saw the publication also of a pair of poems in which, as Mr. Stanhope, Bond sang the praises of King George I and the Prince of Wales. His Majesty naturally received primacy of praise, in *The Governour, a Poem on the Present Posture of Affairs: presented to the King*. It celebrates the achievements of George I in peace and war, in opposing his enemies abroad, especially Russian designs in the Baltic, and in rebellion and peace at home.[80] In *An Epistle to his Royal Highness the Prince of Wales, Occasion'd by the State of the Nation*, Bond praised the Prince, who "shone the *Guardian-Angel* of our Isle" both when his father went abroad in war and when he won a victory himself at Oudenard. Since he had less personal material here, Bond turned his attention to the national scene, where he found speculation rife, merit often neglected, and effrontery successful, even in poetry:

> HERE, those, that on his Menials joy'd to wait,
> With *South-Sea* Squibs, besiege a Duke's Estate;

> For *Cyper-Scrolls* his *Rent-Rolls* they command.
> He gets their *Paper,* and they get his *Land.*[81]

In 1722 Bond revised Edward Jones's translation of George
Buchanan's *History of Scotland,* advertising it as "Revised and
Corrected from the LATIN Original" and dedicating it, "against his
consent," to his cousin John Hervey first Earl of Bristol, as a
"known Lover and Encourager of Learning."[82] Bond's work was
evidently slipshod. At any rate, John Watkins, who translated and
edited Buchanan in 1829, remarked that though Bond "professed
to have corrected the translation by the original, it is evident on
comparison that he did this very slightly, for the numerous errors
which disfigured the folio [Jones' translation] were suffered by him
to pass unamended. . . ."[83]

Late in 1722, probably, and again as H. Stanhope, Bond published his *The Case Stated, in a Letter to Archibald Hutcheson,
Esq.* Clearly and logically argued, the pamphlet attempted to re-
store public faith in the good will of George I and to take severely
to task those who questioned his good faith. In the autumn of this
same year he contributed the Prologue to Mrs. Centlivre's *Artifice.*
Here he asks the indulgence of the critics especially:

> *But, oh! ye* Criticks! Comic-Bards *are few,*
> *And we've no* Wit *beneath the Sun, that's* New:
> *Ask not, in such a* General Dearth, *much Wit,*
> *If she your Taste in* Plot, *and* Humour *hit:*
> Plot, Humour, Business, *form the Comick Feast,*
> *Wit's but a* higher—relish'd Sawce, *at best;*
> *And where* too much, *like* Spice, *destroys the Taste.*
> ([London, 1723], Sigs.
> [A3] verso-[A4] recto)

Bond's part in Edward Jessup's *Life of the Celebrated Monsieur
Pascal* (1723) was a minor one. The novice author, Bond explained,
felt that he needed an introduction by some veteran friend, but
Bond's Preface is little more than a translation of the biography of
Pascal by his sister Madame du Perier, taken from Pierre Bayle's
Nouvelle de la République des Lettres (pp. 531–533) for December
1684. During 1723 also was published another unnoticed performance of Bond—his translation of Pliny's panegyric of the Emperor
Trajan, in Pliny the Younger's *Epistles and Panegyrick,* translated
by Addison, John Hughes, Bond, and others, and published in 1724
in two volumes by Mears. According to the editor, John Henley,
only the first 92 of the 142 pages were translated by Bond, "*Mr.
Bond being hinder'd by a Fitt of Sickness, from proceeding with
the Translation any farther. . . .*"[84]

A little-noticed performance of 1724 was *An Odaic Essay in Commemoration of the Nativity of our Lord*, a folio poem of some eleven pages addressed to Lady Gage of Hengrave-Hall. The apparently unique copy at the University of Texas contains, as a cancel insert, a commendatory poem signed with his favorite pen name, H. Stanhope, and addressed to himself:

> The sound Philosopher in ev'ry Line,
> With the persuasive Orator you join,
> And with the sweet Tongu'd Bard, the deep Divine.
>
> (Sig. b recto)

From March 23, 1724, until May 7, 1725, Bond published his last major work of the decade—with Aaron Hill he wrote *The Plain Dealer*. It appeared twice a week. It has been praised by Bonamy Dobree as "almost up to *Spectator* standard," but the old canard of Savage, given currency by Johnson, is still quoted that the two editors, Hill and Bond, were "the two contending powers of light and darkness."[85] Since Savage had every reason to remember Hill gratefully and no known cause to speak kindly of Bond, he was rather a prejudiced witness. Miss Dorothy Brewster, Hill's biographer, found the task of discriminating between the essays no easy matter.[86] Indeed this writer's impression is that most of the stodgy essays are Hill's and the sprightly ones Bond's.

Otherwise Bond seems to have produced only occasional poetry for the rest of the decade, evidently forced by his illness to retire to Bury St. Edmonds, which until 1733 became his regular address. These occasional poems appear over his own name. In 1725, for example, Pack's *New Collection of Miscellanies in Verse and Prose* opened with Bond's "The Muses's Choice, or the Progress of Wit, an Elegiac Epistle to Major Pack." This rather considerable piece praises not only Pack, but "Garter'd Campbell" (Argyll), Stanhope, and the beauty of Bury women (pp. 21, 28). During the following year, probably, Bond wrote *Verses Sacred to the Memory of Henrietta Late Duchess of Grafton*. Here the late death of the Countess (August 9, 1726) is bemoaned by Piety, Fortitude, and Fame.[87] After this poem occurs a silence of some five years—unless Bond had a hand in Curll's edition of Bishop Parker's *History of his own Times* (1728).[88] The silence was broken in 1730 with *Cobham and Congreve, an Epistle to the Lord Viscount Cobham in Memory of his Friend the late Mr. Congreve.*[89]

In 1733 Bond reappeared in London both as Mr. Stanhope and under his own name. As Stanhope he published *The Patriot: an Epistle to the Most Noble Philip Earl of Chesterfield*. The poem celebrates Chesterfield's zeal for liberty, his eloquence, liberality, patriotism, and concern for England's trade. The poet was obviously in poor health:

> Tho' low and humble are my Muse's Strains
> Of Thought, impair'd, the poor and last Remains. . . .
> . . . .
> An *Addison*, or *Pope*, your Praise shou'd sing. (p. 4)

The year 1733 saw also the production of Bond's only play, *The Tuscan Treaty, or Tarquin's Overthrow*, first performed at Covent Gardens on August 20, 1733.[90] Though called a "tragedy" on the title page, it was much more accurately described in Bond's Dedication to the Duchess Dowager of Marlborough as a "dramatic poem," for the only "tragic" scene is the sentimental demise of a minor character, Vario. Though Bond received a benefit performance, and though Aaron Hill furnished Prologue and Epilogue, sent some free tickets, and attended himself, the play was not and did not deserve to be a success. Cousin Hervey gave Bond two guineas, but took no tickets.[91]

On Wednesday, May 28, 1735, Hill's tragedy *Zara* was finally rehearsed, before a "great Appearance of Nobility and other Persons of Distinction," in Sir Richard Steele's Great Room in the York Buildings. "A Sett of Gentleman and Gentlewomen, who never acted before," devoted their services by playing their roles gratis, for Bond's benefit.[92] Bond himself played the role of Lusignan, but he was weak and felt premonitions of disaster. On June 6 Hill published in *The Prompter* a letter which he had just received from Bond complaining against the theatre managers for their refusing, during a period of two years, to bring on his play. Now he fears death through the effects of want: ". . . shou'd I chance to *die*, in *Earnest*," he contemplated, "while I am *acting* Death. . . ." His fears were realized. Attending the theatre for a third performance, Hill heard "that the Gentleman had acted *Lusignan*, the first Night only: having filled himself so powerfully with a Sense of That Similitude, between his own Condition and Those Afflictions which are so strongly, and so passionately, *painted*, in the *Character* that He had fainted on the Stage, incapable of the *too animated* Misery; and, being carried home, directly, in his Chair, had *really died*, next Morning."[93]

The funeral notice in *The London Magazine* for June 1735 was brief: "Mr. *William Bond*, a near Relation to the Lord Viscount *Gage*, and Author of several poetical Pieces."[94] He must have aged rapidly during his recent and frequent illnesses. Thirty-five years later a correspondent writing to the *Gentlemen's Magazine* remarked, "He was then about sixty."[95] During his last months, he must have been working at his translation, *The Manual of Epictetus*, which appeared the year after his death.

VIII | Dickory Cronke

ERHAPS THE MOST CONFUSING among the supernatural works
attributed to Defoe is *The Dumb Philosopher*. This sixty-
eight page pamphlet, which appeared on October 13, 1719,
carries a lengthy but informative title:

> *The Dumb Philosopher, or Great Britain's Wonder; containing: I. A*
> *faithful and very surprising Account how Dickory Cronke, a Tinner's son,*
> *in the County of Cornwall, was born Dumb, and continued so for Fifty-*
> *eight Years; and how, some days before he died, he came to his Speech:*
> *with Memoirs of his Life, and the Manner of his Death. II. A Declaration*
> *of his Faith and Principles in Religion; with a Collection of Select Medita-*
> *tions, composed in his Retirement. III. His Prophetical Observations*
> *upon the Affairs of Europe, more particularly of Great Britain, from 1720*
> *to 1729. The whole extracted from his Original Papers, and confirmed by*
> *unquestionable Authority. To which is annexed his Elegy, written by a*
> *Young Cornish Gentleman, of Exeter College in Oxford, with an Epitaph*
> *by another Hand. "Non quis, sed quid."*[1]

In 1790 it was assigned to Defoe by George Chalmers, who perhaps
suspected that he had authored all the contemporary biographies
of deaf and dumb seers.[2] The pamphlet was reprinted by Walter
Scott in his edition of Defoe in 1810, and it has remained a standard item in editions of Defoe ever since.[3]

Although Defoe scholars have unanimously assigned to Defoe
the authorship of *The Dumb Philosopher*, they have disagreed
widely about its basis and its significance. Of the veridity of the
"faithful account" provided in the first part of the pamphlet there
has existed considerable difference of opinion. The biographical
section of some twenty-two pages provides rather precise detail.

Dickory, "Restoration Dick," the son of a tin miner in Cornwall, was born May 29, 1660, in a little hamlet near St. Colomb (Major), a hamlet within "four or five miles" of Padstow. His infirmity of dumbness went undetected until he was three, it would seem, but he was then carefully taught and proved a wonderfully apt scholar, and subsequently a teacher, showing a keen and inquisitive mind. A delicate boy, he proved unfit for work in the tin mines, but after he became twenty he took service with a Mr. Owen Parry, a Welsh gentleman, whom he served until his master died twenty years later. He then served Mrs. Mary Mordaunt, in Bath and Bristol, until her death four years later. Then Dickory returned to Cornwall, but found none of his family alive except his youngest sister, who lived at a little town called St. Helen's, "about ten miles further in the country" (p. 9). With her Dickory spent the rest of his life, an uneventful one until May 27, 1718. After a seizure of apoplexy the previous day, he then gained the power of speech—a gift which was on the following day taken from him. The next day, his fifty-eighth birthday, he died, leaving behind him some pious and practical meditations and some prophecies. These he entrusted to his and Mr. Parry's friend Mr. Anthony Barlow, a Welsh gentleman whom Dickory designated as his literary executor.

In 1818 George Smeeton reprinted the biographical section of *The Dumb Philosopher,* and in 1820 he included it in his *Historical and Biographical Tracts*—along with the account of another Cornish notable, Hugh Peters the regicide, who was executed the same year Dickory was born. But Cornish antiquarians like George Clement Boase subsequently rejected the narrative and Dickory as fictitious.[4] In 1895 George Aitken, after a study of Cornish authorities and the registers of St. Columb Major, was undecided. "I am inclined to think that Dickory Cronke was a real person, and that Defoe threw off this pamphlet after hearing of his death in 1718. I have, however, not been able to find any reference to Cronke in contemporary newspapers or elsewhere. . . ." Although he admitted that the account might be fictitious, Aitken was hopeful: "it would be rash to express a positive opinion on the matter. Cronke may yet turn out to have been well known locally in his day."[5] Aitken's inclination to regard the story as at least in part veridical surprised Mr. John Robert Moore, who rejected the detailed biography as circumstantial justification for the prophecies.[6] But there is a possibility that Dickory did have some recent pattern and that Aitken was checking the wrong registers or the wrong names. Although the name Cronke seems absent from Cornish parish registers so far published and may in fact represent the author's German designation for a boy born ill, or dumb, parish registers in Surrey record the name Cronke as extending far back and still surviving there; and the name Dickory was popular with Cornish families in the 1660's.[7]

The pamphlet is ambiguous about the extent of its own veridity. We are cautioned on the title page itself by the disconcerting motto *"Non quis, sed quid."* Then the Preface further warns us "that it is an indication of ill nature or ill manners, if not both, to pry into a secret that is industriously concealed" (p. iii). What secret? Perhaps the editor is suggesting that the names and other details have been deliberately altered; but to conceal the identity of an obscure Cornish lad? Only a sister survives him, and she would stand to gain by the disclosure.

Moreover the narrative varies considerably about the nature and extent of the editor's contributions. We are assured that "though the language is something altered, and now and then a word thrown in to help the expression, yet strict care has been taken to speak the author's mind" (p. iv). At one point we are informed that "the meditations following" (p. 20) are the fruit of six hours of special inspiration during the hours immediately following Dickory's gift of speech and represent the special discourse which he had intended to deliver orally to his sister and her friends. It would seem to have been kept intact. At the end of the narrative, however, it is suggested that the editor played an extensive role: "This is the substance of what he [Dickory] either writ or extracted from his papers . . ." (p. 35). The title page and the Preface suggest, even further, that the editor has selected from a large mass of material: what the reader "has now before him was collected from a large bundle of papers, most of which were writ in shorthand, and very ill-digested" (p. iv).

The narrative itself offers even more convincing evidence that it is incredible. Obviously no mother who gave her son "a double portion of her care and tenderness" could have failed to perceive before "upwards of three years" that her son was dumb (p. 5). Such slipshod and unimaginative writing, such failure to visualize suggests that the author was either no parent or a singularly unobservant one. The supposition that Dickory could at fifty-eight suddenly converse with ease, without being taught to speak, again seems incredible, though this detail is doubtless demanded by the prophetic convention. But it does seem inartistic that, having been suddenly endowed for a day with the power of speech, Dickory should, instead of being allowed to sing his swan song, be forced to retire, voiceless again, to his chamber and there utter his oracular pronouncements in shorthand.

Defoe scholars have disagreed not only about whether *The Dumb Philosopher* had any factual basis; they have differed even more over the significance of the pamphlet. Walter Wilson in 1830 dwelt upon its circumstantiality, as critics have done ever since, pointed out its effortlessness, and remarked upon its moral purpose:

> In this, as in all the author's narratives, there is an unsuspicious air of truth running through all its circumstances, that sets scepticism itself at defiance. . . .
> . . . .
> In this simple story, De Foe has put in practice, without any apparent effort, the same peculiarity of invention that distinguishes his other performances. Although the incidents of the narrative are few in number, they are told in the same unpretending manner, and with so much exactness, that it is difficult for the reader to persuade himself that it is any other than a real history. . . . and when he lays a tax upon . . . credulity, it is levied with an air of seriousness that extorts belief, and finds ample remuneration in the moral lessons with which it is accompanied. His purpose of reformation, he unfolds at the outset: . . ."[8]

William Hazlitt was content to echo Wilson,[9] but in 1869 William Lee thought that he perceived a parallel between Defoe's spiritual autobiography in *Robinson Crusoe* and Dickory Cronke's biography in *The Dumb Philosopher*:

> Cronke was, in a certain sense, like Crusoe, isolated, and shut out from intercourse with mankind, for a great portion of his life. Both were afterwards enabled to enjoy the blessings of human intercourse. Both were reflective and religious men, and wrote meditations worthy of being published to the world. . . . There is the same atmosphere of truth surrounding all the details of both, so that the reader lives in the reality of each story, and scepticism itself is set at defiance. In Crusoe, the Author has declared that the history of his own life is allegorically enclosed; and, though I will not positively affirm, that portions of his inner life are contained in Dickory Cronke, yet I believe so. It is noticeable that Cronke's life is made to begin about the same time as Defoe's,—to terminate at the author's age when writing this book; and that, like himself, Cronke had a fit of apoplexy.[10]

Later Thomas Wright elaborated upon Lee and pronounced, "It is unlikely that all these coincidences are accidental."[11]

These parallels George Aitken dismissed as "a fanciful suggestion," and John Robert Moore called such interpretations "fantastic surmises." Instead Mr. Moore regarded the story and the meditations as realistic groundwork and found in the final eight pages the entire purpose and significance of the pamphlet. ". . . If one omits the prophecies," he remarked, "this tract becomes the most pointless writing in the whole range of Defoe's works."[12] The seventeen prophecies in the third section of *The Dumb Philosopher* cover the period from 1720 until 1729, and most years are allotted two predictions. The first year, 1721, is, however, given five; and the two years, 1724–1725, only one. Most of the prophecies are political in nature, covering foreign and domestic affairs. Several, for 1721 and 1722, are concerned with international peace and threats thereto. Others foretell Jacobite plots and their failure. One curious prediction concerns a German alchemist:

> 3. In the year 1721, a philosopher from lower Germany shall come, first to Amsterdam in Holland, and afterwards to London. He will bring with him a world of curiosities, and among them a pretended secret for the transmutation of metals. Under the umbrage of this mighty secret he shall pass upon the world for some time; but at length he shall be detected, and proved to be nothing but an empiric and a cheat, and so forced to sneak off, and leave the people he has deluded, either to bemoan their loss, or laugh at their own folly. N. B. This will be the last of his sect that will ever venture in this part of the world upon the same errand. (pp. 31–32)

English readers were accustomed, after Philip Horneck's *High-German Doctor* (1714–1715), to interpret alchemical terms as political ones, and this prophecy, as Mr. Moore suggests, probably concerns the importation of John Law's Mississippi Bubble and the South Sea venture, which was gradually building up to a collapse. There are other interesting prophecies, especially some concerning the Church of England, but consideration of these is best deferred.

In drawing attention to its prophetical nature Mr. Moore has helped to set *The Dumb Philosopher* in its proper light: it certainly fits into the tradition of English political prophecy. By the eighteenth century the Galfridian patterns had changed,[13] but the political prophecies persisted in old and new forms. The old prophecies, like those of Merlin, were retold; there was an edition in 1718—the year before publication of *The Dumb Philosopher*—and his memory was perpetuated not only in the many ephemerides which borrowed their titles from him, but his effigy was on exhibit in Merlin's cave and hermitage at the popular resort of Richmond. In 1715 there was again imported the famous Nostradamus: *The Prophecies of Michael Nostradamus concerning the Fate of all the Kings and Queens of Great Britain since the Reformation, particularly King George*. These are but samples of the persistence of the old prophecies.

Among new prophecies and new types, apart from the fanatical ravings of the French prophets in London at the end of the first decade, the most interesting and important here is *The Cheshire Prophecy* (1714), by John Oldmixon. Although Dickory Cronke would have been forgotten long ago but for his attribution to Defoe, Robert Nixon, the Cheshire prophet, was to become famous, to be immortalized in *Tom Jones* and *Pickwick Papers*, and to obtain his niche, as if he had been an actual person, in the *Dictionary of National Biography*.[14] Perhaps he was more real because he was more vividly imagined. Perhaps Robert Nixon, rather than Robinson Crusoe, is glanced at in the Preface of *The Dumb Philosopher*: "Indeed the public has too often been imposed upon by fictitious stories, and some of a very late date . . ." (p. iii). The resemblances between Robert Nixon and Dickory Cronke seem too close to owe their similarities merely to the conventions of the general prophetic type, though these conventions seem to be especially strong in *The Dumb Philosopher*. These resemblances appear not so much in the prophecies themselves as in the biographical sections of the narratives and their editorial assurances. Nixon (here the reverse of Cronke) is an idiot, but except for his inspired utterances, he is practically dumb: "They could seldom get any Thing out of him but *Yes* and *No*; and if he spoke much more, 'twas unintelligible; nay, he would hardly say *No* and *Yes*, unless he was pinched by *Hunger*." Indeed, "our Clown of a Prophet, after he came to Court, was entirely dumb."[15] Moreover, trances precede his utterances and follow them just as apoplexy precedes those of Dickory. Nixon's first prophecy occurs after a "Trance for the Space of an Hour," and a similar trance follows. Indeed a trance is for Nixon a necessary concomitant: "It must be observed that *Nixon* could not speak, except it was immediately after he was come out of his Trance, and never could be brought to pronounce a sensible Word, more than *Ay* or *No* as hath been said, unless when he was pronouncing his Oracles" (p. 20).

Not only is the sibylline trance a frequent characteristic of the prophet from classical and Hebrew times; so even more was the seer's abstinence. Christ himself, one remembers, was by some distrusted as a prophet because he did not follow the rigid pattern of self-denial observed by John the Baptist and his predecessors. Here Dickory reverts to the prophetic type in contrast to the glutton Nixon. Nixon "had a very good Stomach; and the Report was, that he would eat up a Shoulder of Mutton at a Meal, if they would let him, and a good Luncheon of Bread and Cheese after it" (p. 14). As for Dickory, "The chief part of his sustenance was milk, with a little bread boiled in it. . . . Dinners he never eat any; and at night he would only have a pretty large piece of bread, and drink a draught of good spring water . . ." (pp. 10–11). The last two days of his life—the period of prophecy—Dickory evidently lived on water alone. Moreover, as seer, Dickory pays the penalty often exacted of the true prophet. Teresias was blind. Duncan Campbell was deaf and dumb. Nixon was an idiot doomed to eventual starvation. Cronke was dumb and doomed to die immediately after his swan song. The children of *Vox Infantis* (1649) all die or are translated as soon almost as they have prophesied. In Norfolk the infant prophet survives her birth "not above two houres," and one in Buckinghamshire "not above three dayes." The special prophet of Commonwealth doom, discovered in the middle of a field in Herefordshire, on July 16, 1649, appearing "not to bee a quarter of a yeare old," speaks her prophecy, gives some wholesome moral advice, and is translated.[16]

But *The Dumb Philosopher* interpreted as prophecy leaves out of account the far larger section which is devoted to homely wisdom and moral and spiritual advice. This aspect of the work indeed prompted the title and was entirely the point of the elegy and the epitaph which close the pamphlet. In these poems Dickory's prophetic nature is completely ignored, and his wisdom instead is celebrated. The Preface chooses to emphasize the same aspect: "Here is a dumb philosopher introduced to a wicked and degenerate generation, as a proper emblem of virtue and morality; and if the world could be persuaded to look upon him with candour and impartiality, and then to copy after him, the editor has gained his end, and would think himself sufficiently recompensed for his present trouble" (p. iv). Dickory Cronke, we must remember, is presented mainly as philosopher, not prophet.

Either emphasis, however, obscures a union of the two natures —prophet and moralist—which characterized the Hebrew prophet and even the contemporary astrologer. Doubtless the moral admonitions of the Hebrew prophet were ignored by his listeners, as were his prophecies also; but lack of morality was one of the most shocking aspects of the French prophets who plagued London during the first decade of the century.[17] The eighteenth century reader of ephemerides was as familiar with homely wisdom and moral admonition along with the prophecies in his almanac as was the American reader in *Poor Richard's Almanac* in the 1730's.

The devotional and moral section of *The Dumb Philosopher* is subdivided into two parts, first, "An Abstract of his Faith, and the Principles of his Religion," six general statements of doctrine followed by a strong avowal of Anglican faith, and secondly, "Meditations and Observations relating to the Conduct of Human Life in general," forty statements of practical, gnomic, religious, and spiritual advice which are far-ranging in depth and coverage, but generally suitable to the sphere of life in which Dickory has allegedly been involved. Many statements are of the worldly type of Poor Robin: "If you would live at your ease, and as much as possible be free from the incumbrances of life, manage but a few things at once, and let those, too, be such as are absolutely necessary. By this rule you will draw the bulk of your business into a narrow compass, and have the double pleasure of making your actions good, and few into the bargain" (p. 24). Others are more moral in nature: "If a man does me an injury, what is that to me? It is his own action, and let him account for it. As for me, I am in my proper station, and only doing that business the Providence has allotted; and withal, I ought to consider that the best way to revenge, is not to imitate the injury" (p. 25). Some of these reflections are political in nature, hardly suitable for one in Dickory's retired sphere of life: "When a prince is guarded by wise and honest men, and when all public officers are sure to be rewarded if they do well, and punished if they do evil, the consequence is plain; justice and honesty will flourish, and men will always be contriving, not for themselves, but for the honour and interest of their king and country" (p. 27). But all of these reflections, one must recall, partake of the inspiration which characterizes the prophecies.

All of these types of reflection can be matched in the popular almanacs of the day, where political prophecies are intermingled with such apothegms. In his ephemerides, for example, John Partridge affixed atop each page of his yearly calendar, six verses of gnomic or moral philosophy. The practice became a conventional feature of many almanacs, as for example John Tanner's *Angelus Britannicus*. John Wing in his *Olympia Domata* for 1720 and 1722 incorporated practical wisdom instead of political predictions where he had space on the recto pages. For June 1720, he offered, for example:

> *Of all the Sins the Devil yet made choice,*
> *Revenge and Malice are his Master piece;*
> *False Friendship Cheating Luxury and Pride,*
> *And many more than might be nam'd beside.*[18]

Such moral advice was even more popular in Scottish almanacs, where astrologers were more cautious to offer political predictions. Perhaps the most unbelievable melange of practical wisdom and political prophecy came in the monthly predictions of *The Milan Predictions for 1703*, where in February, for example, is foreseen "A horrid Attempt; Apparitions appear to a people, every one is an Artisan of his own Fortune. A *Monster* satiated with Blood."[19]

Incongruous as it may seem, the infant in *Vox Infantis* of perhaps three months that suddenly appeared in Herefordshire to foretell doom for the Commonwealth, after it has prophecied to those who found, fed, and listened to it, "wished them all to love one another, and relieve the oppressed, and succour the fatherlesse and widdow, feare God and hee will blesse your Labour, bee no time-servers, meddle not with them that are given to change: observe these sayings, your reward shall bee in Heaven; My time is set; I have no more to say, but now shall leave you Uttering these words; *Glory bee to God on high, peace on earth, etc.* and so vanished away" (pp. 8–9). Under such circumstances, spiritual advice is impressive. So was it with another child: "*William Withers,* born at *Walsham* in Sussex, being a child of eleven years of age, did *An.* 1581 lye in a trance ten days without any sustenance, and at last coming to himself, uttered to the standers by many strange speeches against pride and covetousness, coldness of charity, and other outrageous sins."[20]

Perhaps one other reason why the moral reflections of Dickory are apt is that they authenticate the reliability of his spiritual views and his prophetic utterances. The French prophets had been very untrustworthy in their behavior, as had Robert Nixon. Moreover the author of *The Dumb Philosopher* doubtless knew that he must make an especially exemplary figure of Dickory, because a controversy existed within the church as to whether the dumb should be admitted to communion, as they could not verbalize their belief. In his *Compleat History* William Turner strongly defended their admission:

> I suppose, no one that righly considers the Circumstances . . . will make a Scruple about the Lawfulness of admitting such Persons to participate in the Holy Mysteries of Christ's Kingdom. All judicious *Casuists* determine, that those who are either born, or by any accident made Deaf and Dumb, if their Conversation be blameless, and they able by signs . . . to declare their Knowledge and Faith; may as freely be received to the Lords supper . . . . *Balduinus* in his Cases of Conscience, *Lib.* 2, *Chap.* 12, does confirm this, by producing several Instances of Dumb Persons admitted to the Communion. . . .
>
> . . . .
>
> *Ecclesiastical Story,* informs us of several Confessors of the Truth, who after their Tongues were cut out by bloody Persecutors, could still bear witness to the Truth.[21]

Perhaps the most obvious Cornish pattern for Dickory could have been found originally in Richard Carew's *Survey of Cornwall* (1602), though later writers, like Thomas Fuller and William Turner, repeated the story:

> These examples [of remarkable men] I thrust out before me, to make way for a not much less strange relation, touching one Edward Bone, sometimes servant to the said Master [Peter] Courtney [of Ladock, Cornwall]: which fellow (as by the assertion of divers credible persons I have been informed) deaf from his cradle, and consequently dumb, would yet be one of the first to learn, and express to his master, any news that was stirring in the country; especially, if there went speech of a sermon, within some miles distance, he would repair to the place with the soonest, and setting himself

> directly against the preacher, look him steadfastly in the face, while his sermon lasted; to which religious zeal, his honest life was also answerable; for, as he shunned all lewd parts himself, so, if he espied any in his fellow servants (which he could and would quickly do) his master should straightways know it, and not rest free from importuning, until, either the fellow had put away his fault, or their master his fellow. And to make his mind known, in this, and all other matters, he used very effectual signs, being able therethrough to receive and perform any enjoined errand. Besides, he was assisted with so firm a memory, that he would not only know any party, whom he had once seen, for ever after, but also make him known to any other, by some special observation and difference.[22]

Perhaps scholars have been looking in Cornwall for the wrong pattern, for a dumb prophet, which Bone is not, rather than a deeply moral and religious man. Like Bone, Dickory had "a mind composed and calm, and entirely free from the ordinary disturbances of human life. He never gave the least sign of complaint or dissatisfaction at anything, unless it was when he heard the tinners, swear, or saw them drunk; and then, too, he would go out of the way as soon as he had let them see, by some significant signs, how scandalous and ridiculous they made themselves; and against the next time he met them, would be sure to have a paper ready written, wherein he would represent the folly of drunkenness, and the dangerous consequences that generally attended it" (p. 11).

But these facts do not entirely explain the significance of Dickory's Confession of Faith and his apology for his failure to attend religious services, as his actual Cornish prototype Edward Bone had so eagerly done. This confession of faith is motivated in the account by the desire of Dickory's sister that he should clear himself of the charge of neglect: "that he would do well to make some declaration of his faith and principles of religion, because some reflections had been made upon him upon the account of his neglect, or rather his refusal, to appear at any place of public worship" (p. 19).

This opportunity the author utilized to the full to have the dumb prophet-philosopher strongly affirm the Trinitarian doctrine and recommend the principles of the Church of England. In "An Abstract of his Faith," the dumb philosopher is emphatically Trinitarian. Principles III, and VI for example, make his orthodoxy abundantly clear:

> 3. I believe and am fully and entirely satisfied, that God the Father, out of his infinite goodness and compassion to mankind, was pleased to send his only Son, the second person in the holy and undivided Trinity, to mediate for him, and to procure his redemption and eternal salvation.
> ....
> 6. I believe that these three persons are of equal power, majesty, and duration, and that the Godhead of the Father, of the Son, and of the Holy

Ghost is all one, and that they are equally uncreate, incomprehensible, eternal, and almighty; and that none is greater or less than the other, but that every one hath one and the same divine nature and perfections. (pp. 21–22)

After this avowal of orthodoxy, Dickory proceeds to the *"Principles of his Religion"* and attests to the authority of the Anglican Church:

As to my principles in religion, to be as brief as I can, I declare myself to be a member of Christ's church, . . . and among these I look upon the Church of England to be the chief and best constituted.

The Church of England is doubtless the great bulwark of the ancient Catholic or Apostolic faith all over the world; a church that has all the spiritual advantages that the nature of a church is capable of. From the doctrine and principles of the Church of England, we are taught loyalty to our prince, fidelity to our country, and justice to all mankind; and therefore, as I look upon this to be one of the most excellent branches of the Church Universal, and stands, as it were, between superstition and hypocrisy, I therefore declare, for the satisfaction of you and your friends, as I have always lived so I now die, a true and sincere, though a most unworthy member of it. (pp. 22–23)

The reader of today may find it difficult to understand the importance of this profession of faith. But viewed in the light of political and ecclesiastical events of the two years which preceded the publication of *The Dumb Philosopher*, the statement of faith assumes major significance. To understand it, one must return to the sequence of events touched off by a sermon preached before the King by Benjamin Hoadly, Bishop of Bangor, on March 31, 1717. Hoadly's liberal attitude toward the dissenters prepared for a bill introduced in Parliament to remove some of the penalties under which they labored, a bill which was by many viewed as tantamount to "comprehension," though this term is ordinarily reserved for the unsuccessful attempt in 1660 to include the dissenters within the Church of England. It led also to a furious pamphlet warfare, the Bangorian controversy. ". . . All the topics in dispute between whig and tory, high and low churchmen, were brought into the controversy, and an unusual amount of heat and bitterness animated the writers. The number of the tracts was prodigious, amounting probably to near two hundred."[23] Among the numerous disputants was evidently Daniel Defoe, who came to the defense of Hoadly's liberal position in hopes of helping to secure concessions in Parliament for the dissenters. Among the Bangorian pamphlets which Defoe is supposed to have published during the year 1717 are *A Declaration of Truth to Benjamin Hoadly; A Reply to the Remarks upon the Lord Bishop of Bangor's Treatment of the Clergy and Convocation; A Letter to Andrew Snape, occasion'd by the Strife that lately appeared among the People called Clergy-men*; and *A Vindication of Dr. Snape, in Answer to Several Libels lately publish'd against him. In these*

Defoe was far from defending Snape and Sherlock, but was supporting Hoadly's suggestion that the government had no right to regulate religious matters at all. Late in 1718 a bill "for strengthening the Protestant interest," or removing some of the impositions upon the dissenters, was introduced into Parliament, passed, and given royal assent in February 1719.

It was not too soon, for a new controversy had broken out among the dissenters in Devon and Cornwall, had spread to London, and threatened to engulf the dissenters in a controversy which might undo all that Hoadly and the King had done for them. The central figure in the dispute was Dr. James Peirce, of Exeter. When he and several other dissenting ministers departed from conventional Trinitarian doctrines in their sermons and statements and thereby alarmed some of their brothers and their congregations, the Exeter Assembly, composed of Presbyterian and Independent divines of Cornwall and Devon, took the matter under advisement. The matter was also referred to the general meeting of dissenters at Salters Hall in London, and to the public as well by the dispossessed Dr. Peirce and his disputants. The author of *The Annals of King George, Year the Fifth* devoted 116 of his 434 pages to this controversy and commented, "But it could hardly have been expected to what a strange Excess those Heats have been since carried; the Pulpit, the Press, and all Means of Publication have been almost engrossed in their Quarrels. . . ." "A great Number of Pamphlets indeed it produced . . . that abound too much with Biterness and Personal Recrimination to deserve any particular Regard; but they were most founded upon the Conduct of the Dissenters about *Exeter*. . . ."[24] Defoe himself evidently entered the controversy with a pamphlet, but to pacify, rather than to exacerbate, for he realized what harm the controversy was liable to cause the dissenters. In his *Letter to the Dissenters* (1719), he deliberately avoided the "Doctrinal Points in which they have differ'd." ". . . 'tis none of my Business here," he explained; "I avowedly put it out of the Question. . . ." Instead he urged, "*Consider the TOLERATION*." "Why do ye appeal against one another in Print? Why do ye Impeach your Brethren on one Side and on the other before the Judicature of common Fame? Printing Books and Advertisements full of reproaches and recriminations, charging and condemning one another before your Enemies? . . . Do you not in this put yourselves into the very Hands of your Enemies, and give them occasion to wound you with your own Weapons?"[25] The whole pamphlet is a tactful, wise argument, not even naming Peirce and his disputants.

In the light of these disputes—the Bangorian controversy which began in 1717 and still reverberated; the bill of 1718 and 1719 for "strengthening the Protestant interest"; and the Exeter controversy of 1718 and 1719—it is obvious that any confession of faith would be controversial in 1719, especially one which goes to such pains to call attention to its importance, and particularly one which supposedly emanated from the territories of the Exeter Assembly and carried such supernatural sanctions.

The more carefully one examines *The Dumb Philosopher* the more apparent it becomes that Daniel Defoe could have had nothing to do with it. Not a shred of external evidence has been produced to saddle him with it. The internal evidence points away from him. Concerning the authorship of *The Dumb Philosopher* Mr. Moore has remarked with disarming disingenuousness: "There has been no question of authorship; the tract has been reprinted in nearly all collections of Defoe's works since Scott included it in 1810."[26] There has been no question of authorship only because the question has not earlier been raised. Defoe had that same year, in his *Letter to the Dissenters,* carefully avoided mentioning doctrinal matters. Would he then in *The Dumb Philosopher* have provided us with an Anglican confession of faith, supernaturally sanctioned, and in the prophecies themselves have rejected any further efforts toward "comprehension"?

> 15. Great endeavours will be used about this time [1727] for a comprehension in religion, supported by crafty and designing men, and a party of mistaken zealots, which they shall artfully draw in to join with them; but as the project is ill-concerted, and will be worse managed, it will come to nothing; and soon afterwards an effectual mode will be taken to prevent the like attempt for the future. (p. 34)

Defoe doubtless foresaw the failure of any further attempts at comprehension; but this important difference existed between Defoe and the pamphlet: *The Dumb Philosopher* was opposing further attempts to strengthen the dissenting position. In his remarks in *Considerations on the Present State of Affairs in Great Britain* (1718), just as in his *Letter to the Dissenters* the year following, Defoe was hoping to consolidate and further the dissenters' gains. As Mr. Moore has pointed out, "He had contended that a reasonable plan for religious comprehension could be worked out ...."[27] Similarly support in *The Dumb Philosopher* for the Church of England as "the great bulwark of the ancient Catholic or Apostolic faith all over the world" seemed to Thomas Wright as "noteworthy" "coming as it does from one of the staunchest of Dissenters."[28] It is not only "noteworthy"; it is incredible. A Moderate Whig, Defoe could support a moderate Tory position. But that he would betray the church for which he had taken grave risks and undergone serious suffering to support instead its persecutor, the Church of England—this seems incredible.

But the final prophecy would be even more shocking, if it came from Defoe.

> 17. About this time [1728] a new scaffold will be erected upon the confines of a certain great city, where an old count of a new extraction, that has been of all parties and true to none, will be doomed by his peers to make his first appearance. After this an old lady who has often been exposed to danger and disgrace, and sometimes brought to the very brink of destruction, will be brought to bed of three daughters at one, which shall be called Plenty, Peace, and Union; and these three shall live and grow up together, be the glory of their mother, and the comfort of posterity for many generations. (pp. 34–35)

Undoubtedly Mr. Moore is correct in interpreting this prophecy as a call for the execution of Robert Harley, Earl of Oxford, Defoe's old benefactor. ". . . No one seems to have realized how complete the final break between the two men became," Mr. Moore commented.[29] In 1714, even after Harley was dismissed from his office, Defoe had written to him, ". . . I am and shall be Ever Watchfull for your Lordships Interest. . . ."[30] He had in 1714 and 1715 risked danger in publishing the three parts of his *Secret History of the White Staff*, which was, according to Harley's biographer E. S. Roscoe, "a strikingly able and effective defence of his patron's political conduct."[31] His *Account of the Conduct of Robert Earl of Oxford* (1715) he reissued in 1717 as *Memoirs of Some Transactions during the Ministry of Robert Earl of Oxford*. "It would seem that in 1715 and 1717 alike Defoe expected this tract to be of service to the defence of the Earl of Oxford," Mr. Moore remarked.[32] After 1717 Harley took comparatively little part in current politics. His stands in 1717, opposing the Court Martial bill and the standing army, seem to be favourably reported in *A History of the Last Session of the Present Parliament* (1718), which Mr. Moore assigns to Defoe. In 1719 Harley seems to have taken a leading part in opposing the Peerage Bill, but it is difficult to see how this action could have angered Defoe, who evidently opposed it also.[33] Indeed it is difficult to see how Defoe could have become so enraged with his former friend that he now wanted to see him executed and even recommended that such an execution was necessary for the peace and prosperity of England! Lee remarked concerning Defoe's defense of Harley: ". . . we are constrained to admire the courage, the faithfulness and gratitude of Defoe. . . . He could never forget the benefactor who had taken him out of a dungeon, and procured him the royal favour,—nor hold his peace while that benefactor was threatened with destruction."[34] If Defoe wrote *The Dumb Philosopher*, then Mr. Moore aptly called the pamphlet a scorpion with a sting in its tail.[35] Never before did Defoe display such inveterate venom. But we bemonster Defoe by fathering upon him such an unnatural offspring. It does not fit in with his known ideas and attitudes; and if we retain it in the Defoe canon, we do violence to the man's religious sincerity and personal integrity.

There are additional reasons why Defoe is unlikely to have written *The Dumb Philosopher*. Instead of anticipating the prophetic nature of *The Dumb Philosopher*, Defoe's vaticinations in the early 1710's, like *The Highland Visions*, are all yearly predictions and entirely lack the moral wisdom and spiritual advice which characterize *The Dumb Philosopher*. Their prophetical relationship to the pamphlet is like that of Drew Pearson to the prophet Amos. Moreover the pamphlet does not fit into the patterns of exposition and narrative which Defoe exhibited about the same time in *The Family Instructor* and the three parts of *Robinson Crusoe*. Especially does it lack the vivid dialogue of which Defoe was by this time a master. It was perhaps this comparatively colorless and undistinguished style of the biographical section which made Mr. Moore comment, "There is nowhere else in Defoe a story so dull as this."[36]

Possibly Chalmers ascribed *The Dumb Philosopher* to Defoe because he thought that Defoe had written *The History of the Life of Duncan Campbell* (1720). Although their only obvious similarity is the exhibition of a mute hero, perhaps they were written by the same man; but if so they are the work not of Daniel Defoe but of William Bond. The possibility that Bond wrote *The Dumb Philosopher* as well as *Duncan Campbell* deserves consideration. He had time for it, as Defoe, busy writing the three parts of *Robinson Crusoe* and many other pieces, did not, for Bond had by this time well-nigh finished his biography of Campbell, and he and Curll were evidently waiting for subscriptions to accumulate before releasing it. The same publisher who issued *The Dumb Philosopher*, Thomas Bickerton, was, evidently on behalf of Edmund Curll, to publish Bond's *Mr. Campbell's Packet* the year following. The defense of the Church of England, especially against any further concessions to the dissenters, would be plausible for Bond, who was a strong Trinitarian. Many of the leading articles in his *Weekly Medley* during 1719 were directed against the dissenters of Salters Hall; Hoadly was especially attacked; and in the issue for October 3–10, 1719, Defoe was himself abused because of his defense of dissenting meeting-houses:

> Is not the Saturday's Post worse than the Flying-Post in Defense of Presbyterianism? It is really very unlucky that this Fellow should make me his Adversary: After I had prov'd him a *FOE* to Politics, a *FOE* to Religion,

and given him good Advice to be converted, by predicting to him that otherwise the *Saturday's Post* would be look'd upon with a more Evil Eye than the *Flying-Post*; what does he do but the vary same Instant publish a *Saturday's Post* more *vile* and more *Presbyterian* than the Flying-Post had done, and so by proving my prediction true, turn a very *FOE* to himself at last?

Pray, Sir, to use your familiar Way of Speech, why should a Man be call'd a villanous Presbyterian for blaspheming before he enters a Presbyterian Conventicle, unless you would have the common People conclude it to be a Holy Place? You should rather have pointed against the whole Doctrine of Presbyterianism, by owning that he had by Blasphemy fitted himself to go to the Conventicle, where they do scarce any thing else but blaspheme against the Holy Trinity; then you would have done something: You would have follow'd my Advice, and push'd the Point home upon the Body of Dissenters . . . thou should'st have told them it was the *House of the Devil*, where the Lord our Saviour Jesus Christ's Divinity is oppugn'd by a Set of Pseudo-Teachers the Members of Antichrist.[37]

Whether Bond, a disappointed Jacobite, was still violently resentful of the ambiguous role Harley played in betraying the Jacobites is less certain, but he owed Harley no favors, as Defoe did.

In addition, there are some coincidences that make the authorship of Bond worth considering. The two poems commending Cronke, the dumb philosopher, were allegedly written, first, by a J. P., a Cornish gentleman of Exeter College, Oxford; and the second, by a gentleman who chanced to go to the church yard where he was buried. The only possible identification for "J. P.," if all the information given in the pamphlet is correct, seems to be John Phillipps, son of Sam Phillipps, gentleman, of Poughill (now Broomhill), Cornwall. He matriculated at Exeter College March 10, 1718, at age eighteen.[38] The home of this Phillipps is some distance from St. Columb, and the date of the elegy—August 25, 1719—would seem to suggest as author of the poem a fellow residing in the college rather than a young boy spending his first summer vacation there. This John Phillipps, or J. P. (or both), may be the J. Philips who the following year contributed a poem to Bond's *Mr. Campbell's Packet*. Or if this Cornish ancestry is fictitious, "J. P." could have been John Porter, of Hart Hall, still officially Exeter College, who wrote critical letters prefixed in 1720 to Bond's and Martha Fowke Sansom's *Clio and Strephon*. The epitaph at the end of the pamphlet is unsigned; but it is at least interesting that a young nobleman admirer of Bond came from Dickory Cronke's village. In his *Tour through England and Wales* (1724–1726), Defoe was to comment concerning St. Columb that it was "eminent for nothing but its being the antient estate of the famous Arundell of Trerice."[39] John Arundell, Baron Arundell of Trerice, who was born November 21, 1701, and matriculated at Balliol College, Oxford,[40] was evidently author the following year (1720) of *The Directors*, the most glowing poem ever published in Bond's praise. Perhaps it was Arundell who helped to popularize the dumb philosopher by his epitaph. Possibly, after visiting the churchyard where Cronke's prototype was buried, he wrote Bond about the dumb philosopher and included the epitaph in his praise. For this conjecture it is unnecessary to assume that the picture of Cronke in *The Dumb Philosopher* is accurate. But there may have been a more recent Edward Bone in Cornwall. Bond, one recalls, published another Cornish story in his *Mr. Campbell's Packet* the following year—the apparition of Dorothy Dingley, as related by the Reverend Mr. Ruddle. He obviously had some Cornish source for this story. From his *Weekly Medley* for the first week in 1719, it would appear that he had a correspondent in Padstow about this time (No. XXIV, p. 141). Moreover Bond was, in September of 1719, evidently donning the garb of prophet as "Jonathan Foresight" (pp. 356–357, 363). But these bits of evidence tend to suggest that Bond could have written *The Dumb Philosopher*; they constitute no actual proof that he did.

If Bond did not write the pamphlet, an obvious possibility is John Oldmixon, creator of the famous Robert Nixon. Oldmixon might have taken time out from his labors at *The History of England*, a work on which he was engaged for four years, in an attempt to repeat his earlier success of *The Cheshire Prophecy* and tide himself over financially by writing *The Dumb Philosopher*. The Anglican bias there does not exclude Oldmixon: though brought up as a nonconformist, and a frequenter during the decade of Presbyterian and Anabaptist conventicles, he had by 1718 begun to attend the Anglican Church. It would probably be a mistake, however, to lay much stress upon the fact that Oldmixon had married Elizabeth Parry in 1703.[41] Dickory, one recalls, served "Mr. Owen Parry" faithfully for twenty years. Such a parallel is probably accidental, and there is little evidence to show that Oldmixon may have been the author.

Just who wrote *The Dumb Philosopher* must remain uncertain, then, until more evidence can be accumulated and examined for the various possible ascriptions. One thing we can be morally certain of about its authorship, however—Daniel Defoe did not write it.

A Note on Authorship

Although none of his four major occult works appeared under Defoe's name, the ascription is made easy by external and internal evidence. They are among the first works attributed to Defoe, being assigned to him only about a score of years after his death in Theophilus Cibber's, or Robert Shiels', *Lives of the Poets of Great Britain and Ireland* (1753), where he was identified as "Moreton." *The History of Apparitions* had already been attributed to Defoe by William Oldys or Samuel Johnson in *Catalogus Bibliothecae Harleianae* (1743–1745, II, 922). *A System of Magick* was in some of the papers advertised under Defoe's favorite pen name "Andrew Moreton," and *The History of Apparitions* was reissued over this name. There is ample internal evidence. A poem on the origin of evil which appears in *The History of the Devil* (pp. 60–61) Defoe had already printed as his, in *Jure Divino* (folio edition of 1706, Bk. VI, pp. 11–14), and in the *Review* for August 27, 1709. Another section of *Jure Divino* (VII, pp. 6–7) appears in *The History of the Devil* (p. 96).

Moreover the whole series of occult works—"A Vision of the Angelick World," *The History of the Devil, A System of Magick,* and *The History of Apparitions*—is tied to *Robinson Crusoe* and tightly knit by "puffs" as well as by similarities of style, subject matter, and ideas. Thus in *Serious Reflections of Robinson Crusoe,* Crusoe puffs the subjoined "Vision": ". . . I abhor superstitious and sceptical notions of the world of spirits, of which I propose to speak hereafter, either in this work or in some other by itself . . ." (p. 183). The "Vision" forecasts *The History of the Devil*: "It would take up a long tract by itself to form a system of the devil's politics, and to lay down a body of his philosophy" (p. 271). In *The History of the Devil* itself (pp. 323–324) Defoe seems to refer to his "Vision." Then near the end of the book he seems to anticipate his *System of Magick*. Speaking of the new or "other measures" which the Devil now takes, the author comments, ". . . but I must adjourn that to a time and place by itself" (p. 365). In his *History of the Devil* he seems also to promise his *History of Apparitions*: ". . . all those pretenses of frenziful and fanciful people, who tell us they have seen the Devil, I shall examine, and perhaps expose by themselves" (p. 42). The account of Owke Mouraski, detailed at length in *The History of Apparitions* (pp. 61–74), Defoe actually began in his *History of the Devil*, then cut short with the comment: "This account has an innumerable number of diverting incidents attending it; but they are equal to all the rest in bulk, and, therefore, too long for this book" (p. 268). Again, in discussing the apparitions of the Devil, he apologized that "this is out of my way at this time, and does not relate at all to the Devil's history" (p. 327), as if he were then planning his book on apparitions. In his *System of Magick*, finally, he twice puffed his *History of the Devil*: ". . . I am not now upon the proof of the reality and existence of the Devil; that has been worthily undertaken, and historically, mathematically, and enthusiastically enough performed by a late writer in another place . . ." (p. 53). The "late writer" who in *The History of the Devil* taught him "to except, our own people, our own countrymen, and country worthies" (pp. 57–58) from religious criticism was of course Daniel Defoe.

Notes

INTRODUCTION

1. *Journal*, ed. F. W. Macdonald, Everyman edition (London, 1922), IV, 215.
2. Richard S. Westfall, *Science and Religion in Seventeenth-Century England* (New Haven, 1958), pp. 78, 83–92, 201, 113–114.
3. Sir Leslie Stephen, *History of English Thought in the Eighteenth Century*, Harbinger ed. (New York, 1962), I, 161.
4. *The Doctrine of Divine Providence Opened and Applyed* (Boston, 1684), Sig. [A3] recto.
5. *An Essay for the Recording of Illustrious Providences* (1684), Sig. [A3] verso.
6. *James Janeway's Legacy* (London, 1683), p. 102.
7. *The Storm*, Sigs. [A5] verso– [A6] recto.
8. *Defoe's Review Reproduced from the Original Editions*, ed. Arthur Wellesley Secord (New York: Columbia University Press, 1938), II, 90, second pagination. Subsequent page references to *The Review* are made to this edition and will be shown in the text.
9. *The Shortest Way with the Dissenters and Other Pamphlets* (Oxford: Blackwell, 1927), p. 194. Subsequent page references to *An Appeal* are made to this edition and are shown in the text.
10. *The Life and Strange Surprizing Adventures of Robinson Crusoe* (Oxford: Blackwell, 1927), I, 14–15. Subsequent page references are made to this edition and will be shown in the text.
11. *The Reluctant Pilgrim: Defoe's Emblematic Method and Quest for Form in Robinson Crusoe* (Baltimore, 1966), p. 184. Mr. Hunter's chapter "The 'Providence' Tradition" is especially helpful for the Puritan literature of this subject.
12. *The Farther Adventures of Robinson Crusoe* (Oxford: Blackwell, 1927), II, 174. This novel appears together with *Robinson Crusoe* in three volumes. Subsequent page references to it are made to this edition and will be shown in the text.
13. Charles Gildon, *The Life and Strange Surprizing Adventures of Mr. D---De F---*, ed. Paul Dottin under the title *Robinson Crusoe Examin'd and Criticis'd* (London: J. M. Dent, 1928), pp. 88–89. Subsequent page references to Gildon are made to this edition and will be shown in the text.
14. *The History and Remarkable Life of the truly Honourable Col. Jacque* (Oxford: Blackwell, 1927), I, 205; II, 152–153. Subsequent page references are made to this edition and will be shown in the text.
15. *A Journal of the Plague Year* (Oxford: Blackwell, 1928), p. 236. Subsequent page references are made to this edition and will be shown in the text.
16. From a note by Chalmers among the George Chalmers manuscripts in the Miriam Lutcher Stark Library of the University of Texas. From these MSS. one learns that the collection was sent by Duncan to T. Chapman in late 1783 or

early 1794. With Duncan's permission, Chapman in June of 1784 sent the collection along to George Chalmers, volunteering to publish it under Chalmers' auspices (Chalmers MSS, cited with the kind permission of the Miriam Lutcher Stark Library, University of Texas).

17. Walter Wilson, *Memoirs of the Life and Times of Daniel De Foe* (London, 1830), III, 646, n. Z.

18. Daniel Defoe, *Serious Reflections of Robinson Crusoe*, in *Romances and Narratives by Daniel Defoe*, ed. George A. Aitken, 2nd. edition (London, 1899), III, 189–190, 190. All subsequent page references are made to this edition, without the volume number, and will be incorporated in the text.

19. *Memoirs of a Cavalier* (Oxford: Blackwell, 1927), p. 309.

20. William Turner, *A Compleat History of the Most Remarkable Providences* (1697), Bk. I, ch. XV, pp. 70–71.

21. For a discussion of Defoe's ideas concerning second sight, see chapters V and VI.

22. The Reverend Sabine Baring Gould, *Curiosities of Olden Times*, rev. ed. (Edinburgh, 1896), p. 263.

23. *Historical Applications* (1670), pp. 91, 90.

24. *Pseudodoxia Epidemica, or Enquiries into Vulgar Errors*, Bk. V, ch. XXIII, sec. 7, in *Works*, ed. Geoffrey Keynes (Chicago, 1964), II, 395; Thomas Woodcock (?), *An Account of Some Remarkable Passages in the Life of a Private Gentleman*, 2nd ed. (London, 1711), p. 87.

25. Hunter, p. 159.

CHAPTER I

1. In his *Robinson Crusoe and its Printing* (New York: Columbia University Press, 1925), p. 124, Henry C. Hutchins cites the annotation in Taylor's Sales Catalog regarding lot 36 (*Serious Reflections of Robinson Crusoe*) marking the first impression of 1,000 copies as "not sold."

2. Richard Baxter, *The Certainty of the Worlds of Spirits* (London, 1691), pp. 222–223; Joseph Glanvill, *Some Discourses, Sermons, and Remains*, ed. Anthony Horneck (London, 1681), p. 194.

3. Signed respectively "WHITE-WITCH," "E. S.," and "T. E.," the first two of these three letters appeared in Mist's *Weekly Journal*, Numbers 59 and 62 (January 16 and February 6, 1720) and the last two in Mist's *Collection of Miscellany Letters* (London, 1722 [probably 1721]–1727), I, 162–169. They were claimed for Defoe by William Lee and printed in Lee's *Daniel Defoe: His Life and Recently Discovered Writings* (London, 1869), II, 182–184, 193–199, though Lee, printing the third letter from the *Collection*, failed to perceive that this letter, promised in Number 63 (February 13, 1720), p. 374, had evidently never been printed in *The Weekly Journal* itself. The fact that it was preserved and included in Mist's *Collection* and the close similarity of ideas and methods in these three letters and those of Defoe in the "Vision" may strengthen Lee's ascription of them to Defoe.

4. Daniel Defoe, "A Vision of the Angelick World," in *Serious Reflections of Robinson Crusoe, Romances and Narratives by Daniel Defoe*, ed. George A. Aitken, 2nd edition (London, 1899), III, 238. Subsequent page references to the "Vision" are made to this edition, without the volume number, and will be shown in the text.

5. Isaac Ambrose, *Ministration of and Communion with Angels*, in *Compleat Works* (London, 1674), p. 94. All subsequent page references are made to this edition and will be shown in the text. Concerning Protestant reluctance to discuss some aspects of angelic ministry, see Robert Hunter West, *Milton and the Angels* (Athens: University of Georgia Press, 1955), pp. 100–101.

6. Richard Baxter, *Christian Directory*, in *Practical Works* (London, 1830), V, 235; Karl Barth, *Church Dogmatics*, trans. G. W. Bromily and R. J. Ehrlich (Edinburgh: Clark, 1961), Vol. III, Part III, p. 369.

7. Defoe, *An Essay on the History and Reality of Apparitions*, in *The Novels and Miscellaneous Works of Daniel De Foe* (Oxford, 1840–1841), XIII, 127–128. Subsequent page references to the "Essay" are made to this edition without the volume number, and will be shown in the text.

8. George Bull, *Some Important Points of Primitive Christianity Maintained and Defended* (London, 1713), II, 434.

9. For examples, see Ambrose, pp. 104–105, and Bull, II, 438.

10. For the fullest explanation of this doctrine, see Arthur O. Lovejoy, *The Great Chain of Being* (New York: Harpers, 1960).

11. Katherine M. Briggs, *The Anatomy of Puck: an Examination of Fairy Belief among Shakespeare's Contemporaries and Successors* (London: Rutledge and Kegan Paul, 1959), p. 169.

12. All references to this library are based upon a microfilm copy of the apparently unique British Museum copy of Olive Payne's sale catalogue (1731) of the libraries of Defoe and of Phillips Farewell. The author is in process of preparing an edition of this catalogue.

13. Joseph Glanvill, *Sadducismus Triumphatus*, 4th ed. (London, 1726), p. 28. The Defoe-Farewell Library included a copy of the second, 1682 edition. The Glanvill essay cited originally appeared as "Against Modern Sadducism in the Matter of Witches and Apparitions," in *Essays on Several Important Subjects in Philosophy and Religion* (London, 1676).

14. Glanvill, *A Blow at Modern Sadducism* (1668), pp. 56–57; Henry More, *An Antidote against Enthusiasm*, in *A Collection of Several Philosophical Writings*, 4th ed., (London, 1712), p. 131. Concerning such spirits, see West, p. 85.

15. Increase Mather, *Angelographia, or a Discourse concerning the Nature and Power of the Holy Angels* (Boston, 1696), Sig. [A5] recto. Subsequent page references will be made to this edition and will be shown in the text.

16. Defoe, the *Review*, "Supplement to the Advice from the Scandal Club" for November 1704, pp. 6–7. For the fullest treatment of angelic corporeity, see West.

17. Thomas Shepherd, *Several Sermons on Angels* (London, 1702), p. 42; Henry Hallywell, *A Private Letter of Satisfaction to a Friend* (London, 1667), p. 22; and Thomas Tryon, *A Treatise of Dreams and Visions*, 2nd. ed. (London, 1689), p. 181 ff. In his *Inquiries concerning the State and Oeconomy of the Angelical Worlds* (London, 1723), Reynolds was quite confused on this point and finally suggested that the issue could not be solved "this Side the Light of another World" (p. 223).

18. See Henry Lawrence, *Of our Communion and Warre with Angels* (Amsterdam[?], 1646), p. 32; John Webster, *The Displaying of Supposed Witchcraft* (London, 1677), p. 215 ff., in echo of Lawrence; Ambrose, p. 128; Joseph Hall, *The Invisible World Discovered* (London, 1659), pp. 29–30; Benjamin Camfield, *A Theological Discourse of Angels and their Ministries* (London, 1678), pp. 29–30; and Richard Saunders, *Angelographia, or a Discourse of Angels* (London, 1701), p. 53.

19. *History of Apparitions*, p. 4. See also pp. 34, 60, 218, and 260.

20. John Aubrey, *Miscellanies*, 2nd ed. (London, 1721), p. 124. A copy of this edition was in the Defoe-Farewell Library.

21. Thomas Heywood, *The Hierarchy of the Blessed Angels* (London, 1635), p. 442. See also West, p. 47.

22. John Beaumont, *An Historical, Physiological and Theological Treatise of Spirits* (London, 1705), p. 79; and *Gleanings of Antiquities* (London, 1724), pp. 191–192.

23. John Heydon, *Theomagia, or the Temple of Wisdom* (London, 1663), III, 214; Shepherd, p. 12.

24. Noel Taillepied, *A Treatise of Ghosts*, trans. Montague Summers (London: Fortune Press, 1933), p. 122.

25. Defoe, *The Consolidator, or Memoirs of Sundry Transactions from the World in the Moon*, in *The Earlier Life and the Chief Earlier Works of Daniel Defoe*, ed. Henry Morley (London: Routledge, 1889), pp. 317–318.

26. *The Political History of the Devil*, in *Novels and Miscellaneous Works* (Oxford, 1840–1841), X, 221. See also his *System of Magick*, in *ibid.*, XII, 278. Subsequent page references are made to this edition and will be shown in the text.

27. West, pp. 57–58, citing Reginald Scot, *A Discourse of Devils and Spirits*, ed. Brinsley Nicholson (London, 1886), p. 424; Samuel Freeman, "The Worship of Angels and Saints Departed," in *Popery not Founded on Scripture* (London, 1688), I, 220–222; Shepherd, pp. 80, 85; Camfield, p. 73 ff.; Hall, p. 19 ff.; Glanvill, *Sadducismus Triumphatus*, p. 35; Reynolds, *Inquiries*, pp. 176–178; Lawrence, p. 20; Increase Mather, *Angelographia*, Sig. [A3] verso—[A4] recto; West, p. 50, citing John Salkeld, *A Treatise of Angels* (London, 1613), p. 251 ff.; West, p. 4; Hallywell, p. 53; Robert Dingley, *The Deputation of Angels, or the Angell-Guardian* (London, 1654), passim; Heydon, III, 195; Matthew Smith, *The Vision, or a Prospect of Death, Heav'n, and Hell* (London, 1702), offering (on p. 72 ff.) the confirming opinions of Peter Martyr and Zanchy as well as those of his contemporaries; Mary, Lady Chudleigh, *Essays upon Several Subjects in Prose and Verse* (London, 1710), p. 51; Beaumont, *Treatise*, passim. The only American copy of *Scala Naturae* (1695) is too fragile to allow photographic reproduction, and it has not been used for this study.

28. "Vision," pp. 295–314. See the letter from Defoe to Robert Harley, *ca.* November 6, 1705, in *The Letters of Daniel Defoe*, ed. George Healey (Oxford: Oxford University Press, 1955), p. 111, n. 2. Defoe referred to this same incident involving Duckett in *HA*, p. 7, and in the *Review* for October 9, 1705.

29. Lawrence, p. 45; Isaac Barrow, *Theological Works*, ed. Alexander Napier (Cambridge, 1859), I, 229.

30. Hall, pp. 25–26; Shepherd, p. 89. According to West, p. 40, the Puritans "acknowledged that in the prosecution of moral warfare angels have certain powers over the elements."

31. See below, pp. 77–78.

32. See West, pp. 56–57.

33. Defoe, *The Fortunes and Misfortunes of the Famous Moll Flanders* (Oxford: Blackwell, 1927), I, 163–164. Subsequent page references will be made to this edition and will be shown in the text.

34. Aubrey, *Miscellanies*, pp. 110–116; William Turner, *A Compleat History of the Most Remarkable Providences* (London, 1697), Part I, ch. V, pp. 40–43; Increase Mather, *Angelographia*, pp. 69–70; Beaumont, *Treatise*, chs. V, VI.

35. Ambrose, p. 129, ff.; Bull, II, 489–490; Saunders, p. 137; Beaumont, *Treatise*, ch. VIII, p. 251.

36. Defoe, *The Life, Adventures, and Pyracies of the Famous Captain Singleton* (Oxford: Blackwell, 1927), pp. 215–216, 219. Subsequent page references will be made to this edition and will be shown in the text.

37. In his excellent study, *Defoe and Spiritual Autobiography* (Princeton: Princeton University Press, 1965), Mr. G. A. Starr has recognized this incident as "a turning point" in Crusoe's "spiritual career": ". . . only the appearance of an angel, brandishing a sword and threatening his destruction, finally forces him to repent" (pp. 60, 100). This vision, Mr. Starr comments, "however fanciful it may seem, has various precedents" (p. 106). But he cites only that of Balaam's vision of the threatening angel; and nowhere else in Defoe does he seem to recognize the ministry of the blessed angels, through dreams, hints, or other media. See especially pp. 89–90, 118–119. In his *Reluctant Pilgrim*, which has appeared since this study was completed, Mr. J. Paul Hunter has, with sensitive perception, shown the centrality of Providential care and angelic ministry in *Robinson Crusoe*.

38. Bull, II, 488.

39. Defoe, *Shortest Way*, p. 194.

40. *The Consolidator*, p. 319.

41. Walter Wilson, *Memoirs of the Life and Times of Daniel De Foe* (London, 1830), III, 556–557; Lee, I, 409; George A. Aitken, Introduction to *Robinson Crusoe*, in Defoe, *Romances and Narratives*, 2nd. ed. (London, 1899), I, lxiii.

42. Charles Gildon, *The Life and Strange Surprizing Adventures of Mr. D . . . . De F . . .* , ed. Paul Dotton, as *Robinson Crusoe Examin'd and Criticis'd* (London: J. M. Dent, 1923), pp. 68, 85, 105–106, 118.

43. The Defoe-Farewell Library included a copy of *The History of the Life and Surprizing Adventures of Mr. Duncan Campbell* (1720).

44. Defoe, *The Fortunate Mistress* (Oxford: Blackwell, 1927), I, 57–58, 60–61.

CHAPTER II

1. The failure to recognize the power of the Adversary unfortunately mars Mr. Starr's *Defoe and Spiritual Autobiography*.

2. *The Doctrine of the Passions Explained and Improved*, in *The Works of the late Reverend and Learned Isaac Watts*, ed. D. Jennings and P. Doddridge (London, 1753), II, 618 (Section XXI, 8).

3. Barth, Vol. III, Bk. III, p. 519.

4. Anthony Collins, *Discourse of Free-Thinking* (London, 1713), p. 28.

5. Roland Stromberg, *Religious Liberalism in Eighteenth-Century England* (Oxford: Oxford University Press, 1954), p. 72.

6. *Little Review*, No. 1, p. 2.

7. A second edition of the former, retitled simply *The History of The Devil*, was published by Warner the following year—a page for page reprint, with a Preface replacing the original Dedication. The third edition, a duodecimo, appeared shortly after the second. J. Brinsley, Olive Payne, and others reissued the second edition in 1734; Joseph Fisher published the fourth edition in 1739; and John Atkinson, the fifth, a duodecimo, in 1754. Subsequent eighteenth century editions appeared in London and the provinces in 1770, 1772 (a Birmingham edition with *Anecdotes of a Scoundrel, or Memoirs of Devil Dick*), 1777, 1790 (at Berwick), 1793, and 1794. In addition to the *Journal of the Plague Year* it seems to be the only volume of non-fiction by Defoe currently available in paper-backed format. A French translation appeared in Amsterdam in 1729; and a German translation, the following year. The former prompted a twenty-two page critique in the *Bibliotheque Raisonée des Ouvrages de Savans de l'Europe* for 1729 (III, Part i, 149–171). The *System of Magick* did not enjoy similar success. The advertised or alleged new editions from 1728 through 1731 are merely reissues of the unsold sheets of the first edition, printed in large supply for a similarly brisk sale, and refurbished with a new title page. The 1840 Oxford edition seems actually to have been the second edition.

8. Glanvill, *Sadducismus Triumphatus*, p. 21.

9. D. P. Walker, *The Decline of Hell: Seventeenth Century Discussions of Eternal Torment* (Chicago: University of Chicago Press, 1964), p. 75. (Compare the scholastic position as delineated in West, pp. 62, 200.)

10. Charles Leslie, *The History of Sin and Heresy*, in *The Theological Works of The Reverend Mr. Charles Leslie* (London, 1721), I, 783.

11. Isaac Ambrose, *War with Devils*, in *Compleat Works* (London, 1674), p. 5.

12. *HD*, Ch. VI; Increase Mather, "A Disquisition concerning Angelical Apparitions," separately paginated in *Angelographia*, pp. 35–36.

13. *SM*, p. 116. Compare Richard Baxter, *Christian Directory*, in *Practical Works*, III, 304.

14. Edward Langton, *Supernatural: the Doctrine of Spirits, Angels, and Demons from the Middle Ages* (London: Rider, 1934), p. 219, quoting *Table Talk*, DLXXIV.

15. Ambrose, p. 5. See also William Turner, *Compleat History*, Part I, chs. 96, 84; Richard Saunders, *Angelographia*, p. 213; Richard Boulton, *A Compleat History*

of Magick (London, 1715–1716), I, 16, and his *Possibility and Reality of Magick* (London, 1722), p. 176; John Reynolds, *Inquiries concerning the State and Oeconomy of the Angelical Worlds* (1723), p. 209, and his *View of Death* (1725), p. 74.

16. N. Orchard, *The Doctrine of Devils Proved to be the Grand Apostacy of these later Times* (London, 1676), p. 23. In his *Question of Witchcraft Debated* (1669), John Wagstaffe objected (p. 48 ff.) to assigning too much power to the Devil, as did John Webster, pp. 17–18.

17. John Spencer, *A Discourse concerning Prodigies* (London, 1665), pp. 1–2.

18. Francis Bragge, *Works* (Oxford, 1833), II, 340.

19. Hall, pp. 154–155.

20. Samuel Freeman, in *Popery not Founded*, p. 207.

21. Martin Luther, *Table Talk*, trans. William Hazlitt, Bohn ed. (London, 1857), p. 255, sec. DXCIV.

22. I. Mather, *Angelographia*, Sig. [A5] recto.

23. Cooper, in *The Mystery of Witchcraft* (London, 1617), maintained that God reveals some things to Satan, but alone knows the future (p. 131); See also Goodwin, *The Mystery of Dreames, Historically Discoursed* (London, 1658), p. 64; Saunders, *Angelographia*, pp. 55, 171; Spencer, ch. VII.

24. Turner, Part I, ch. III, pp. 16–34, and ch. XCVII.

25. *The Universal Spectator and Weekly Journal*, vol. II, No. *CCIX*, p. 1.

26. *Table Talk*, p. 257, sec. DXCVIII.

27. Jean François Baltus, *An Answer to Mr. de Fontenelle's History of Oracles* (London, 1709), p. 142.

28. *Sadducismus Triumphatus*, p. 51.

29. Ambrose, p. 6.

30. Patrick Hume, *Annotations on Milton's Paradise Lost*, in *The Poetical Works of Mr. John Milton* (Oxford, 1695), p. 164.

31. Defoe, *The Family Instructor*, Vol. II, in *The Novels and Miscellaneous Works* (Oxford, 1840), XVI, 144. Subsequent references to *The Family Instructor* will cite this edition, omitting the volume number, and will be incorporated in the text.

32. Richard Gilpin, *Daemonologia Sacra, or a Treatise of Satan's Temptations* (London, 1677), p. 77. Subsequent references will be incorporated in the text.

33. *Several Discourses*, 2nd ed. (London, 1726), p. 223. This was evidently the volume listed in the Defoe-Farewell Library as "Sermons." Listed also was Collier's sermon "God not the Origin of Evil," which was added to this volume in 1726.

34. Defoe, *The True-Born Englishman*, in *The Shortest Way with the Dissenters* (Oxford: Blackwell, 1927), p. 33.

35. Francisco Gomez de Quevedo Villegas, *The Visions*, trans. L'Estrange, 11th ed. (London, 1715), p. 103. A copy of this edition was in the Defoe-Farewell Library.

36. Maximilian Novak, however, has explored this aspect of Defoe's thought in his *Defoe and the Nature of Man* (Oxford: Oxford University Press, 1963).

37. For a somewhat limited study of this subject, see Walther Fischer, "Defoe und Milton," *Englische Studien*, XLVIII (1924), 213–227.

38. *HD*, p. 60. These lines first appeared in *Jure Divino* (folio ed. of 1706, Bk. VI, pp. 11–14), then *The Review* for August 27, 1709 (VI, 250). See my article "Blake's 'Tyger': the Nature of the Beast," *Philological Quarterly*, XLVI (1967), 488–498.

39. Milton, *Paradise Lost*, ed. Hume (Oxford, 1695), V, 603–604; and Hume, *Annotations*, p. 187.

40. West, p. 125.

41. In the Preface to his *History of Sin and Heresie* (1698) Charles Leslie had objected that the subject of the Fall had been "*degraded at last into a Play, which was design'd to have been acted upon the Stage: And tho' once happily prevented, yet it has pass'd the Press, and become the entertainment of prophane raillery*" (*Theological Works*, I, 777).

42. Walter Raleigh, *The History of the World* (London, 1614), I, 71, Bk. I, ch. v. This edition was in the Defoe-Farewell Library.

43. Richard Bovet, *Pandemonium*, ed. Montague Summers (Aldington, Kent: Hand

and Flower Press, 1951), p. 7. "For the next thing we meet with in the sacred Story, is this very *Noah* (who was the only person amongst all mankind, with his Family) whom the Almighty miraculously saved from that Universal Deluge: and from whose Loins the succeeding Generations of Men were to be derived: we see this very *Noah* exposing his shame through intemperance with Wine."

44. "After the Flood, how soon did *Nimrod* and the builders of *Babel* declare their Pride; and the whole World receiv'd this principle of the Devil, and govern'd themselves by it . . ." (*Theological Works*, I, 805).

45. See Raleigh's folding map after I, 178, and Samuel Bochart, *Geographia Sacra* (Frankfort, 1681), p. 70 ff., Bk. I, ch. XVI ff. This edition of Bochart was in the Defoe-Farewell Library.

46. Ross, *Pensebeia*, 4th ed. (London, 1664), pp. 103, 113.

47. Joseph Pitton de Tournefort, *A Voyage into the Levant*, trans. John Ozell (London, 1718), which Defoe paraphrased in *HA*, ch. XIV; Aaron Hill, *The Ottoman Empire* (1709). In the Defoe-Farewell Library two books could have supplied him with additional information: John Covel's *Some Account of the Present Greek Church* (1722), largely a theoretical attack, and the eighth edition (1723) of Humphrey Prideaux's *The True Nature of the Imposture in the Life of Mahomet*.

48. Frank E. Manuel, *The Eighteenth Century Confronts the Gods* (Cambridge: Harvard University Press, 1959), p. 22.

49. Albert L. Caillet, *Manuel Bibliographique des Sciences Phychiques ou Occultes* (Paris: Dorbon, 912), II, 90, giving the date as April 29, 1744. In *Banned Books*, however, Anne Lyon Haight gave the date as 1743 and added that it was still so listed (New York: R. R. Bowker, 1935, p. 28).

50. Bennet, 2nd ed. (Cambridge, 1701), Sig. a 1 verso. As Defoe's spokesman remarks in *A New Family Instructor*, "I have a great many very good Tracts, in my Library, wherein, all that has or can be said, on both Sides, is, I believe, summ'd up, and disputed" (p. 34). ". . . I had their own *Legends, Missals, Church-Registers*, or other authentick *Books*, written by their own Authors, to support?" (p. 108). These included not only such general attacks as Bartholomaeus Sacchi de Platina's *Apud de Vitis ac Gestis . . . Pontificium* (Cologne, 1568) and Sir Paul Rycaut's translation and continuation *The Lives of the Bishops and Popes* (1684), but R. Hospinianus's *Historia Jesuitica* (1627); the anonymous *Pyrotechnica Loyolana, Ignatian Fire-works* (1667), maintaining that the Jesuits had burned London and were now advocating the cause of Satan; Jean Claude's *Catholic Doctrine of the Eucharist in All Ages* (1683, 1684); Thomas Bennet's *Confutation of Popery*, F. Boyer's *Parallel of the . . . Pagans with . . . the Jesuits, and Unigenitus*, translated by S. Whatley (1726); and the undated *True Legend of Priests and Monks Life*, so designated in the Payne catalogue for lack of a title page. It may well have been the *Fables of Monkery* which Defoe cited derisively in *SM* (p. 127) or perhaps Gabriel d'Emiliane's recent *Frauds of Romish Monks Set Forth in Eight Letters* (1691, 1725, with a sequel that same year). Though there was evidently no copy in the Defoe-Farewell Library, Defoe seems to have drawn heavily upon Henry Wharton's *Enthusiasm of the Church of Rome Demonstrated in Some Observations upon the Life of Ignatius Loyola* (1688).

51. Gerald Robertson Cragg, *From Puritanism to the Age of Reason: a Study of Changes in Religious Thought within the Church of England, 1660 to 1700* (Cambridge: Cambridge University Press, 1950), p. 76, n. 1.

52. Paul Dottin, Notes, in Gildon, p. 180.

53. Montague Summers, *Witchcraft and Black Magic* (London: Rider, 1946), p. 215; Edwin Beresford Chancellor, *The Hell Fire Club* (London: Philip Allan, 1925), p. 3.

54. Notices signed "W. L.," "Orthodox," and "Antloethiops," which appeared in issues of *Applebee's Journal* for May 6, 13, and 20, 1721, admit that despite a diligent search, nothing of these societies can be found. All these notices are attributed to Defoe by William Lee (II, 371–373, 373–374, 377–378).

55. Summers, *Witchcraft and Black Magic*, p. 218.

56. Ronald Fuller, *Hell-Fire Francis* (London: Chatto and Windus, 1939), p. 53. See also Summers, *Witchcraft and Black Magic*, p. 220.

57. Of Kircher's books, the Defoe-Farewell Library contained *Ars Magna Lucis et Umbrae* (Amsterdam, 1671), *China Monumenta* (Amsterdam, 1677), *Iter Exstaticum Coeleste* (Rome, 1656), *Mundus Subterraneus* (Amsterdam, 1668), and *Physiologia Kircheraina Experimentalis* (1680).

58. *Marlowe's Doctor Faustus, 1604–1616*, ed. W. W. Greg (Oxford: Clarendon Press, 1950), p. 178.

59. The Defoe-Farewell Library contained a copy of Giovanni Battista Casali's *De Profanis et Sacris Veteribus Ritis* (1664), which examined the religious customs of the Egyptians, Romans, and Christians, and it contained also a number of books concerning the Sybyllines oracles: David Blondel's *Des Sibylles Celebrees* (1646), which exposed the oracles as impostures and castigated the doctrines they voiced; Isaac Voss's *De Sibyllinis* (1679); and Sir John Floyer's translation *The Sibylline Oracles* (1713), which Defoe cited in *SM* (p. 193). In Floyer, Defoe knew at least one defender of the old tradition; and he probably knew also the work of Baltus. Even if he failed to notice the contemporary controversy created in England by the translation of Baltus in 1709 and 1710, he could hardly have been unaware of its continuation in 1713–1716, when there appeared translations of the Oracles by defenders, Floyer and Whiston, and subsequently vindications of their authenticity by both.

60. Matthew Smith, p. 3.

61. Cecil L'Estrange Ewen, *Witchcraft and Demonianism* (London: Heath Cranton, 1933), pp. 381–384, cites printed accounts based upon a letter from "Ralph Davis of Northampton to William Simons of London, Merchant." The account is regarded as a hoax by Wallace Notestein, *A History of Witchcraft in England from 1558 to 1718* (Washington: American Historical Association, 1911), pp. 375–383.

62. Edward Arber, ed., *The Term Catalogues, 1668–1707* (London, 1903–1906), III, 130. This is probably the same pamphlet as *Love's True Oracle, or a New and Curious Fortune Book . . . To which is Added, the Signification of Dreams and Moles*, which, the 1965 BM Catalogue hazards (XXIII, 1076), might have been published at Newcastle about 1810.

CHAPTER III

1. Defoe, *Serious Reflections*, pp. 295–296. In July of 1956 Mr. Coleman O. Parsons published a brief account of English ghost collections anterior to Defoe's, "Ghost Stories before Defoe," in *Notes and Queries*, CCI, 293–298. See also Mr. Parsons's Introduction to the facsimile reproduction of Joseph Glanvill's *Sadducismus Triumphatus*, 3rd ed. (Gainesville, Fla.: Scholars' Facsimiles and Reprints, 1966), pp. xiv–xv.

2. Lee, I, 426–427. A second issue with the same title was sold the following year by A. Millar. On November 23, 1728, J. Peele and others advertised it as *The Secrets of the Invisible World Disclos'd; or, an Universal History of Apparitions*, above Defoe's pseudonym Andrew Moreton; and on February 13, 1729, an issue bearing this same title was advertised by John Clarke, A. Millar, and J. Green. The so-called third and fourth editions of 1738 and 1740 are in fact merely reissues of the second edition. The 1840 edition is thus the third and last.

3. The editor of *A View of the Invisible World: or, General History of Apparitions* (1752) included a new Introduction, excised most of the expository matter, and provided a score of new stories to match the score from Defoe. But the new stories take up only about a third of the space devoted to Defoe's. *The Secrets of*

the *Invisible World Laid Open* (1770) includes entire chapters from Defoe; and although the early sections were rewritten to condense and combine Defoe's materials, few new stories were added. The most notable is that of the apparition of Mrs. Veal, in the Payne version rather than in Defoe's more familiar account. *Visits from the World of Spirits* (1791), based upon the 1770 compilation, contains a new preface and some additional stories, but most of the material comes from Defoe.

4. As late as 1836, T. Ottway's *Spectre, or News from the Invisible World* used eight.

5. Boulton, *Compleat History*, I, 263–270.

6. See above, pp. 46–47.

7. See above, p. 27.

8. The Author has assumed that the "Joseph Beaton," Defoe's Boston co-partner according to Chancery records, was really Joseph Beacon. Distinguishing *c* and *t* in contemporary legal script is sometimes a difficult matter. See James R. Sutherland, "Some Early Troubles of Daniel Defoe," *Review of English Studies*, IX (1933), 279–280.

9. Eliott O' Donnell, *Ghosts with a Purpose* (London, 1951), pp. 117–118. O'Donnell credits "T. Charley" with the story.

10. Deodat Lawson, *Christ's Fidelity the only Shield against Satan's Malignity*, 2nd ed. (Boston, 1704), pp. 98–100.

11. *A Strange, but True Relation* (London, 1678), p. 5.

12. For details, see Moore, *Daniel Defoe*, pp. 30–31.

13. Bovet, p. 121.

14. Defoe to Robert Harley, *ca.* November 6, 1705, in *Letters*, p. 111.

15. Baxter, *Certainty*, p. 7.

16. Hall, Bk. II, sec. 7, pp. 121–128; and Hallywell, p. 62.

17. Thomas Hobbes, *Leviathan*, Part III, ch. XXXIV, in *English Works*, ed. Sir William Molesworth (London, 1839–1845), III, 388.

18. Ludwig Lavater, *Of Ghosts and Spirites Walking by Nyght*, trans. R. H. (London, 1572), p. 171.

19. William Drage, *Daimonomageia*, a *Small Treatise of Sicknesses and Diseases from Witchcraft* (London, 1665), p. 20.

CHAPTER IV

1. Much of the first part of this chapter is quoted or adapted from the author's "Defoe and Mrs. Bargrave's Story," *Philological Quarterly*, XXXIII (October 1954), 388–395, by kind permission of the editor.

The Apparition of Mrs. Veal was evidently first published by Benjamin Bragg on July 5 or 6, 1706, a few days after Defoe in *The Review* turned aside from economic, legal, and political subjects and considered in a series of issues, "the invisible Agency of supernatural Operations" (III, 313, for July 2, 1706). Probably because of the fact that the title page carries the date 1705—that of the séance—as well as 1706—that of publication—a number of early bibliographers dated it 1705; and in his *Checklist of the Writings of Daniel Defoe* (Bloomington: University of Indiana Press, 1962, pp. 43–44), Mr. John Robert Moore agreed, suggesting that Bragg's edition was pirated. But Bragg's 1706 edition gives every bibliographical indication of being a first edition, especially with its blank final page. Moreover Bragg alone advertised *The Apparition of Mrs. Veal* in the periodicals and in the Term Catalogue. He evidently first advertised it in *The Daily Courant* for July 6, 1706 (Arthur Scouten, "*The Loyal Post*, a Rare Queen Anne Newspaper, and Daniel Defoe," *Bulletin of the New York Public Library*, LIX, 1955, 196, n. 2). In November 1706 he advertised it in the

Term Catalogues (III, 525). In *The Daily Courant* for April 9, 1707, Bragg advertised the "3rd Edition" (Moore, *Checklist*, p. 43). It seems inconceivable that if Bragg's edition had been pirated he alone would have advertised it—or even advertised it at all—and that the publishers of Drelincourt would have acquired and used his edition, for on September 30, 1706, Bragg's edition became part of the late 1706 issue of the fourth edition of Drelincourt.

2. The letters of E. B. and of Stephen Gray were printed by Frank Higenbottam in "The Apparition of Mrs. Veal to Mrs. Bargrave at Canterbury, 8th of September, 1705: Two New Contemporary Manuscript Sources," *Archaeologica Cantiana*, LXXIII (1959), 154–166. That of Miss Luykn was published by C. E. Firth in "Defoe's *True Relation of the Apparition of Mrs. Veal*," *Review of English Studies*, VII (January 1931), 1–6; and the article in *The Loyal Post* was reprinted by Arthur S. Scouten in "An Early Printed Report on the Apparition of Mrs. Veal," *RES*, n.s., VI (1955), 259–263. Details of the 1714 interview were published by George A. Aitken, in "Defoe's 'Apparition of Mrs. Veal,' " *Nineteenth Century*, XXXVII (January 1895), 95–100. The "Spavan" account is quoted from Charles Drelincourt, *The Christian's Defense against the Fears of Death*, trans. and abridged by J. Spavan (Boston, 1744). Payne's account is cited from the author's reprint: "*The Apparition of Mrs. Veal*: a Neglected Account," *PMLA*, LXIX (June 1954), 523–541. All quotations from these sources will be taken from these editions, and references will be incorporated in the text, without volume numbers. All these accounts are available in *Accounts of the Apparition of Mrs. Veal*, Augustan Reprint Society Publication No. 115 (1965). Unfortunately the editor, Mr. Manuel Schonhorn, does not indicate the provenance of his typescripts.

3. George Chalmers, *The Life of Daniel De Foe* (London, 1790), p. 74.

4. See Chapters VI and VII.

5. A more detailed analysis of the material here summarized is provided in the author's "Defoe and Mrs. Bargrave's Story."

6. Dorothy Gardiner, "What Canterbury Knew of Mrs. Veal and Her Friends," *RES*, VII (1931), 197.

7. *The Penny London Post*, No. 171 (May 30, 1726), p. 4. For permission to quote from the unique copy of this number the writer is indebted to the Library of Harvard University.

8. She was interviewed there by Payne. See my article "*The Apparition of Mrs. Veal*: a Neglected Version," *PMLA*, LXIX (1954), 523–541.

9. James Sutherland in his *Defoe* (Philadelphia, 1938), p. 243n., so quotes *Read's Journal* for November 1, 1718.

10. Information from P. Long, Esq., of the Bodleian, citing Baker's own annotated copies of the periodical.

11. *The Universal Spectator*, No. CCIX (October 7, 1732), p. 1. The late Mr. George Sherburn graciously allowed me the use of his private file.

12. *Ibid.*, No. CCCXX (November 23, 1734).

13. Henry Fielding, *Tom Jones*, Book VIII, chap. i (London, 1749), II, 174.

14. Augustus M. Toplady, *Works* (London, 1825), III, 278.

15. *Ibid.*, VI, 234.

16. James Boswell, *Life of Johnson*, ed. G. B. Hill and L. F. Powell (Oxford: Clarendon Press, 1934), II, 163.

17. See John Lyon, *The History of the Town and Port of Dover* (Dover, 1813), I, 98–116.

18. Arthur W. Secord, "A September Day in Canterbury: the Veal-Bargrave Story," *Journal of English and Germanic Philology*, LIV (1955), 648.

19. Arthur H. Scouten, "At that Moment of Time: Defoe and the Early Accounts of the Apparition of Mistress Veal," *Ball State Teachers College Forum*, II (Winter, 1961–1962), 45, 50.

20. Tanner MSS. in the Bodleian, as quoted by the Rev. C. Eveleigh Woodruff, "Letters relating to the Condition of the Church in Kent," *Archaeologica Cantiana*, XXI (1895), 177–178.

21. Paul Dottin, *Daniel Defoe et ses Romans* (Paris, 1924), I, 159. See also John Robert Moore, *Daniel Defoe: Citizen of the Modern World* (Chicago: University of Chicago Press, 1958), p. 169. Subsequent page references are made to this edition and will be shown in the text.

22. Defoe to Robert Harley, April 1706 (?), in *Letters*, pp. 115, 118.

23. This possibility is asserted as a certainty by Mr. Scouten in his "At that Moment," p. 48.

24. In his interesting study "John Norris and the Veal-Bargrave Story," *Modern Language Notes*, LXXV (1960), 646–651, George B. Wasserman suggested that the striking parallels between some of Norris's work and Mrs. Bargrave's story seem to show that Defoe, or Mrs. Bargrave, used Norris partly as a pattern. The appearance of the Norris material in Gray's letter to Flamsteed of course eliminates Defoe from suspicion on this point.

25. This conventional aspect of the ghost story seems exaggerated by Mr. Coleman O. Parsons in his "Ghost Stories before Defoe," *Notes and Queries*, CCI (July 1956), 293–298.

26. See note 3 of this chapter.

27. *Life of Johnson*, II, 164, n. 4.

CHAPTER V

1. Eustace F. Bosanquet, *English Printed Almanacks and Prognostications: a Bibliographical History to the Year 1600* (London, 1917), p. xii.

2. Defoe advertised as ready for sale "Andrews," probably *News from the Stars*, though William Andrews, who had begun astrological predictions in 1656 with a Preface contributed by William Lilly, was of course long dead; "Chapman," probably *The English Chapman's and Traveller's Almanack*; "Coley," or *Merlinus Anglicus Junior*, though Henry Coley himself probably died about 1695; *Culpepper Revived*; "Dade," though John Dade had begun publishing almanacs as early as 1591, and William Dade at least as early as 1640; *Dove, Speculum Anni*, which Jonathan Dove had founded by 1640; *Fly, an Almanac*, *Speculuum Uranicum, or an Almanac and Prognostication*, by Thomas Fowle; "Gadbury," evidently *Ephemeris, or a Diary*, probably then edited by John Gadbury, though the famous Job Gadbury lived until 1715; Francis Moore's *Vox Stellarum*, which enjoyed an existence stretching into the present century; the even more famous John Partridge's *Merlinus Liberatus*; *Perkins*, first published by Samuel, then F. Perkins; *Pond, an Almanack*, founded early in the previous century by Edward Pond and now, in 1705, issued from Saffron Walden, doubtless by a relative; *Rose*, originally begun by George Rose about 1660; William Salmon's *London Almanack*, a "prophetic" almanac; Richard Saunders' *Apollo Angelicanus: the English Apollo*; *Swallow, an Almanac*, begun at least as early as 1634 by John Swallow; John Tanner's *Angelus Britannicus*; John Tipper's *Ladies Diary, or the Women's Almanack*, the third issue, by a Coventry schoolmaster; Thomas Trigge's *Calendarium Astrologicum*; T. White's *White, a New Almanacke and Prognostication*; *Olympia Domata, or an Almanack*, begun by Vincent Wing about 1652 and continued by John Wing (a nephew), Tycho Wing, and Vincent Wing, Jr.; *Poor Robin*, begun about 1664 by William Winstanley and continued by others, but now, in 1705, devoid of political predictions; *Woodhouse, a New Almanack and Prognostication*, begun about 1604 by W. Woodhouse and now carried on by John Woodhouse.

3. In addition to these twenty-five advertised by Defoe as ready on November 13, 1705, at least eighteen others were available during this year or by the time Defoe began his prophecies: J. Chattock's *Celestial Observations, or a Complete Ephemeris* (London, 1708), later (1710) entitled *Telescopium Anglicanum, or*

an *Ephemeris*; William Cookson's *Manolologion, or an Ephemeris of the Coelestial Motions*; Andrew Crumpsty's *New Almanack . . . fitted for the Meridian of Dublin*; M. F.'s *Almanack*; *Mercurius Oxoniensis, or the Oxford Intelligencer*, published by M. G. in London in 1707; Richard Gibson's almanacs, which shifted title about this time, from *Astrologus Britannicus*, in 1707, to *Vox Solis*, printed in Gosport in 1711; *Gloria in Excelsis, or Good News from the Stars* (Aberdeen and Edinburgh); John Goldsmith's *Goldsmith, an Almanack*, which appeared from 1674 until 1838; *The London Oracle, being a New Year's Gift*; *Merry Andrew, or an Almanack after a New Fashion* (Edinburgh); *The Oxford Almanack*, a folio sheet printed at Oxford and prompting, in successive years, *An Explanation of the Designs of the Oxford Almanack for 1711* and *The Oxford Almanack of 1712 Explain'd, or the Emblems of it Unriddl'd* (Steele dedicated his *Bickerstaff's Predictions for the Year 1712*, one recalls, to the editor of this almanac); George Parker's *Merlinus Liberatus*, which continued publication until about the middle of the nineteenth century; Rider's *British Merlin*, begun about 1674 by Cardanus Rider and continued by William and Cardanus Rider; John Thomson's *Torryburn's New Almanack* (1711) and *Edinburgh's New Almanack* (1712–1714); John Tipper's *Great Britain's Diary, or the Union Almanack*; and John Whalley's "prophetic" almanacs, called about this time *Astrologus Britannicus*.

4. Francis Moore, *Vox Stellarum, being an Almanack for . . . 1708* (London, 1707). Since these almanacs were unpaginated and some have lost their signatures through cropping or crumbling, it is sometimes easiest to refer to the month.

5. Job Gadbury, *Ephemeris, of a Diary for . . . 1708* (London, 1707), Sig. [A6], recto.

6. John Partridge, *Merlinus Liberatus, being an Almanack for . . . 1708* (London, 1707), Sig. [B4] recto; Gadbury, Sig. [B5] recto.

7. *The Prose Works of Jonathan Swift*, ed. Herbert Davis (Oxford, 1939), II, 138, 142. Subsequent references to Swift will cite this edition and be incorporated in the text.

8. Button to Defoe, *ca.* December 25, 1710, in Defoe, *Letters*, p. 304. The editor, Mr. George Healey, kindly sent me his photostat of the original letter for comparison. The brackets are Mr. Healey's.

9. Defoe, *The British Visions, or Isaac Bickerstaff's Twelve Prophecies for the Year 1711*, Sig. [A2], recto. Except where otherwise specified, the first edition, printed at Newcastle, is cited. It consists of twelve leaves and seems to be a 16mo printed in half sheets. The title page carries a crudely designed head, centered. Sigs. [A1] recto and [B4] verso are blank. There is a copy in the Boston Public Library. The first London printing, of which there is a copy in the Harvard College Library, has a slightly different title: *The British Visions, or Isaac Bickerstaff, Sen., being Twelve Prophecies for the Year 1711*. It is a single octavo sheet, like the second London printing, which carries the same title except that the "Sen." of the first London printing is altered to "Senr." There is a copy in the Boston Public Library.

10. It would be a mistake to infer that the Newcastle printing was published there, for Button was probably never intended to act as publisher of this second prophecy. In *The Review* Defoe implied that it had been offered to Baker in February; and on April 26, 1711, he speaks of "the true Copy, which I had directly from *Newcastle*, and which was first Publish'd by the Publisher of this Paper [Baker]" (VIII, 54).

11. *The British Visions*, p. 7. He also refers to himself, as "I, *Bickerstaff* the Aged" (p. 22). It is also so signed and so introduced, for the persona in passing refers to his successful prediction of Partridge's death (p. 3), and so entitled.

12. Perhaps Defoe was aping Swift's prediction: "The Affairs of *Poland* are this Month [August] entirely settled: *Augustus* resigns his Pretensions . . ." Swift, *Prose Works*, (II, 148). It is also barely possibly that Defoe accidentally predicted the death of the Dauphin by imitating Swift here also.

13. Button to Defoe, in *Letters*, p. 304.

14. In the *Review* of August 12, 1712, Defoe replaces the March death of General

Catinate with the August death of the Duke de Vendôme, as satisfying the prediction of the July demise of the "great *French* General."

15. Defoe, *The Highland Visions, or the Scots New Prophecy, Declaring in Twelve Visions what Strange Things shall Come to Pass in the Year 1712* (London, 1712), p. 3. Subsequent references will be incorporated in the text.
16. Defoe, *The Second-Sighted Highlander, or Predictions and Foretold Events, especially about the Peace, By the famous Scots Highlander, being Ten new Visions for the year 1713*, (London, 1713), Sig. [A2] recto.
17. S. A. Mitchell, *Eclipses of the Sun*, 4th ed. (New York, 1935), pp. 58, 128.
18. Edmund Halley, *A Description of the Passage of the Shadow of the Moon, over England, in the Total Eclipse of the Sun, on the 22d. Day of April 1715 in the Morning* (London, 1715).
19. Moore, *Checklist*, p. 123.
20. Defoe, *The Second-Sighted Highlander, being Four Visions of the Eclypse, and Something of what may Follow* (London, 1715), pp. 42, 44, 45,
21. William Peterfield Trent, "Daniel Defoe" in *CHEL*, IX, 425.
22. Joseph Addison, *The Freeholder* (London, 1758), pp. 189–190.

CHAPTER VI

1. *The Works of Daniel Defoe*, ed. G. H. Maynadier (New York: Sproul, 1903), IV, xvii; Wright, *The Life of Daniel Defoe* (London: C. J. Farncombe, 1931), p. 268. Despite the intervening scholarship, Mr. Wright here made only stylistic changes from his first edition of 1894, though his 1931 Preface advertised that the new edition had been "almost entirely re-written."
2. "A Remarkable Passage of an Apparition," in *Romances and Narratives of Daniel Defoe*, ed. George A. Aitken (London: J. M. Dent, 1895), IV, 239–240.
3. "Bibliographical Notes on Defoe," *The Nation* (London), LXXXIV, No. 2188 (June 6, 1907), 516n.
4. "A Catalogue," p. 5, bound with Margaret Pennyman, *Miscellanies in Prose and Verse* (London: Curll, 1740).
5. Mrs. Anna Eliza Bray, "General Preface," *The White Hoods: an Historical Romance* (London, 1845), pp. xxx–xxxi; *Trelany of Trelawne* (London, 1845), p. 435.
6. Lee, "Passages of an Apparition," *Notes and Queries*, 3rd ser., X (November 24, 1866), 417–418.
7. Jago-Arundell, *The Gentleman's Magazine*, LXXX (1810), Part II, p. 103; *Notes and Queries*, 2nd ser., XI (1861), 410; W. P. Courtney, "Francis Arundell," in *DNB*.
8. Hawker, "The Botathen Ghost," *All the Year Round*, XVII (May 18, 1867), 503.
9. Alfred Farthing Robbins, "A Cornish Ghost Story," *The Cornish Magazine*, I (1898), 290; S. Baring-Gould, *Cornish Characters and Strange Events* (London: John Lane, 1909), p. 73.
10. The letter quoted, of November 27, 1850, is in C. E. Byles, *The Life and Letters of R. S. Hawker* (London: John Lane, 1905), p. 212. See also pp. 65–66, 90, 489, 440.
11. *Ibid*, p. 99.
12. Baring-Gould, *Cornish Characters*, facing p. 72, and p. 79. My colleague John Talmadge kindly drew my attention to this gem.
13. Dyer, *The Ghost World* (London, 1893), p. 202.
14. Summers, *The History of Witchcraft and Demonology* (New York: University Books, 1956), pp. 232–233.
15. Robbins, "Defoe's 'Remarkable Passage of an Apparition,'" *Notes and Queries*, 8th ser., VIII (November 2, 1895), 350.

16. "Dorothy Dingley," *The Speaker*, XII, 394, 395.
17. Robbins, "Defoe's 'Remarkable Passage of an Apparition,' " p. 350.

CHAPTER VII

1. Chalmers, *Life* (1790). It was not included among the attributions of the earlier versions of the biography in 1785.
2. *The Spectator*, ed. Donald F. Bond (Oxford: Oxford University Press, 1965), I, 129. Subsequent page references to *Spectator* are made to this edition and will be shown in the text.
3. *The Tatler*, ed. George A. Aitken (London, 1898), I, 126–127.
4. Moore, *A Defoe Checklist*, p. 173.
5. *The Weekly Medley*, p. 168, from a microfilm of the evidently unique complete file at the Bodleian. All subsequent page references to *The Weekly Medley* are made to this edition and will be shown in the text.
6. *In October next will be publish'd, A very Entertaining and useful History, containing an Account of the Birth, Education and Profession of the celebrated Mr. Duncan Campbell, the famous Dumb Gentleman, famous for his writing down the Name of any Stranger at the first Sight; setting forth the various surprizing Adventures of his Life, and the wonderful and mysterious Methods of Prediction, which he hath made use of for the information of Persons of all Stations of Life, that have consulted him, from the time he was five or six Years of Age, to this present Year, written by a Scotch Gentleman. NB. Mr. Campbell for the Conveniency of Persons of Quality who please to consult him, resides still in the Spring-Gardens, at the back-side of the Ship-Tavern Charing-Cross"* (p. 354).
7. Under the mistaken heading "Shortly will be published, Proposals for printing by Subscription, a Number of Books, entitled A History of the Life" the long advertisement was repeated, but it announced that publication was "now put off for a small time longer. He lives at the Corner of Exeter-Change in the Strand" (p. 444). This confusion was cleared up the following week in the issue for December 19–26, 1719, under the proper heading: "Very speedily will be published." All data concerning the proposals were omitted, and there was added at the end, "Mr. Campbell lives at the Corner of Exeter Court by Exeter-Change in the Strand, where he now gives Attention to those Gentlemen and Ladies that please to consult him" (p. 448). This advertisement was included in the next three issues, omitted only in the final number of *The Weekly Medley*.
8. Just before the biography actually appeared there was produced on the London stage an afterpiece which may well have been an attempt to exploit it. On March 24, 1720, there was presented at King's Theater, Spring Garden, *Harlequin a Sham Astrologer*. It doubtless profited from the popular notice which had been given the forthcoming biography of the seer. On April 5 evidently the same afterpiece was advertised for Lincoln's Inn Fields as *Harlequin the Sham Astrologer*. *The London Stage*, Part 2 (1700–1729), ed. Emmett Avery (Carbondale: Southern Illinois University Press, 1960), II, 574–575.
9. Lee, I, 323n. No W. Langley then residing in Oxford appears in Joseph Foster's *Alumni Oxonienses 1715–1886* (Oxford, 1888–1892).
10. It was published by T. Bickerton.
11. Moore, *Checklist*, p. 174. Sheets from the second corrected edition can be easily distinguished from those of the first edition by means of the press numbers at the foot of certain leaves. The first edition lacks press numbers except for *1* at the foot of leaves [A5] verso, a verso, [R8] verso, S verso, [T7] verso, [T8] recto, X2 verso, and [X7] recto. The second edition shows several different presses at work, and each sheet is marked, sometimes differently for inner and

outer forms. Press number *1* appears at the foot of leaves C verso, [G8] recto, [I8] recto, [P8] recto, [Q7] verso, [S7] verso, [T5] verso, [U7] verso, and [X6] recto; *2* appears at the foot of leaves A3 verso, B verso, [D7] verso, [E8] recto, F verso, H verso, [L8] recto, [M6] recto, [N7] verso, O verso; press number *4*, on [a3] verso, [K7] verso, [08] verso, [P8] verso, R2 verso, [S6] verso, and T2 verso. Sheets of the inserted *Mr. Campbell's Packet* show no press numbers.

12. William Bond and Martha Fowke, *Clio and Strephon, being the Second Part of the Platonic Lovers* (London, 1732), p. 15n. Copies of the *Supernatural Philosopher* at Harvard and the Boston Public Library lack Steele's commendation. Either the cancel leaf bearing this advertisement escaped the notice of the binders of these copies, or Steele gave his commendation for the second state of this issue, the so-called second "edition" of it mentioned by Mr. Moore (*Checklist*, p. 174) as appearing July 23, 1728.

13. Thus the Trent copy of the 1739 issue in the Boston Public Library is the second edition except for sheets A, R, and U–X, which are first edition; and the Trent copy of the 1748 issue there is the second edition except for sheets H and I, which are first edition. These data are pointed out by John Alden in his *Catalog of the Defoe Collection in the Boston Public Library* (Boston: G. K. Hall, 1966), p. 55.

14. William Bond, *The History of the Life and Adventures of Mr. Duncan Campbell*, in Daniel Defoe, *The Novels and Miscellaneous Prose Works of Daniel Defoe* (Oxford, 1840–1841), XIX, 224–225. Subsequent page references to *Duncan Campbell* are made to this edition, omitting the volume number, and will be shown in the text.

15. George Frisbie Whicher, *The Life and Romances of Mrs. Eliza Haywood* (New York: Columbia University Press, 1915), pp. 80–81.

16. Eliza Haywood, *A Spy upon the Conjuror, or a collection of Surprising Stories* (London, 1724), p. 1. For details of publication, see Whicher, pp. 80–83.

17. Duncan Campbell, *The Friendly Daemon, or the Generous Apparition* (London, 1726), p. 9. Subsequent references will be shown in the text.

18. Duncan Campbell, *Secret Memoirs of the late Mr. Duncan Campbel, the Famous Deaf and Dumb Gentleman, written by Himself* (London, 1732), p. 3, Sig. [A3] recto and verso. Further references will be incorporated in the text.

19. Robert Halsband, *The Life of Mary Wortley Montagu* (Oxford: Oxford University Press, 1956), pp. 118–119, citing Joseph Spence, "Anecdotes," Huntingdon Library MS., f. 380.

20. Great Britain, *Calendar of State Papers, Domestic Series, of the Reign of Queen Ann,* vol. II (1703–1704) (London, 1924), ed. Robert P. Mahaffy, p. 323, citing State Papers, Domestic, Entry Book, 387, p. 351.

21. Charles Dalton, *English Army Lists and Commission Registers, 1661–1714* (London, 1892–1904), IV, 44; George Aitken, Notes, in *The Spectator,* ed. Aitken (London: Nimmo, 1898), V, 10, n. 2.

22. Compare *Duncan Campbell*, pp. 7–8, with Martin Martin, *A Description of the Western Islands of Scotland* (Glasgow, 1884), p. 371.

23. Compare *Duncan Campbell*, pp. 16, 18, with Johannes Scheffer, *The History of Lapland* (London, 1704), pp. 282–292, 283.

24. At least Campbell's name does not appear in the Readex microcard *English Newspapers and Periodicals: Index* for 1700.

25. William P. Trent, for example, in his *Daniel Defoe: How to Know Him* (Indianapolis: Bobbs Merrill, 1916), took refuge behind a general statement: "Whether Defoe wrote the *History* of the Scotch fortune-teller alone or in collaboration is a tangled point in his bibliography which cannot be discussed here . . ." (p. 212). Nor elsewhere, evidently, for he dismissed the problem briefly in his "Bibliographical Notes on Defoe": "I have . . . little intention of . . . endeavouring to clear up a slight doubt that hangs over the authorship of 'The Life and Adventures of Mr. Duncan Campbell' " (*Nation* [London], June 6, 1907, p. 517).

26. Paul Dottin, "Daniel De Foe et les Sciences Occultes," *Revue Anglo-Americaine*, I, 105 (December 1923).

27. Dottin, *Daniel De Foe et ses Romans*, I, 261.

28. H. C. Hutchins, Defoe bibliography, *CBEL*, II, 506.

29. Moore, pp. 173–174.

30. Whicher, pp. 78–79.

31. John Aubrey, *Miscellanies* (London, 1696), pp. 178–180. This edition of Aubrey is used only for this chapter.

32. Thomas Dych and William Pardon, *A New General English Dictionary*, 8th ed. (London, 1754), under "S."

33. Louis Moréri, *The Great Historical, Geographical, Genealogical and Poetical Dictionary*, 2nd ed., enlarged by Jeremy Collier (London, 1701), II, under "T."

34. *The Spectator*, "Volume the Ninth" (London, 1753), p. 162. Subsequent page references to *The Spectator* are made to this edition and will be shown in the text.

35. *The Plain Dealer* (London, 1724–1725), No. VII, verso.

36. Moore, *Checklist*, p. 173.

37. Indeed Curll and Campbell may have intended interesting the gullible Beaumont in the undertaking, but if so, Beaumont's rustication or perhaps his disillusionment with the seer prevented his making satisfactory progress with the projected biography. Or Curll and Campbell may have intended merely to borrow largely from Beaumont without actually employing him, and brought in Bond only when it became apparent that Campbell could not complete the book himself. Already in 1715–1716 Curll had been a party to wholesale pilfering from Beaumont, in Richard Boulton's *Compleat History of Magick, Sorcery, and Witchcraft*.

38. Lee, II, 32, quoting Mist's *Weekly Journal* for April 5, 1718. See also Ralph Straus, *The Unspeakable Curll* (London: Chapman and Hall, 1927) pp. 79–82.

39. Edmund Curll, *The Curliad* (London, 1729), pp. 24–25. See also Straus, pp. 133, 263. Defoe's alleged authorship of the biography of Daniel Williams, published by Curll in 1718, has not been argued anywhere and can thus hardly be used as a valid datum here.

40. Rushbrook Parish, *Rushbrook Parish Registers, 1567 to 1850, with Jermyn and Davers Annals*, ed. S. H. A. H. (Woodbridge, 1903), p. 66.

41. *The Theatre*, with an Introduction by John Loftis (Ann Arbor: Augustan Reprint Society, 1948), reproducing No. XXIV, verso (May 7, 1720).

42. *Mercuris Politicus*, May 1720, pp. 44–45; July 1720, pp. 60–61. Subsequent page references are made to this edition and are shown in the text.

43. The subtitle is changed from *Monthly Observations on the Affairs of Great Britain, with the most Material Occurrences in Europe* to *A Monthly Historical Account of the Most Material Occurrences in all Parts of the World, and more particularly of the Affairs of Great Britain*. A new printer as well as new editor seems indicated by change from continuous signatures and pagination to those separate for each issue and by the replacement of the hitherto standard headpiece by a variety of narrower ones. Shifts in the treatment of material include the division of foreign reports by countries, a detailed calendar of particular events, with sections ranged under such topics as Fires, Robbers, Weekly Papers, Stocks, and a gradual refinement of some of these sections into such subsections as Murders, Self-Murders, Accidental Deaths, and Sudden Deaths: Gone now is the resemblance, marked before, to Defoe's *Review*. In the May 1720 issue Defoe's *Manufacturer* and *Commentator* are singled out for severe criticism (pp. 45–46), as the former was in the March issue (p. 48).

44. Here again there is a change in the method of reporting foreign news, with editorial remarks supposedly appended to the news and clearly designated "Remarks" for each country. Though no external evidence would suggest that perhaps the last may have been Bond himself. His *Weekly Medley*, defunct early the same year, is not entirely different.

45. The *DNB* article was contributed by E. S. Shuckburgh. For Pope's references see *The Dunciad*, Twickenham 2nd edition (London: Methuen, 1953), pp. 110–111, 164, 111n., 41. Apparently James Sutherland, like previous editors of Pope, was unaware of the fact that Bond's 1728 *Progress of Dulness* was merely a reprint of "The Parallel," in *Mr. Campbell's Packet* (1720).

46. Straus, p. 287.

47. *Secret Memoirs*, pp. 26–32. According to correspondent "M. R.," "He now writes Hackney against the Government, being employed and paid by one H--s, a Nonjuring Parson; but when the Government desired to speak to him for some of his wry Steps, the Slippery Wretch step'd out of the way, and put a poor Man, one *Hardwick* to own the Paper in his Room . . ." (*Thursday's Journal*, October 8–15, 1719, p. 2).

48. See Ralph M. Williams, *Poet, Painter, and Parson: the Life of John Dyer* (New York: Bookman Associates, 1956), pp. 41–44.

49. Bond, *Verses Sacred to the Memory of the most Noble Henrietta, late Duchess of Grafton* (London?, 1726?), p. 14n.

50. Mrs. Eliza Haywood, *Memoirs of a Certain Island Adjacent to the Kingdom of Utopia*, 2nd ed. (London, 1726), II, 104, and "Key," II, 2.

51. W. P. Courtney, "Richardson Pack," in *DNB*; Dalton, V, 189; *Rushbrook Parish Registers*, p. 369; Pack, "Bury Toasts," in *The Lives of Miltiades, and Cimon, with Poems on Several Occasions* (London, 1725), pp. 29–35; Pack, *A New Collection of Miscellanies in Verse and Prose* (London, 1725).

52. Aaron Hill, *The Works of the late Aaron Hill, Esq.*, 2nd edition (London, 1754), I, 194–195; Hill, *The Prompter*, No. LX (June 6, 1735), 1–2; *The London Stage, Part 3: 1729–1747*, ed. Arthur Scouten (Carbondale: University of Southern Illinois Press, 1961), I, 495, 496; David Erskine Baker, *Biographia Dramatica* (London, 1812), I, 45.

53. Where no other source is given, details of the Bond family are drawn from David Elisha Davy, "Suffolk Collections," British Museum Additional MS. 19119, fol. 229, from a microfilm copy, and from John Burke and John Bernard Burke, eds., *A Genealogical and Heraldic History of the Extinct and Dormant Baronetcies of England, Ireland, and Scotland* 2nd ed. (London: 1841), pp. 70–71.

54. John Evelyn, *Diary*, ed. E. S. de Beer (Oxford: Oxford University Press, 1955), IV, 93, 258; Defoe, *A Tour through England and Wales*, Everyman ed. (London: Dent, 1928), I, 168.

55. The poet is so identified, for want of other possibilities, by "S. H. A. H." (Sydenham Henry Augustus Hervey) in *Letter Books of John Hervey* (Wells, 1894), III, iv; but the will of the William Bond, who died in 1696, was proved in the Prerogative Court of Canterbury in 1697 (Probate Act Book 42, fol. 49). *Index to Wills Proved in the Prerogative Court of Canterbury* (London. British Record Society, 1960–), XII, 43.

56. Count Anthony Hamilton, *Memoirs of the Count Grammont*, ed. Gordon Goodwin (Edinburgh, 1908), II, 190; John Gage Rockewode, *The History and Antiquities of Suffolk: Thingoe Hundred* (London, 1838), p. 209, n. "f."; Edmund Malone, *A Life of John Dryden*, in *The Critical and Miscellaneous Prose Works of John Dryden*, ed. Malone (London, 1800), I, Part I, 396, n. 7.

57. She was buried in St. Edmund's Chapel, at the right hand of the Duchess of Gloster's tomb, August 11, 1696. *The Marriage, Baptismal, and Burial Registers of the Collegiate Church or Abbey of St. Peter, Westminister*, ed. Joseph Lemuel Chester (London: Harleian Society, 1876), p. 240.

58. *Complete Baronetage*, ed. G. E. C. (Exeter, 1900–1906), III, 20; *CSP, Dom., 1697*, pp. 125; *CSP, Dom., 1698*, p. 311.

59. John Hervey, first Earl of Bristol, to Secretary Boyle, July 7, 1710, in *Letter Books of John Hervey*, I, 268; and Hervey to Lady Bond, May 19, 1712, I, 329–330.

60. Rockewode, p. 209n; W. A. Copinger, *The Manors of Suffolk* (Manchester, 1908–1911), VII, 58.

61. Bond and Martha Fowke, *The Platonic Lovers, Consisting of Original Letters in Prose and Verse*, 3rd ed. (London, 1732), p. xxiii.

62. Copinger, VI, 334.
63. *Rushbrook Parish Registers*, p. 87.
64. *Ibid.*, pp. 347–348.
65. *Ibid.*, pp. 164–172.
66. This genealogy of William Bond is of course based partly upon conjecture, but it seems less likely that he was a younger son of Sir Thomas Bond or an illegitimate son of Thomas Bond. In *Thursday's Journal* for October 8–15, 1719, M. R. remarked sarcastically, "But don't you really know, *Good Lack*, that he is a *Gentleman*, nay that he is of *Quality too*, for he comes of a whole Generation of Clowns in the Isle of Eli . . . He says he is nearly related to the Bonds of Norfolk, that his Uncle and Sir Henry Bond's Mother in law were Cousin Germans only twice remov'd . . ." (p. 2).
67. Passes for Holland were approved for "Thomas Bond, esquire, and Anselme Dumats, his servant," on May 6; and for William Bond, "a protestant," on June 21, 1697 (*CSP, Dom. 1697*, pp. 146, 206). According to M. R., Bond "was educated a Papist" (p. 2).
68. *Rushbrook Parish*, p. 164. If he wrote *The Creed of an Independent Whig* (1720), he was unfortunately married. "*I Believe* that all Men have Portions in *this World*: and therefore I advise them to follow my Example, and each Man take to him a Wife." "*I Believe* it is better to Marry than Burn; yet Marriage produces many a *Heart Burn*" (p. 20). Though there seem to be no references in Bond's certainly identifiable writings to his marriage or wife, there are scattered references to the miseries of unhappy marriages, especially those dictated by parents.
69. Although George Sewell is generally named as Bond's collaborator, only one number is signed "S." Earlier, during 1714–1715, Bond had evidently written for Robert Mawson's *Weekly Journal, with Fresh Advices Foreign and Domestick*. According to M. R., he "was lately for a considerable time a *Runner*, or *Devil*, or *Footman* . . . to one Mawson a Journalist, to collect Paragraphs of Street News for him, at seven Shillings a Week Wages" (p. 2).
70. Alexander Pope to William Broome, February 10, 1715, in *Letters*, ed. George Sherburn (Oxford: Oxford University Press, 1956), I, 276–277.
71. Mr. Berry to James Stuart, September 15, 1718, in *Calendar of the Stuart Papers*, ed. F. H. Blackburne Daniell (London, 1902–1923), VII, 287. In *Thursday's Journal*, M. R. remarked, "Ye Jacobites, behold your Champion" (p. 3).
72. *Evening Post*, No. 1366 (May 3–6, 1718), p. 3.
73. Bond and Fowke, *The Epistles of Clio and Strephon, Being a Collection of Letters* (London, 1728), p. 23. Subsequent page references are made to this edition.
74. Campbell, *Secret Memoirs*, p. 32. It was probably Rogers, not Bond, who was attacked, beaten almost to death, and then imprisoned at the suit of M—s—n, "a Proprietor of the Saturday's Post." Details are given in *The Weekly Medley*, Nos. XXXVII (March 28–April 4, 1719), p. 220; XLI (April 25–May 2), pp. 241–242; XLII (May 2–9), p. 249; and XLIV (May 16–23), p. 259. Although Bond had spent much of the winter in Sussex following the death of his brother Thomas, he must have been recalled to London by this attack and imprisonment.
75. In the leading article for December 19–26, 1719, the editor noted at the close, "I have just now had word sent me, that one of the Booksellers, that had his Name to the Book, is subpoena'd to appear in the Crown Office about some Passage in it, which I am told is for a Quotation out of Mr. Dryden . . ." (p. 446). The offensive quotation was obviously selected by Bond. In the following issue of *The Medley* the pamphlet was not advertised. No further issue of the weekly appeared.
76. Hill to Martha Fowke (?), in Works, I, 41; *Clio and Strephon*, 117–121; 27n. Since no copy of a separate and early edition of *Buckingham House* is listed in the BM Catalogue or in the National Union Card Catalogue, one might assume that Bond may have had only a few gift copies printed.
77. In Bond's *The Case Stated, in a Letter to Archibald Hutchison*, published under his pseudonym Stanhope, a catalogue of books recently printed for E. Curll in-

cludes "*Priestianity, or a View of the Disparity* . . . By Mr. Stanhope" (p. 38); and this pamphlet itself advertises on its title page that it was written "By the author of the Creed of an Independent Whig." Through confusion with *The Character of an Independent Whig, The Creed* is sometimes assigned to Thomas Gordon. *The Creed* pleads for religious toleration and opposes a regimented belief (pp. xii, 9), though it supports an Established Religion (pp. 17–18). In its evident sympathy for the Non-juror it quotes Defoe: "*I Believe* that *Daniel de Foe* was in the Right when he said, *Of all the Plagues with which Mankind are Curst* Ecclesiastick *Tyranny's the worst*" (pp. 20–21). Perhaps Bond had become a Whig out of reaction to his former Jacobitical principles, perhaps out of opportunism. *Priestianity* attacks the morals and behavior especially of the chaplains in aristocratic or wealthy families. It would perhaps be unwise to rely too heavily upon these attributions to Bond.

78. Bond and Fowke, *The Platonic Lovers* (1732), pp. xx–xxi. In 1732 Curll published also *Clio and Strephon, Being the Second and Last Part of the Platonic Lovers, consisting of Love Epistles & c. by William Bond, Esq: of Bury St. Edmonds, and Mrs. Martha Fowke . . . to which is added a Collection of Miscellanies.* It is a shameless piece of bookmaking, for it contains no new work by either poet, and certainly no new love letters.

79. Bond, "The Parallel," in *Duncan Campbell*, pp. 250, 248–249.

80. Printed for Edmund Curll, this poem advertises (Sig. [A4]) the new engravings for the Campbell biography: the Vandergucht portrait and the good Genius. According to Straus (p. 264), the first edition of the poem was advertised in *The Post Boy* on November 26, 1720; and the second "edition," four days later, in *The Daily Post*.

81. *An Epistle to his Royal Highness*, pp. 4–5. According to Straus (pp. 263–264), four "editions" appeared, on October 31, November 2 (according to *The Post Boy*), November 4, and November 15, 1720. On December 5 *The Post Boy* advertised "A Key to Mr. Stanhope's Epistle" (Straus, p. 263).

82. In his "Book of Expenses" Hervey recorded his payment of £21 to his "cousin Mr. William Bond" on October 29, 1721 (*Diary* [Wells, 1894], p. 93). The offending dedication was subsequently removed, perhaps as a condition of the gift. *Buchanan's History of Scotland*, 2nd ed., trans. Bond (1722), Sig. A3 recto, A4 recto.

83. John Watkins in the Preface to his translation of George Buchanan, *The History of Scotland* (London, 1831), p. 3.

84. *Pliny's Epistles and Panegyrick* (London, 1724), II, 97n.

85. Bonamy Dobrée, *English Literature in the Early Eighteenth Century.* Oxford History of English Literature, Vol. VII (New York: Oxford University Press, 1959), p. 396.

86. Dorothy Brewster, *Aaron Hill, Poet, Dramatist, Projector* (New York: Columbia University Press, 1913), pp. 156–157.

87. Since the only copy of *Verses Sacred to the Memory of the most Noble Henrietta, late Duchess of Grafton* known to the present writer lacks any imprint and is printed on white satin, evidently as a presentation copy, the poem may have been designated for presentation only rather than for publication.

88. The suggestion is made in Straus, p. 115. This edition should not be confused with Thomas Newlin's 1727 translation.

89. It is advertised as by William Bond, Esq., in Curll's list (p. 4) appended to Margaret Pennyman's *Miscellanies*.

90. *The London Stage, Part 3: 1729–1747*, I, 311–312.

91. Hill to Benjamin Victor, August 18, 1733, in Victor, *The History of the Theatres of London and Dublin* (London, 1761), II, 195–197. Hervey recorded his gift, on January 30, 1732/33, in his *Diary*, p. 158.

92. *The London Stage, 1729–1747*, I, xxxiii, 495, 496, 497.

93. Hill, *The Prompter*, No. LX (June 6, 1735), pp. 1–2.

94. *The London Magazine*, June 1735, p. 334.

95. *The Gentleman's Magazine*, XL (September 1770), 406.

CHAPTER VIII

1. *The Dumb Philosopher*, in *The Novels and Miscellaneous Works of Daniel De Foe* (Oxford, 1840–1841), XIX, i. Subsequent references will be incorporated in the text and will omit the volume number. The publisher, Thomas Bickerton, announced a second edition on May 27, 1720 (Moore, *Checklist*, p. 169), but the advertisement may have been merely a conventional attempt to boost flagging sales. The four copies at Harvard and the Boston Public Library seem to be identical. Could an otherwise unrecorded edition be represented by the transcript in William Freeman's *Incredibe De Foe* (London: Herbert Jenkins, 1950, p. 251): "*The Dual Philosopher, or Great Britain's Wonder, containing a Faithful and very Surprising Account how Dickery Cronks, a Turner's Son . . .*"?
2. Chalmers, *The Life of Daniel De Foe*, pp. 77–78.
3. It has also been attributed to him in all the Defoe bibliographies.
4. George Clement Boase and William Prideaux Courtney, *Bibliotheca Cornubiensis* (London, 1874–1882), I, 99, 113.
5. See the introduction to Aitken's edition of Defoe's, *Romances and Narratives*, (1895), XV, xiii, xiv.
6. John Robert Moore, "Defoe's Political Propaganda in *The Dumb Philosopher*," *Huntington Library Quarterly*, IV, 108 (October 1940).
7. The nonexistent "St. Helen's" could not, as Aitken conjectured, have been intended for Helland, since it is in the wrong direction—east northeast from St. Columb Major, whereas Dickory was travelling southerly from Padstow. Ten miles south southeast of St. Columb, however, is St. Allen, for which "St. Helen's" seems a more likely mistake—if there was a mistake. But the Reverend J. R. Crothers, Rector of St. Erme and Priest-in-charge of St. Allen, has kindly written, September 3, 1965, that no burial is recorded there anywhere near the date May 29, 1718. Inquiries to parishes adjacent to St. Columb have elicited prompt responses, but no trace of any Cronke, from the Reverend M. C. Browning, Vicar of St. Ewal and Rector of St. Ervan and from the Reverend Bernard de S. Scott, recently Priest-in-charge, St. Issey. According to the latter, the name Diggory or Dickery appears four times in the decade in the parish baptismal records.
8. Wilson, *Memoirs*, III, 468, 471.
9. William Hazlitt, "The Life of Daniel De Foe," in Defoe, *The Works of Daniel De Foe* (London, 1840), I, cix.
10. Lee, *Daniel Defoe*, I, 311.
11. Wright, p. 264.
12. Aitken, in Defoe, *Romances*, XV, xiv; Moore, "Defoe's Political Propaganda," IV, 107, 117.
13. Rupert Taylor, *The Political Prophecy in England* (New York: Columbia University Press, 1911), p. 133.
14. C. W. Sutton, "Robert Nixon," *DNB*.
15. John Oldmixon, *Nixon's Cheshire Prophecy at Large*, 10th ed. (London, 1740), pp. 14, 20. Subsequent references will cite this edition and will be incorporated in the text. All of them derive from a purported letter dated Nantwich, March 14, 1714, and signed "W. E."
16. *Vox Infantis, or the Propheticall Child* (1649), as reprinted in *Reprints of English Books, 1475–1700*, No. 49, ed. Joseph Arnold Foster (East Lansing, 1945), pp. 5, 6. Subsequent quotations will be incorporated in the text.
17. For a convenient, brief discussion, see James Sutherland, "John Lacy and the Modern Prophets," *Background for Queen Anne* (London: Methuen, 1939), pp. 36–74.
18. John Wing, *Olympia Domata, or an Almanack for . . . 1720*, Sig. [B2] recto.
19. "Signior Piscatore," *The Milan Predictions for 1703* (London, 1703), p. 21.
20. Nathaniel Wanley, *The Wonders of the Little World* (London, 1678) Bk. VI, ch. XVIII, p. 595.
21. William Turner, *Compleat History*, Part III, ch. III, pp. 3–4.
22. Richard Carew, *Carew's Survey of Cornwall*, ed. Thomas Tonkin and Francis de

Dunstanville (London, 1811), pp. 326–327. The story is found also in Thomas Fuller, *The History of the Worthies of England*, ed. P. Austin Nuttall (London, 1840), I, 319–320; and in William Turner, Part III, p. 5.

23. The Rev. G. G. Canon Perry, "Benjamin Hoadly," in *DNB*.
24. *The Annals of King George, Year the Fifth* (London, 1720), pp. 265, 378.
25. Daniel Defoe, *A Letter to the Dissenters* (London, 1719), pp. 8, 9, 11–12.
26. Moore, "Defoe's Political Propaganda," IV, 107.
27. Moore, *Checklist*, p. 115, quoting Defoe, *Considerations on the Present State of Affairs* (1718), p. 22.
28. Wright, p. 264.
29. Moore, "Defoe's Political Propaganda," IV, 117.
30. Defoe to Harley, September 28, 1714, in Defoe, *Letters*, p. 447.
31. Edward Stanley Roscoe, *Robert Harley, Earl of Oxford* (New York: Putnam's, 1902), p. 70.
32. Moore, *Checklist*, p. 127.
33. Moore, *Defoe*, p. 209.
34. Lee, I, 239.
35. Moore, "Defoe's Political *Propaganda*," IV, 117.
36. *Ibid.*, IV, 108.
37. William Bond, *The Weekly Medley* (London, 1718–1720), Nos. XL, XLVIII, LXII, pp. 237, 286, 367 (April 18–25, June 13–20, Sept. 19–26, 1719).
38. Foster, *Alumni Oxonienses, 1715–1886*, III, 1108. These volumes and the earlier series were checked for all contemporary Cornish J. P.'s attending Exeter College.
39. Defoe, *Tour*, I, 256.
40. Foster, I, 33; *The Complete Peerage*, ed. G. E. C. and Vicary Gibbs (London, 1910), I, 263.
41. George A. Aitken, "John Oldmixon," in *DNB*.

Index

Boston Public Library, 211, 214, 219

Boswell, James: *Life of Johnson*, 94, 105, 209, 210

Botelar (Justice of the Peace), 149

Boufflers, Louis François, Duc de, 116

Boulton, Richard: 82; *A Compleat History of Magick*, 37, 75, 78, 205, 208, 215; *The Possibility and Reality of Magick*, 37, 205

Bovet, Richard: *Pandemonium*, 53, 56, 64, 69, 81, 85, 105, 206, 208

Boyce, Dr., 97

Boyer, F.: *Parallel of the Pagans*, 206

Boyle, Henry, Baron Carleton, 217

Boyle, Robert, 3, 151

Boyle lectures, 62

Bragg, Benjamin, 107, 108, 208, 209

Bragge, Francis, 42, 205

Bray, Mrs. Anna Elizabeth: *Trelawny of Trelawne*, 133, 134, 212; *The White Hoods*, 212

Bray, Thomas: *Papal Usurpation and Persecution*, 60

Breval, John Durant, 167

Brewster, Dorothy: *Aaron Hill*, 179, 218

Briggs, Katherine M.: *The Anatomy of Puck*, 17, 202

Brinsley, J., 204

The British Journal, 145

Broome, William, 217

Brown, Tom: *Amusements*, 151

Browne, Sir Thomas: 39; *Pseudodoxia Epidemica*, 10, 201

Browning, Rev. M. C., 219

Brutus, Marcus Junius, 75

Buchanan, George: *The History of Scotland*, 178, 218

Budgell, Eustace, 138

Bull, George: *Some Important Points*, 13, 16, 26, 29, 202, 203, 204

Bunyan, John: *Grace Abounding*, 10; *The Holy War*, 51

Burnet, Gilbert: *Some Letters*, 83

Burthogge, Richard: *Essay upon Reason*, 14

Button, Joseph, 112, 113, 116, 119, 211, 212

Byles, C. E., 134, 212

Cabalists, 160

Caesar, Julius, 75

Caillet, Albert L.: *Manuel Bibliographique des Sciences Phychiques*, 206

Cain, 55–56

Calendar of State Papers, 214, 217

Calvin, Johannes: 15; *Harmonie*, 22

Camfield, Banjamin: *A Theological Discourse of Angels*, 23, 89, 202, 203

Campbell, Dr., 147

Campbell, Archibald (father of seer), 143, 151

Campbell, Archibald, first Duke of Argyll, 147, 151, 170, 179

Campbell, Daniel, 147

Campbell, Duncan (seer): 70, 137–151, 164, 165, 176, 186, 213, 215; ancestry and biography, 143–144, 148–151; portrait, 144; writings—*The Friendly Daemon*, 137, 146–147, 148, 156, 160, 161, 214; *Secret Memoirs*, 147–148, 151, 153, 156, 158, 160, 161, 214, 216, 217

Campbell, Duncan, of Holborn: *Times Telescope*, 148

Campbell, Capt. Duncan, 149

Campbell, Ensign Duncan, 149

Campbell, Sir James, 147

Campbell, John, 147

Campbell, John, Lord Lorne, 149

Carew, Richard: *Survey of Cornwall*, 189, 220

Carr, Col., 144

Cartwright, Francis, 79

Casali, Giovanni Battista: *De Profanis et Sacris Veteribus Ritis*, 207

Casaubon, Meric: *Of Credulity and Incredulity*, 4, 71

Catinate, Nicolas: *Mareschal*, 119, 212

Centlivre, Mrs. Susanna: 169; *The Artifice*, 178

Chalmers, George: 201; *The Life of Daniel De Foe*, 92, 105, 132, 133, 137, 181, 195, 209, 213, 219

Chancellor, Edwin Beresford: *The Hell Fire Club*, 206

Chapman, T., 8, 201

Charles II, King of England, 108

Charles IV, King of France, 75, 89

Charlotte Caroline of Brandenburg-Anspach, 144

Chattock, J.: *Celestial Observations*, 211; *Telescopium Anglicanum*, 211

Chesterfield, Earl of. See Stanhope, Phillip Dormer, fourth Earl of Chesterfield.

Christ, 24, 54, 56, 106, 196

Chudleigh, Lady Mary: *Essays upon Several Subjects*, 23, 203

Church of England, 61, 185, 190–193, 195

Churchill, Sarah, Duchess of Marlborough, 180

Cibber, Theophilus: *Lives of the Poets*, 170, 198

Cicero, Marcus Tullius: *De Divinations*, 21

Clarendon, Earl of. See Hyde, Edward, first Earl of Clarendon.

Hall, Joseph, 23: *The Invisible World Discovered*, 43, 86, 88, 202, 203, 205, 208
Halley, Edmund: 3, 163; *A Description of the Passage of the Shadow*, 125, 212
Hallywell, Henry: *A Private Letter of Satisfaction*, 19, 23, 86, 202, 203, 208
Halsband, Robert: *The Life of Mary Wortley Montagu*, 214
Hamilton, Count Anthony: *Memoirs of the Count Grammont*, 171, 173, 216
Hammond, Anthony, 169
Hamond, George, 14
Hardwick (pretended editor of *Weekly Medley*), 216
Harlequin a Sham Astrologer, 213
Harley, Robert, Earl of Oxford, 115, 118, 194–195, 196, 203, 208, 210, 220
Harsnett, Samuel: *A Declaration of Egregious Popish Impostures*, 82–83
Harvard University, 209, 211, 214, 219
Hawker, Claude, 134
Hawker, Robert Stephen, 134–135, 212
Haywood, Mrs. Eliza: 152, 153, 169, 170; *The Dumb Projector*, 137, 146, 148, 156; *Memoirs of a Certain Island*, 216; *A Spy upon the Conjuror*, 137, 145–146, 148, 156, 160, 214
Hazlitt, William (the younger), 106, 132, 184, 219
Head, William: *The English Rogue*, 78
Healey, George, 211
Hell, 39–40, 85–86
Hell-Fire Clubs, 63, 207
Henley, John, 178
Henrietta, Duchess of Grafton, 169
Hervey, John, first Lord of Bristol, 171, 178, 180, 216, 218
Heydon, John: *Theomagia*, 21, 23, 203
Hervey, Sydenham Henry Augustus, 216
Heywood, Thomas: *The Hierarchy of the Blessed Angels*, 21, 203
Higenbottam, Frank, 209
Hill, Aaron: 58, 169, 170, 176, 179, 180, 216, 219; *The Ottoman Empire*, 165, 206; *The Plain Dealer*, 170, 172, 179; *The Prompter*, 180, 216, 219; *Zara*, 180
Hill, Thomas, 144
hints. See promptings.
History of the Empires in the Sun and Moon Worlds. See Cyrano de Bergerac, Savinien.
Hitchens, Fortesque: *The History of Cornwall*, 133
Hoadly, Benjamin: *Bishop of Bangor*, 191–192, 193, 195

Hobbes, Thomas: 61, 81, 82, 88; *Leviathan*, 88, 208
Hogarth, William, 63
Homer, 174, 175
Hopkins, Matthew, 65
Horace, 175
Horneck, Anthony: *The Ascetick*, 104
Horneck, Philip: 169; *The High German Doctor*, 185
Hospinianus, R.: *Historia Jesuitica*, 206
Howard, Anne, 171
Howard, Henry Stafford, Earl of Stafford, 169
Hughes, John, 178
Hughs (dissenting minister), 168, 216
Hume, Patrick, 48, 54, 205
Hunt, Robert, 65
Hunter, J. Paul: *The Reluctant Pilgrim*, 5, 100, 200, 201, 204
Hutchins, Henry C.: 132, 152, 215; *Robinson Crusoe and its Printing*, 201
Hutchinson, Francis: *An Historical Essay concerning Witchcraft*, 37, 64, 82
Hyde, Edward, first Earl of Clarendon, 75
hypochondria, 24, 96

idolatry, 57–58
Index Expurgatorius, 59
Index to Wills of Canterbury, 216
Inquisition, 61
invocation of the Devil, 65–66

Jacobites, 59–60, 128, 185, 196
Jago-Arundell. See Arundell, Rev. Francis Vyvan Jago.
James II, King of England, 171
James IV, King of Scotland, 75
James Janeway's Legacy, 200
Jarvis, T. M.: *Accredited Ghost Stories*, 133
Jessup, Edward: *The Life of the Celebrated Pascal*, 178
Jermyn, Henry, Baron Dover, 173
Jesuits, 60
Jetzer, 82, 83
Johnson, Samuel, 94, 106, 179, 198
John the Baptist, 186
Jones, Edward, 178
Joseph I, Emperor of Austria, 114
Juvenalis, Decimus Junius, 175

Keller, Helen, 150
Kesel, Leonard, 83
A Key to Mr. Stanhope's Epistle, 218
Kircher, Athanasius: *Ars Magna Lucis et Umbrae*, 206; *China Monumenta*,

227

206; *Iter Exstaticum Coeleste*, 206; *Mundus Subterraneus*, 206; *Oedipus Aegyptiacus*, 64; *Physiologia Kircheraina Experimentalis*, 206
Kirkman, Francis, 78

Mississippi Bubble, 185
Mist, Nathaniel: *A Collection of Miscellany Letters*, 201; *Weekly Journal*, 14, 174, 201
Mitchell, S. A.: *Eclipses of the Sun*, 212
Modest Inquiry into the Opinion concerning a Guardian Angel, 14, 15, 23
Mohammedans, 57, 58–59
Montagu, Edward, third Earl of Sandwich, 63
Montagu, Lady Mary Wortley, 149
Moore, Francis: 110, 210; *Vox Stellarum*, 211
Moore, John Robert: 8, 9, 182, 184, 193, 194–195, 219, 220; *Daniel Defoe*, 208, 210, 220; *Defoe Checklist*, 137, 152, 208–209, 212, 213, 214, 215, 219, 220
Mordaunt, Mrs. Mary, 182
More, Henry: 62, 71, 82; *An Antidote against Atheism*, 19; *An Antidote against Enthusiasm*, 17, 71, 202
Moréri, Louis: *Great Historical Dictionary*, 162, 215
Moreton, Andrew: pseudonym of Defoe, Daniel
Morley, Henry: ed., *The Early Life and Chief Earlier Works of Daniel Defoe*, 203
Moses, 56
Mouraski, Owke, 76, 199

Naudé, Gabriel: *The History of Magick*, 64
Neale, John Mason: *The Unseen World*, 133
New Philosophy, 16
The Newcastle Gazette, 113
Newlin, Thomas, 218
News from the Stars, 210
Newton, Isaac, 3
Nimrod, 206
Nixon, Robert, 185–187, 189, 197
Noah, 56, 206
Norris, John, 104, 105, 106, 210
Nostradamus, 185
Notestein, Wallace: *A History of Witchcraft in England*, 207
Novak, Maximilian: *Defoe and the Nature of Man*, 205

observation of days. *See* day fatalities.
O'Donnell, Eliott: *Ghosts with a Purpose*, 208
Oldys, William: *Catalogus Bibliothecae Harleianae*, 198

Oldmixon, John: *The History of England*, 197; *Nixon's Cheshire Prophecy*, 185–186, 197, 219–220
omens, divine, 31
oracles, 20, 21, 67, 68–69, 71, 138
Orchard, N.: *The Doctrine of Devils*, 42, 88, 205
Ottway, T.: *The Spectre, or News from the Invisible World*, 133, 208
The Oxford Almanack, 211
Ozell, John: translation of Tournefort, 83

Pack, Richardson: 169, 170, 179; *The Lives of Miltiades, and Cimon*, 216; *A New Collection*, 216
pagan worship, 57–58, 61
palmistry, 9, 71
Paracelsus. *See* Bombast.
Pardon, William. *See* Dych, Thomas.
Parker, George: *Merlinus Liberatus*, 211
Parker, Samuel, Bishop of Oxford, 179, 218
Parkins, F.: *Parkins*, 210
Parry, Elizabeth, 197
Parry, Owen, 182
Parsons, Coleman O.: 207, 210; edition of Glanvill's *Sadducismus Triumphatus*, 207
Partridge, John: 109, 110, 111, 139, 188, 212; *Dr. Partridge's Prophecy for 1713*, 112; *Merlinus Liberatus*, 210, 211; *Mr. Partridge's Most Strange and Wonderful Prophecy for 1704*, 112; *The Right and True Predictions for 1704*, 112
Pascal, Blaise, 197
passions, as diabolical avenue, 48–51
Payne, Rev., 91, 95, 96, 97, 102, 105, 106, 208
Payne, Olive, 202, 204
Pearson, Drew, 111, 195
Peckham, 171
Peele, J., 207
Peirce, Rev. James, 192
Peliott, Charles: *Baron de la Garde*, 171
The Penny London Post, 92–93, 209
Pennyman, Margaret: *Miscellanies in Prose and Verse*, 212
Pepys, Samuel, 151, 218
Perier, Gilberte, 178
Perkins, Samuel: *Perkins*, 210
Perkins, W.: *Discourse of the Damned Art of Witchcraft*, 86
Perry, Rev. G. G. Canon, 220
Peter Martyr. *See* Vermigli, Pietro Martire.
Peter, O. B., 136

Peters, Hugh, 182
Philips, John, 144, 169, 196
Philips, Mary, 71
Phillipps, John, 196
Phillipps, Sam, 196
Philosophical Transactions, 98, 150, 151
Pickwick Papers. See Dickens, Charles.
Piscatore, Signior. *See Milan Predictions.*
plague, 7, 116–117, 120–121, 123, 127
Plenitude, Divine, 16, 202
Pliny (the Younger): *Epistles and Penegyrick*, 178, 218
Pond, Edward: *Pond, an Almanack*, 210
Poole, Matthew, 4, 24, 53
Poor Robin. See Winstanley, William.
Pope, Alexander: 173, 176, 217; *Dunciad*, 167–168, 176, 180, 216
Popiad, 177
Pordage, John, 23
Porter, John, 196
Post-Boy, 149, 218
poverty and prisons as diabolical agents, 51–52
Powell, George, 55
The Present Management of the Customs. See Loggin, Robert.
Price (artist), 144
Prideaux, Humphrey: *The True Nature of Imposture in the Life of Mahomet*, 206
Priestianity, 176
Princess, Royal. *See* Charlotte Caroline, of Brandenburg-Anspach.
Prior, Matthew, 167
promptings: angelic, 11, 14, 16, 19–20, 21, 25, 29–30, 31–33; diabolical, 47–48
prophecies and prophets: 9, 11, 20–21, 109–128, 165, 184–190; French, 142, 185, 189; scriptural, 3
Providence, 3–11, 13, 14, 18, 24, 31, 34, 35, 55, 204
Psalmanazar, George: *History of the Island of Formosa*, 165
Ptolemy (Claudius Ptolemaeus), 16, 163
Purgatory, 85
Pyrotechnica Loyolana, 206
Pyrrhonists, 62

Quevedo. *See* Gomez de Quevedo Villegas, Francisco.
Quiller-Couch, Sir Arthur, 135, 136, 213

R., M., 216, 217
Raleigh, Sir Walter: *History of the World*, 53, 55, 56, 64, 206
Read, James: *Penny London Post*, 93; *Read's Journal*, 209

Reformation, 59, 68
Reynolds, John: *Inquiries concerning the State and Oeconomy of the Angelical Worlds*, 14, 23, 37, 202, 203, 205; *View of Death*, 49, 205
Rich, John, 67
Richmond, Duke of. *See* Stuart, Sir Charles.
Rider, Cardanus, 211
Rider, Cardanus, Jr., 211
Rider, William: *Rider's British Merlin*, 211
Robbins, Alfred Farthing: 132, 134, 135, 136, 212, 213; *Launceton: Past and Present*, 135
Robbins, E., 135
Roberts, J., 74
Rochester, Earl of. *See* Wilmot, John.
Rogers (baker), 168, 174, 217
Rogers, Capt. Thomas, 76
Roman Catholic Church, 57, 58–61, 68, 82–83, 206
Rockewode, John Gage: *The History and Antiquities of Suffolk*, 216, 217
Roscoe, Edward Stanley: *Robert Harley, Earl of Oxford*, 194, 220
Rose, George: *Rose*, 210
Ross, Alexander: *Pansebeia*, 58, 206
Rotherham, J., 168, 175
Royal Society, 24
Ruddle, John, 131–136, 197
Ruddle, William, 135–136
Rushbrook Parish Registers, 215, 216, 217
Rutland, Lord. *See* Manners, John.
Rycaut, Sir Paul: *The Lives of the Bishops and Popes*, 206
Ryther, John, 4

St. André, François de: *Lettres au Sujet de la Magie*, 64
Sacchi de Platina, Bartholomaeus: *Apud de Vitis Pontificium*, 206
Sadducism, 13, 81
Salkeld, John: *A Treatise of Angels*, 23, 203
Salmon, William: *London Almanack*, 210
Salters Hall, 192, 195
Sandwich, Lord. *See* Montagu, Edward.
Sansom, Mr., 170
Sansom, Mrs. Martha Fowke: 168, 169, 170, 173–174, 176, 217, 218; *Clio*, 170; *Epistles of Clio and Strephon*, 144, 176, 216; *Mr. Campbell's Packet*, 144
Satanists, 61, 63
Saturday's Post, 196, 217
Saul, 75
Saunders, Richard: *Angelographia*, 14, 26, 44, 202, 203, 205; *Apollo Angli-*

Wilkins (publisher), 167
Williams, Daniel, 215
Williams, Ralph M.: *Poet, Painter, and Parson*, 216
Willis, Thomas, 173
Wilmot, John, second Earl of Rochester, 61
Wilson, Walter: *Memoirs of the Life and Times of Daniel De Foe*, 31, 132, 133, 184, 201, 204, 219
Wing, John: *Olympia Domata*, 110, 188, 210, 220
Wing, Tycho, 210–211
Wing, Vincent, 210
Wing, Vincent, Jr., 211
Winstanley, William: *Poor Robin*, 109, 125, 187, 211
witchcraft: 13, 17, 36, 44, 57, 64, 65–67, 73, 82, 88, 207; white, 71–72; Witch of Endor, 75
Withers, William, 189
Wodrow, Robert, 24
Woodcock, Thomas: 71; *An Account of Some Passages in the Life of a Private Gentleman*, 10
Woodhouse, John: *Woodhouse, a New Almanack*, 211
Woodhouse, W., 211
Woodruff, Rev. C. Eveleigh, 210
Woolston, Thomas, 24, 160
Wright, Thomas: *Life of Daniel Defoe*, 131, 184, 193, 212, 219, 220

Zanchy, Jerome, 203